The *Sams Teach Yourself in 24 Hours* Series

Sams Teach Yourself in 24 Hours books provide quick and easy an
proven step-by-step approach that works for you. In just 24 sessic
or less, you will tackle every task you need to get the results you
experienced authors present the most accurate information to g
answers—fast!

CorelDRAW 9 Toolbox Tools and Flyouts

Tool/Flyout	Tool(s)
	Pick tool
	Shape tool, Knife tool, Eraser tool, Free Transform tool
	Zoom tool, Pan tool
	Freehand tool, Bézier tool, Artistic Media tool, Dimension tool, Connector Line tool, Interactive Connector tool
	Rectangle tool
	Ellipse tool
	Polygon tool, Spiral tool, Graph Paper tool
	Text tool
	Interactive Fill tool, Interactive Mesh Fill tool
	Interactive Transparency tool
	Interactive Blend tool, Interactive Contour tool, Interactive Distortion tool, Interactive Envelope tool, Interactive Extrude tool, Interactive Drop Shadow tool
	Eyedropper tool, Paintbucket tool
	Outline Pen dialog, Outline Color dialog, No outline, Hairline outline, ½ Point Outline, 2 Point Outline, 8 Point Outline, 16 Point Outline, 24 Point Outline
	Fill Color dialog, Fountain Fill dialog, Pattern Fill dialog, Texture Fill dialog, PostScript Fill dialog, No Fill, Color Docker Window

SAMS Teach Yourself **CorelDRAW 9**™ **in 24 Hours**

CorelDRAW KEYBOARD SHORTCUTS

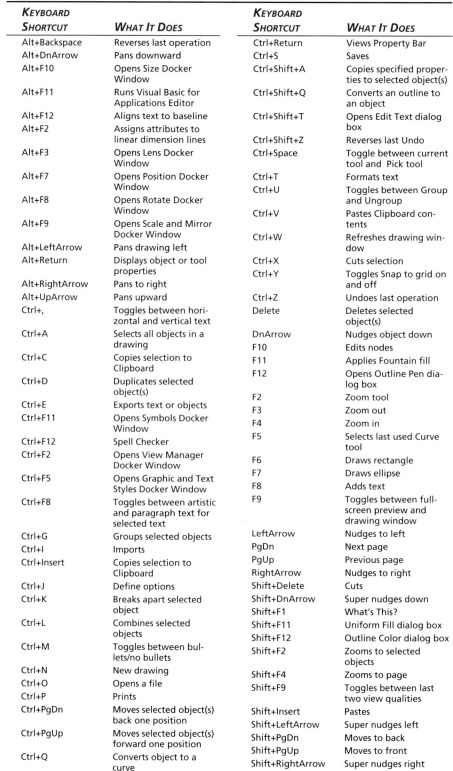

KEYBOARD SHORTCUT	WHAT IT DOES	KEYBOARD SHORTCUT	WHAT IT DOES
Alt+Backspace	Reverses last operation	Ctrl+Return	Views Property Bar
Alt+DnArrow	Pans downward	Ctrl+S	Saves
Alt+F10	Opens Size Docker Window	Ctrl+Shift+A	Copies specified properties to selected object(s)
Alt+F11	Runs Visual Basic for Applications Editor	Ctrl+Shift+Q	Converts an outline to an object
Alt+F12	Aligns text to baseline	Ctrl+Shift+T	Opens Edit Text dialog box
Alt+F2	Assigns attributes to linear dimension lines	Ctrl+Shift+Z	Reverses last Undo
Alt+F3	Opens Lens Docker Window	Ctrl+Space	Toggle between current tool and Pick tool
Alt+F7	Opens Position Docker Window	Ctrl+T	Formats text
Alt+F8	Opens Rotate Docker Window	Ctrl+U	Toggles between Group and Ungroup
Alt+F9	Opens Scale and Mirror Docker Window	Ctrl+V	Pastes Clipboard contents
Alt+LeftArrow	Pans drawing left	Ctrl+W	Refreshes drawing window
Alt+Return	Displays object or tool properties	Ctrl+X	Cuts selection
Alt+RightArrow	Pans to right	Ctrl+Y	Toggles Snap to grid on and off
Alt+UpArrow	Pans upward	Ctrl+Z	Undoes last operation
Ctrl+,	Toggles between horizontal and vertical text	Delete	Deletes selected object(s)
Ctrl+A	Selects all objects in a drawing	DnArrow	Nudges object down
Ctrl+C	Copies selection to Clipboard	F10	Edits nodes
		F11	Applies Fountain fill
Ctrl+D	Duplicates selected object(s)	F12	Opens Outline Pen dialog box
Ctrl+E	Exports text or objects	F2	Zoom tool
Ctrl+F11	Opens Symbols Docker Window	F3	Zoom out
		F4	Zoom in
Ctrl+F12	Spell Checker	F5	Selects last used Curve tool
Ctrl+F2	Opens View Manager Docker Window		
Ctrl+F5	Opens Graphic and Text Styles Docker Window	F6	Draws rectangle
		F7	Draws ellipse
Ctrl+F8	Toggles between artistic and paragraph text for selected text	F8	Adds text
		F9	Toggles between full-screen preview and drawing window
Ctrl+G	Groups selected objects		
Ctrl+I	Imports	LeftArrow	Nudges to left
Ctrl+Insert	Copies selection to Clipboard	PgDn	Next page
		PgUp	Previous page
Ctrl+J	Define options	RightArrow	Nudges to right
Ctrl+K	Breaks apart selected object	Shift+Delete	Cuts
Ctrl+L	Combines selected objects	Shift+DnArrow	Super nudges down
		Shift+F1	What's This?
Ctrl+M	Toggles between bullets/no bullets	Shift+F11	Uniform Fill dialog box
		Shift+F12	Outline Color dialog box
Ctrl+N	New drawing	Shift+F2	Zooms to selected objects
Ctrl+O	Opens a file		
Ctrl+P	Prints	Shift+F4	Zooms to page
Ctrl+PgDn	Moves selected object(s) back one position	Shift+F9	Toggles between last two view qualities
Ctrl+PgUp	Moves selected object(s) forward one position	Shift+Insert	Pastes
		Shift+LeftArrow	Super nudges left
Ctrl+Q	Converts object to a curve	Shift+PgDn	Moves to back
		Shift+PgUp	Moves to front
Ctrl+R	Repeats last operation	Shift+RightArrow	Super nudges right
		Shift+UpArrow	Super nudges up
		UpArrow	Nudges up

David Karlins

with artwork by
Paul Mikulecky

SAMS
Teach Yourself
CorelDRAW™ 9
in 24 Hours

SAMS

201 West 103rd Street, Indianapolis, Indiana 46290

Sams Teach Yourself CorelDRAW™ 9 in 24 Hours

Copyright © 1999 by Sams Publishing

International Standard Book Number: 0-672-31570-X

Library of Congress Catalog Card Number: 99-61033

Printed in the United States of America

First Printing: June 1999

01 00 99   4 3 2 1

Trademarks

Warning and Disclaimer

EXECUTIVE EDITOR
Beth Millett

ACQUISITIONS EDITOR
Beth Millett

DEVELOPMENT EDITOR
Kelly Murdock

MANAGING EDITOR
Jodi Jensen

SENIOR EDITOR
Susan Ross Moore

COPY EDITOR
Nancy Albright

INDEXER
Heather Goens

PROOFREADERS
Mona Brown
Ben Berg

TECHNICAL EDITOR
T. Michael Clark

INTERIOR DESIGN
Gary Adair

COVER DESIGN
Aren Howell

COPY WRITER
Eric Borgert

LAYOUT TECHNICIANS
Brian Borders
Susan Geiselman
Mark Walchle

Contents at a Glance

Contents

About the Author

David Karlins is the author of *Sams Teach Yourself CorelDRAW 8 in 24 Hours, Teach Yourself FrontPage 98 in a Week, Wild Web Graphics with Image Composer,* and many other books on Web graphics and Web design. When he's not writing books, David is a Web site consultant, teacher, and amateur, unpublished movie critic.

Paul Mikulecky is owner of the award winning Electric Design Studio located in Alberta, Canada. He is a graphic designer, illustrator, past contributing editor for *Corel Magazine*, and has also been a speaker at the Corel International Conferences. Paul has won a grand prize and an honorable mention in *Corel Magazine*'s Web Design Contest and is also the recipient of two honorable mentions in the 7th Corel World Design contest. He cowrote and provided illustrations for *Sams Teach Yourself CorelDRAW 8 in 24 Hours*.

Dedication

Dedicated to everyone with a vision to share with the world.

Acknowledgments

Credit for this book, even more than for the previous edition, goes to the CorelDRAW community at large. The lessons and discussion in this book draw on my experiences training students in CorelDRAW, as well as feedback, constructive criticism, and helpful suggestions posted to the book's Web site at www.ppinet.com.

I'm really excited to once again present a set of illustrations from Paul Mikulecky. Paul combines creativity and skill with a unique ability to mesh his drawings closely with the lessons in the book.

Beth Millett did a wonderful job of putting this book together, along with the vast crew at Macmillan Computer Publishing. T. Michael Clark did a dedicated technical edit. Kelly Murdock, Susan Moore, and Nancy Albright contributed thoughtful editing.

Thanks, as well, to my agent Lisa Swayne for making this book happen.

Tell Us What You Think!

As the reader of this book, *you* are our most important critic and commentator. We value your opinion and want to know what we're doing right, what we could do better, what areas you'd like to see us publish in, and any other words of wisdom you're willing to pass our way.

As a Publisher for Sams Publishing, I welcome your comments. You can fax, email, or write me directly to let me know what you did or didn't like about this book—as well as what we can do to make our books stronger.

Please note that I cannot help you with technical problems related to the topic of this book, and that due to the high volume of mail I receive, I might not be able to reply to every message.

When you write, please be sure to include this book's title and author as well as your name and phone or fax number. I will carefully review your comments and share them with the author and editors who worked on the book.

Fax: 317-581-4770

Email: desktop_pub@mcp.com

Mail: John Pierce, Publisher
          Sams Publishing
          201 West 103rd Street
          Indianapolis, IN 46290 USA

Introduction

Teaching yourself CorelDRAW 9 in 24 hours presents a couple of interesting challenges. One of them is that the Corel interface is loaded with complex tools and effects, and the whole package can be a bit overwhelming when you start out. The other challenge comes from DRAW's vector-based drawing system, which has has a different logic and feel than bitmap image programs that some readers may be more familiar with.

Not to worry. Even if you don't know a vector from a tractor, this book will walk you through the process of creating illustrations in DRAW. You'll quickly get introduced to DRAW's most popular and spectacular tools and effects.

I've also aimed this book at professional illustrators who have experience with other drawing packages, but want to add CorelDRAW to their arsenal. We start with the basics, but you'll explore features such as managing layers, printing color separations, and integrating bitmaps and vector images.

For this second edition of *Sams Teach Yourself CorelDRAW in 24 Hours,* I've built on the approach that readers seemed to like in the previous version. The book is filled with illustrations by my artistic collaborator, Paul Mikulecky. Paul is one of the most respected professional Corel illustrators in the world, but what I like best about Paul's drawings is that he manages to create such wonderful, mind-stretching illustrations by using some very basic techniques that mesh with the lessons in this book. If you see an illustration in this book, you'll learn how to create it here.

I've also chosen to include a five-chapter introduction to CorelDRAW's companion, CorelPHOTO-PAINT. My theory is, why pay for two books when we can introduce you to both products in one?

I've been teaching folks like you to use CorelDRAW for 10 years. I think this book provides enough material to take you to a professional level, but doesn't overload you with more than you can digest. This book really will teach you CorelDRAW and PHOTO-PAINT in just 24 hours, but we'll pack plenty of action into that time.

How This Book Is Structured

Each hour in this book includes brief explanations, a few tips, advice, and plenty of To Do exercises that show you how to create effects and illustrations.

The book can function both as a tutorial and a handy reference. A quick look at the thorough index at the back of this book gives you a sense of the scope of features at your fingertips.

The six parts of this book break the material up into bite-sized chunks to help you digest CorelDRAW and PHOTO-PAINT one bite at a time. Each hour ends with a fun project, usually accompanied by a model illustration to challenge you. The projects require only those skills covered in that hour (and previous hours), so you'll build up your skills by actually designing real-life illustrations.

Each hour reinforces your skills with a summary and a quick quiz. Of course we'll supply you with the answers as well, so you can sharpen your understanding as you take the quiz.

Hours 1–3 introduce CorelDRAW. You'll learn to create some pretty complex illustrations combining text and shapes to create logos, icons, and illustrations.

In Hours 4–7, you'll learn to define the CorelDRAW environment for projects ranging from Web graphics to newsletters. And you'll learn to define and apply fills and outlines to your objects.

Hours 8–10 break down the process of defining and controlling curves, the basic building blocks of complex CorelDRAW illustrations.

Hours 11–14 explore the universe of effects that you can apply to objects in CorelDRAW. You'll add lenses, powerclips, blends, contours, and 3D perspective to your stash of effects.

Hours 15–19 cover a number of complex projects, including desktop publishing with text frames and multilayer illustrations. Here, we also examine the process of sending CorelDRAW illustrations to printed output and to the Web.

Hours 20–24 provide a quick introduction to CorelPHOTO-PAINT. Because many of PHOTO-PAINT's tools are similar to those in DRAW, this section starts from the skills you learned in the first 19 hours and builds on them. PHOTO-PAINT is among the elite bitmap image editors, and these chapters add an additional dimension to your array of image editing powers.

What You'll Need

This book assumes only a very basic knowledge of the Windows operating system. Other than that, the book assumes only that you have gotten your hands on a copy of CorelDRAW 9.

Set your copy of CorelDRAW 9 and your copy of this book next to your machine, grab a cup of coffee and maybe a chocolate chip cookie. You've got everything you need to… *teach yourself CorelDRAW 9 in 24 hours*. Have fun!

Conventions Used in This Book

This book uses different typefaces to differentiate between code and regular English, and also to help you identify important concepts.

Text that you type and text that should appear on your screen is presented in monospace type.

```
It will look like this to mimic the way text looks on your screen.
```

A Note presents interesting pieces of information related to the surrounding discussion.

A Tip offers advice or teaches an easier way to do something.

A Caution advises you about potential problems and helps you steer clear of disaster.

New Term icons provide clear definitions of new, essential terms. The term appears in *italic*.

PART I
Diving In

Hour

HOUR 1

Dive In! Having Fun with CorelDRAW 9

CorelDRAW 9 is an enormously powerful graphic design package. With that power comes a fairly complex design environment and an almost infinite combination of tools and effects. In this book, you'll meet and work with all these tools and effects.

CorelDRAW is an encyclopedia vector graphics program. Plus, CorelDRAW 9 comes packaged with Corel PHOTO-PAINT, a powerful program for creating and editing bitmap images. Included as well are a bunch of utilities including the popular Bitstream Navigator for installing fonts. This book includes Hours 20–24 that introduce you to PHOTO-PAINT.

With all that said, you can jump into CorelDRAW 9 with a minimum of preparation and create complex illustrations. Don't be intimidated because there is plenty that you can do with even a beginning understanding of CorelDRAW, and you're going to have fun learning. In this first hour, you'll get acquainted with enough of CorelDRAW's environment to start creating drawings. You also will learn to use lines and line segments to create graphic images.

Welcome to CorelDRAW 9

Before you dive in and start creating your own graphic images, you need to understand a few basic concepts about what CorelDRAW does—both on your screen and behind the scenes. That's what this section is about.

Do you really need to know what's going on behind the scenes in CorelDRAW 9? Not necessarily, but a basic understanding of the unique way CorelDRAW creates images will help you design images and transform those images to hard copy or Web page output.

CorelDRAW is different from bitmap graphic design packages. CorelDRAW is a vector-based program, which means that it creates and handles images as mathematically defined vectors. *Vectors* are objects with both magnitude (size) and direction (angles, curvature, and so on). The files that store CorelDRAW images consist of lists of lines, with information on their location, direction, length, color, and curves, among other things.

The majority of graphic design programs are bitmap-based, which means they define images as enormous lists of dots, called *pixels*. Some of the more popular bitmap-based programs include Photoshop, PHOTO-PAINT, and Image Composer.

Defining images as a series of vectors is a more efficient way to work with them than defining images as a huge number of individual pixels. This is because even a simple object might have thousands of pixels, each individually defined, whereas the same image might be defined more rationally as a small number of curve segments. Therefore, CorelDRAW 9 vector image files are often smaller than comparable bitmapped image files. To give you a quick, simple example of what I'm talking about, I just saved a small illustration in CorelDRAW, and the file size was 12KB. To experiment, I saved the same image as a TIF format bitmap image, and the file size was 2724KB! I could have spent some time adjusting the way I saved the bitmap, and cut the file size down a bit, you can get a sense from this experiment of how much more efficient CorelDRAW vector-based files can be.

In addition to creating more compact files, CorelDRAW's vector-based images have other important advantages. You can easily resize a CorelDRAW image to a thumbnail sketch or icon or a billboard-sized graphic. When you change the size of a bitmap image, you lose quality because the number of dots, or pixels, remains the same even as the illustration is enlarged. That's not the case with CorelDRAW's curve-based illustrations.

Another advantage to working with vector-based images is that smooth curves are easy to define; they will retain their smoothness and continuity even when enlarged (unlike bitmaps). Figure 1.1 shows a Bézier curve defined in CorelDRAW with text fitted to it. These curves are named after a French engineer who developed the math theory for them in the 1970s. That might be more than enough about the mathematics of curves for some of you, but readers with inquiring minds can find out more about Bézier and his curves by checking out the Bézier Curve Web site at `http://www.moshplant.com/director/bezier/index.html`.

The mathematically defined curves generated by CorelDRAW retain their smoothness and continuity even when enlarged. Bitmap images become grainy when enlarged.

FIGURE 1.1

Text fitted to a Bézier Curve in CorelDRAW.

In some ways, however, graphic designers have to live in a bitmap world. This is especially true in the era of the World Wide Web, where much of the target for graphic design is images that appear in, or as, Web pages. Popular Web browsers cannot interpret images in CorelDRAW's native format. And the relatively grainy resolution of computer monitors (generally 72 dots per inch) tends to negate some of the advantages of creating vector-based images. The relatively small, low-resolution images seen on Web sites tend to make curves jagged and grainy regardless of how smooth and high-resolution the original image.

CorelDRAW is a vital and irreplaceable graphic tool capable of creating any graphic image file you will ever need. For one thing, many images are still destined for hard copy, and CorelDRAW's vector-based images are great for printed output. Corel's vector-based tools provide the most powerful array of features for designing images. CorelDRAW can then easily translate those images into bitmap formats. In fact, CorelDRAW has a powerful capacity to transform objects into both of the widely recognized Web-compatible bitmap file formats: GIF and JPEG. So, in that sense, CorelDRAW is the best of both worlds, with unparalleled design tools plus the capability of converting images to bitmap formats as needed.

When you bought CorelDRAW 9, you also bought one of the most powerful bitmap editors available—Corel PHOTO-PAINT 9. Because more and more CorelDRAW users move back and forth between the vector and bitmap worlds, this book includes three hours devoted exclusively to PHOTO-PAINT 9. See Hours 20–22 for detailed information about working with bitmap images.

Taking a Quick Look Around

The CorelDRAW environment can be a bit overwhelming, so I'll introduce you to it one piece at a time. In this first hour, you'll become familiar with just enough of the CorelDRAW 9 window so you can start to create graphic images.

When you launch CorelDRAW 9 (using the Windows Start button or a shortcut button on your Windows desktop), the Welcome to CorelDRAW window appears, as shown in Figure 1.2.

FIGURE 1.2

Starting with the Welcome window.

1

The Getting Started window provides six options for getting started with CorelDRAW 9, as explained in Table 1.1.

TABLE 1.1 STARTING OPTIONS

Icon	Name	What It Does
	New Graphic	Creates a new window in which you can design a graphic
	Open Last Edited	Opens the last graphic image file you worked on
	Open Graphic	Opens the Open Drawing dialog box, enabling you to select from any saved graphic image file
	Template	Enables you to choose from a list of pre-designed page templates that you can use as a basis to begin a design
	CorelTUTOR	Enables you to select from several categories of online help and instructions
	What's New?	Lists and explains new features in CorelDRAW 9

To create a new graphic image from scratch, click the New Graphic icon in the Getting Started dialog box. When you do, you'll see an empty CorelDRAW 9 window, such as the one in Figure 1.3.

The Drawing window is the whole work area in the middle of your CorelDRAW 9 window, excluding the toolbars, toolbox (on the left), and status bar. This Drawing window is where you have fun creating graphics. The section of the Drawing window bounded by the shaded box is called the Drawing page. This is the part of your composition that prints when you send your file to the printer.

You can store graphic images you don't want to print (but do want to save) in the area of the Drawing window *outside* of the Drawing page. The area outside the Drawing page can be a handy storage space when, for example, if you have a file that you use as a template for a publication. You can save logos, blocks of text, and so on, for use in another issue of your publication, but they won't print if they're not on the Drawing page.

The Property Bar tells you information about any selected object in your Drawing window. The Property Bar changes, depending on what object you select in the Drawing window. There is even a special Property Bar that appears when you don't have any object(s) selected. In Figure 1.3, because the Drawing window does not have any objects yet, the No Selection Property Bar displays information about the Drawing page, such as it is Letter page-sized, 8.5-by-11 inches. In Hour 2, "Creating Artistic Text," you'll explore the Property Bar in more detail.

FIGURE 1.3

A clean CorelDRAW 9 Drawing window, ready for you to begin drawing.

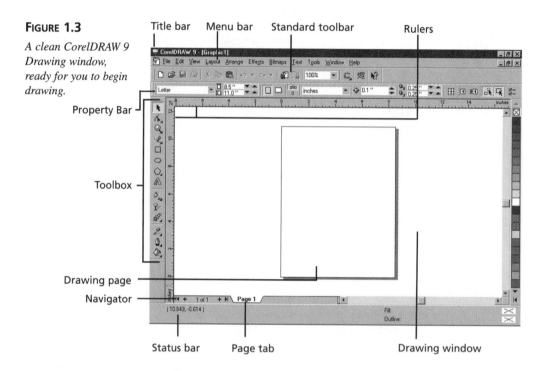

Title bar   Menu bar   Standard toolbar   Rulers

Property Bar

Toolbox

Drawing page

Navigator

Status bar   Page tab   Drawing window

The Property Bar can float over your Drawing window, or you can dock it just below the Standard toolbar (or on either side or the bottom of your Drawing window). When the Property Bar sits below the Standard toolbar, you can drag on any portion of the Property Bar *between* tools and move it onto the Drawing window. If the Property Bar is floating over the Drawing window, you can drag the Property Bar's title bar to move it up below the Standard toolbar, as shown in Figure 1.4.

FIGURE 1.4

Moving the Property Bar off the Drawing window and up beneath the Standard toolbar.

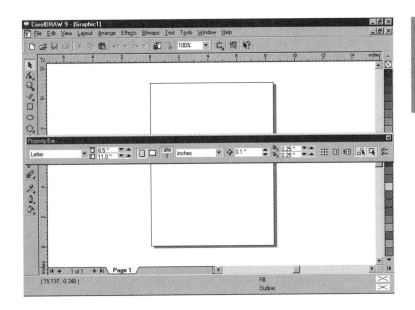

The toolbox is located to the left of the Drawing window. This is where you find all the tools CorelDRAW provides to create and edit graphic objects. When you move your cursor over any of the tools in the toolbox, a ToolTip will appear identifying that tool. In Figure 1.5, the ToolTip identifies the Eyedropper tool.

FIGURE 1.5

When you move your cursor over a tool without clicking, CorelDRAW displays a helpful hint describing the tool.

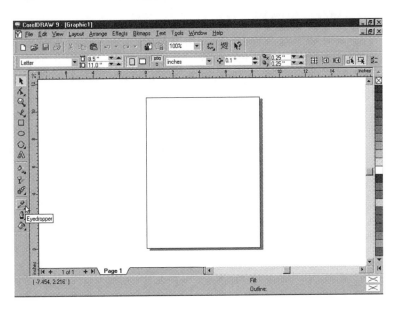

You will explore other tools in the toolbox in this hour, and by the time you complete this book, you will have explored them all. Some tools have a small arrow in the lower-left corner. If you hold your cursor down on these tools, *flyouts* appear, and you can transform these tools into other tools. You'll learn about flyout tools as you need them in later hours.

For your reference, Figure 1.6 shows all the tools in the toolbox. Don't bother to memorize them, please! You can bookmark this page or rely on ToolTips to find the tools you need.

FIGURE 1.6

Toolbox tools.

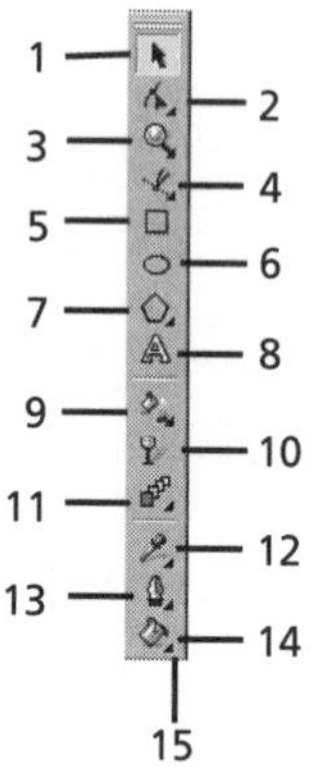

1. Pick tool
2. Shape tool
3. Zoom tool
4. Freehand tool
5. Rectangle tool
6. Ellipse tool
7. Polygon tool
8. Text tool

9. Interactive Fill tool
10. Interactive Transparency tool
11. Interactive Blend tool
12. Eyedropper
13. Outline tool
14. Fill tool
15. Clicking on the black arrow opens a flyout menu with even more options.

Drawing Straight Lines

Now that you've become acquainted with the CorelDRAW 9 toolbox, it's time to experiment with the most basic tool of the bunch: the Freehand tool. You can use this tool to draw designs or straight lines. First, you'll learn to draw straight lines. You'll experiment with using more complex lines to draw shapes in Hour 8, "Drawing and Editing Freehand Curves," of this book.

1.1: Creating Straight Lines

▼ To Do

To create a straight line, complete the following steps:

1. Select the Freehand tool from the toolbox.
2. Click anywhere in the Drawing page to begin your line.

Remember, the Drawing window is the whole work area in the middle of your CorelDRAW 9 window. The section of the Drawing window bounded by the shaded box is the Drawing page. Only objects on the Drawing page print, but because you are just experimenting now, feel free to draw anywhere in the Drawing window.

3. Click again somewhere else in the Drawing window to end your line.

When you click a second time, CorelDRAW draws a straight line from the point where you first clicked to the point where you last clicked. That's it. You've just drawn your first line.

Figure 1.7 shows a line selected, with eight handles appearing around the line. To deselect the line, click on the Pick tool and then click outside the handles. The Pick tool is the first one in the toolbox on the left side of the CorelDRAW window, and you can select it by clicking on it, or by pressing the spacebar.

FIGURE 1.7

Selected lines display handles.

These small black boxes represent handles.

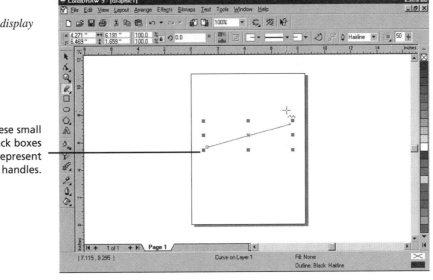

> You can delete a line by clicking on the Pick tool, selecting the line, and pressing the Delete key on your keyboard.

To draw vertical or horizontal lines, hold down the Ctrl key on your keyboard after you click. Your cursor will act as if it were magnetized. It will "stick" to a straight line. Click a second time and then release the Ctrl key to draw horizontal or vertical lines.

Use the Ctrl key technique to draw *crosshairs*, intersecting horizontal and vertical lines (see Figure 1.8).

FIGURE 1.8

Horizontal plus vertical lines.

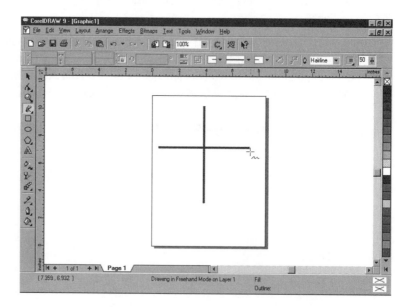

You can also draw lines at 15-degree-angle increments by holding down Ctrl. You'll notice, if you try to draw a slightly off-parallel line, CorelDRAW will "resist" your attempts to angle the line. But if you click once, hold down Ctrl, and then draw a diagonal line at an angle of about 15 degrees, CorelDRAW will *snap* your endpoint at exactly 15 degrees. Other snap points with Ctrl pressed down are at 30 degrees, 45 degrees, 60 degrees, and so on.

You can use the Ctrl key technique to draw parallel lines at different angles, all increments of 15 degrees. Figure 1.9 shows a set of lines rotated 15 degrees.

FIGURE 1.9

Drawing lines at 15 degree angles.

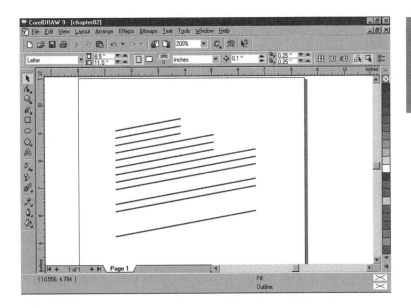

1

You can also draw segmented lines. *Segmented lines* are bent or zigzag lines. They are one object but consist of more than one line. You create segmented lines by clicking once to start the line, but then double-clicking at each node in the line. Each time you double-click, you create a new, attached line segment. You can end your zigzag line by clicking once.

Drawing Curved Lines

CorelDRAW has many options for drawing curved lines. Later in this book, you will spend an entire hour on generating symmetrical bézier curves (Hour 9, "Bézier Curves"), and another hour on editing curves (Hour 10, "Working with Shapes and Curves"). But the simplest way to draw a curve is to use the Freehand tool. With the Freehand tool selected, click and drag to draw a curved line. Release the mouse button when your curve is complete.

The faster you draw a curve, the smoother your curved line will be. In Hour 10, you will see how they are composed of at least two nodes, with curves connecting them. All you need to know to draw a curve is how to hold down your mouse button and draw a curve in the drawing area.

The advanced curve tools that you will explore in Hours 9 and 10 enable you to fine-tune the curves that you draw with the Freehand tool, so as you experiment with curved lines in the following To-Do exercise, don't worry about creating smooth, symmetrical curves.

1.2: Drawing Line Objects

Here's the routine for creating a drawing from lines:

1. Select the Freehand tool in the toolbox.
2. Click in the Drawing area.
3. Double-click on another spot in the Drawing area to create the first node for the object.
4. Double-click at the next node in the object.
5. Keep creating new nodes as needed.
6. Click once (instead of double-clicking) to create your last node.
7. Experiment with a curved line by holding down your mouse key and clicking and dragging to create a curve. Draw a curve quickly, and then draw it slowly. Notice how the curve you drew more slowly reflects your mouse motion in more detail.

If the final node in your line is on top of another node (such as the point where you started to draw your line), your line will become a *closed* object.

Figure 1.10 shows a shape created by drawing a number of lines with the Freehand tool. The shape on the top in Figure 1.10 is referred to as a *closed shape*.

FIGURE 1.10

Create closed objects by ending the last line segment on top of another node in the line.

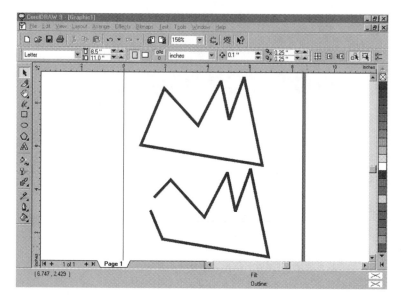

1

When you draw a line, or when you click with the Pick tool to select a line, the lines Property Bar appears under the Standard toolbar. If your line is not closed, you'll see the Auto-Close Curve button in the Property Bar. Clicking on this button closes any selected line objects.

Selecting Objects

The drawings you made with the Freehand tool are *objects*, or they are made up of many objects. You learned that you can delete any selected object by pressing Delete.

Sometimes, it's hard to tell how many distinct objects make up a drawing, let alone select them. When your Drawing window gets crowded, it can be hard to select an object using the Pick tool.

Selecting Objects with the Tab Key

One easy way to select objects is to select the Pick tool, or any shape tool, and then press the Tab key on your keyboard. Try this quick exercise to select objects using the Tab key.

▼ To Do 1.3: Selecting Objects with the Tab Key

1. Create at least three objects using the Freehand tool.
2. Press the spacebar to select the Pick tool. Then, press Tab. One of the objects is selected. You can tell because six black square *handles* appear around the object.
3. Press Tab again. Another object appears selected.
4. Try holding down Shift while you press Tab (Shift+Tab). This selects the previously selected object.

▲ 5. Press Tab until you have selected each object in the Drawing window.

Selecting Multiple Objects

With the Pick tool, you can select more than one object at a time. You can select multiple objects with the Pick tool in two easy ways: Use the Shift+click technique or draw a marquee.

To use the Shift+click technique, hold down Shift while you click with the Pick tool to select more than one object. You can continue to select as many objects as you have in your Drawing window this way. You can even deselect objects that have been selected by Shift-clicking on them.

You can also select more than one object at a time by using the Pick tool to draw a *marquee* (rectangle) around more than one object (see Figure 1.11). Only those objects that are *completely* encompassed by the marquee that you draw with the Pick tool will be selected.

FIGURE 1.11

You can select many objects at once by drawing a marquee around them with the Pick tool.

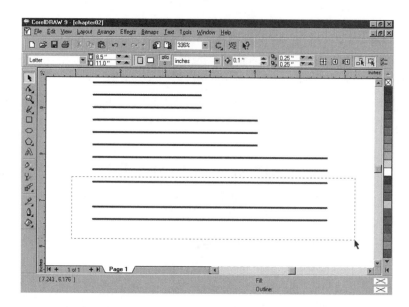

Sometimes, when you work with a complex drawing involving many objects, it becomes difficult to tell how many objects are selected. The status bar helps you by telling you exactly how many objects you selected. Figure 1.12 shows three objects selected.

Now that you know how to select objects, try this magic trick: Select all the objects on your Drawing window, and delete them by pressing Delete. If you created a masterpiece, select Edit, Undo Delete from the menu bar. If not, you have a nice clear screen and you're ready for Hour 2, "Creating Artistic Text." Selecting objects is helpful when you want to delete them. It will be even more useful when you learn to edit objects in the following hours.

You now have a good start with CorelDRAW. You created objects and learned your way around a bit. You're ready to start creating more complex shapes and objects.

Figure 1.12

*The status bar tells
you exactly how many
objects you have
selected.*

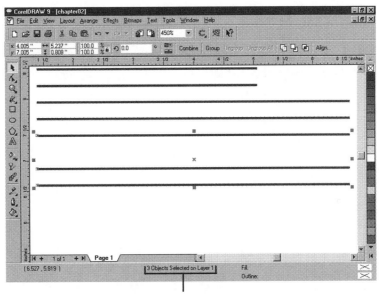

Three selected objects

Summary

CorelDRAW 9 is a powerful, yet easy-to-use, vector-based graphics program. Vector-drawing files save objects by calculating lines and curves. (You'll explore the difference between vector and bitmap-based graphic files in Hour 20, "Diving into PHOTO-PAINT," where you learn to use CorelDRAW's bitmap cousin, Corel PHOTO-PAINT.)

Vectors are objects with both magnitude (size) and direction (angles, curvature, and so on). The files that store CorelDRAW images consist of lists of lines, with information on their location, direction, length, color, and curves. The tools in the toolbox on the left of the Drawing area are used to create drawing objects. You can use the Freehand drawing tool to draw straight or angled lines, or even freehand shapes.

Lines consist of at least two nodes (one at the start, one at the end) and at least one segment. Lines can be drawn with multiple segments and nodes by double-clicking to add nodes and segments as you draw a line.

Workshop

Our resident artist, Paul Mikulecky, has provided a logo for a racetrack that you will learn to create in Hour 2 and Hour 3, "Working with Shapes." To start designing the logo, create a set of parallel horizontal lines. Then, for fun, experiment with drawing a cat using curved lines.

1. Start CorelDRAW 9 and open a new document by clicking on the New button in the toolbar, or by choosing File, New.

2. Draw a horizontal line. Draw several more horizontal lines of different lengths, but parallel to the first line.

3. Somewhere else on your page, practice your skills by drawing some zigzag lines. (Refer to the section "Drawing Lines" if you don't remember how to do this.)

4. Now, move to another place on your page and try re-creating the crude little cat shown in Figure 1.13. This will help you get up to speed at drawing line objects.

FIGURE 1.13

The cat is made mostly from a few curves; the parallel lines were drawn with the aid of the Ctrl key.

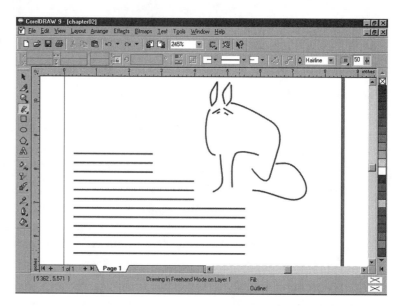

5. Save your file by choosing File, Save. You won't need this file for the workshops in the following hours, but when you reach the end of this book, you might want to go back and see how your drawings have improved.

After that, practice your skills by drawing zigzag lines. Try drawing a closed shape with lines (connected at a single start and finish node).

Take a stab at drawing a design made up of several lines segments, such as the crude little cat in Figure 1.13.

Quiz

The answers to the quiz can be found in Appendix A, "Quiz Answers."

1. How do you select a line?
2. How do you create a 15 degree angle line?
3. How can you tell whether an object is closed?
4. How do you create a closed object composed of straight lines?

HOUR 2

Creating Artistic Text

No program provides more control over the look and shape of text than CorelDRAW. You can edit, format, resize, or reshape text in CorelDRAW 9.

CorelDRAW defines text in two ways: paragraph text and artistic text. Paragraph text is better suited for editing long blocks of text. Artistic text offers you more freedom to assign artistic effects to letters. Later in this book, you'll explore CorelDRAW's array of wild effects and tools. In the process, you will learn to stretch text, twist text, fit it to a curve, and do all kinds of other crazy things. All these effects can be applied to artistic text, but many cannot be applied to paragraph text.

In this hour, you explore artistic text. You will create, edit, and format artistic text, and you will learn to stretch, reshape and resize text objects. You'll experiment with symbols, images that are available from special sets of fonts.

Working with Artistic Text

When you create artistic text, you create a graphic image that can be edited like any other graphic in CorelDRAW 9. You can easily resize or reshape artistic text, you can easily edit the graphical aspects, and you can easily edit the text content and format.

> CorelDRAW 9 also enables you to work with text as paragraph text. When you lay out an article or a substantial amount of text, you'll find it easier to edit that text if you work with it as paragraph text. See Hour 15, "Designing with Paragraph Text," for more information.

Use artistic text for smaller blocks of text. Icons, Web site banners, newsletter mastheads, and other text applications with few characters are ideal for artistic text. You can resize artistic text more easily than paragraph text.

Creating Artistic Text

When you click on the Text tool in the toolbox, you have two options. You can simply click and start typing, or you can drag to draw a text frame and then start typing. If you draw a text frame first and then enter text, as shown in Figure 2.1, your text will be defined as Paragraph text.

FIGURE 2.1

Drawing a text frame before entering text defines your text object as paragraph text.

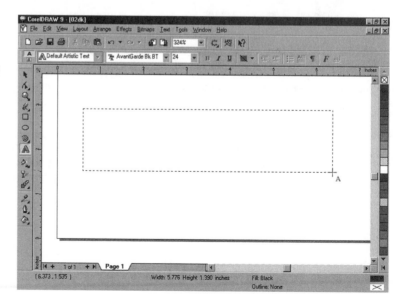

If you create paragraph text, you can convert it to artistic text by selecting the paragraph and choosing Text, Convert to Artistic Text from the menu.

The easiest way to start creating artistic text is to simply select the Text tool, click to place your insertion point in the Drawing page, and type. As you do, the Property Bar becomes theEditing Text Property Bar. Many of the tools in the Editing Text Property Bar are more useful for paragraph text than for artistic text, but some are used with artistic text as well.

After you finish typing text, click on the Pick tool, the arrow at the top of the toolbox. When you click on the Pick tool, your new text will be surrounded with eight small, square black handles. These handles activate whenever you select any object with the Pick tool and change the size and shape of a selected object.

> *Handles* indicate that an object such as artistic text is selected. When a text object is selected, you can change attributes assigned to that object, such as size, color, shape, or location.

The Text Property Bar

One way to change attributes for a selected object is using the Property Bar. When you select Artistic Text, the Text Property Bar becomes active.

The following table explains the Text Property Bar tools and lists.

TABLE 2.1   TEXT PROPERTY BAR TOOLS

Tool	Name	What It Does
	Object(s) Position	Identifies (or changes) the position of the object relative to the lower-left corner of the Drawing page, based on the center of the selected object. X is the horizontal location; Y is the vertical location.
	Object(s) Size	Identifies or changes the exact size of the selected object. X represents the width of the object; Y represents the height of the object.
	Scale Factor	Enables you to resize the height (Y) or width (X) of the selected object proportional to the current size. For example, changing the X setting to 200 doubles the size of the selected text object.

TABLE 2.1   CONTINUED

Tool	Name	What It Does
🔒	Non Proportional Sizing	When you select this button, size changes made to the x-axis Scale Factor spin box do not affect the y-axis, and vice versa.
0.0 °	Angle of Rotation	Identifies and enables you to change the angle to which the text object rotates. Ninety degrees will rotate the text 1/4 turn counterclockwise.
Mirror	Mirror Buttons	The top Mirror button flips the selected text horizontally; the bottom Mirror button flips the selected text vertically.
Courier New	Font List	This drop-down menu enables you to select fonts to apply to the selected text.
23.999	Font Size List	Assigns font sizes to selected text.
B	Bold	Assigns (or turns off) boldface for the selected text.
I	Italic	Assigns (or turns off) italic style for selected text.
<u>U</u>	Underline	Underlines the text in a selected text object.
F	Format Text	Opens the Format Text dialog box.
abl	Edit Text	Opens the Edit Text dialog box.
	Wrap Paragraph	TextEnables you to flow paragraph text around other text frames, including artistic text.
A	Convert Text	Converts selected text objects to paragraph text (or if they are already paragraph text, converts them back to artistic text).
O	Convert to Curves	When you convert text to curves, you can no longer edit it. However, you can edit the individual graphic objects separately.

The Text Property Bar enables you to apply all kinds of formatting to selected text objects. If you want to format individual characters (or words) within a text object, use the Format Text dialog box. Let's explore how to do this.

Formatting Text

You can change text font for an entire selected text object, or you can format only certain characters in an artistic text object.

◄ To Do

2.1: Formatting Text

1. Select a text object.

2. Click on the Text tool; an insertion point cursor appears. You can drag to select part or all of your text to apply new formatting.

3. After you select the text to which you want to apply formatting, pull down the Font List and select a new font. In Figure 2.2, I'm assigning Impact font to my selected text.

FIGURE 2.2

Assigning Impact font to selected text.

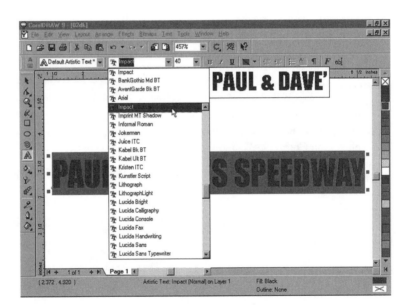

You can assign font size in the same way, by choosing a font size from the Font Size List drop-down menu. In Figure 2.3, I'm assigning a font size of 36 points to my selected text.

FIGURE 2.3

Assigning a font size of 36 points.

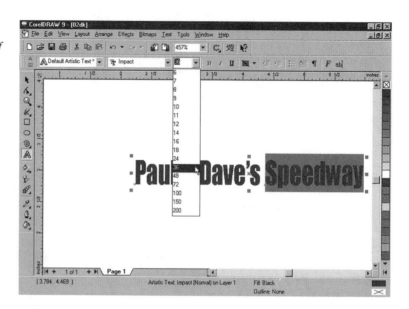

You can also resize and reshape selected text objects by dragging the handles. When you drag a handle in toward the center of the object, you make it smaller. When you drag out, away from the center, you make the object larger. This technique works with all selected objects in CorelDRAW and works with artistic text as well.

If you drag a corner handle, as in Figure 2.4, you maintain the proportion between height and width as you resize your object.

FIGURE 2.4

Resizing text using handles, keeping proportions unchanged.

If you drag on a side or top handle, you will change not only the size but also the shape (or proportions) of the text, as shown in Figure 2.5.

FIGURE 2.5

Changing text shape and size. Notice how the letters are getting wider.

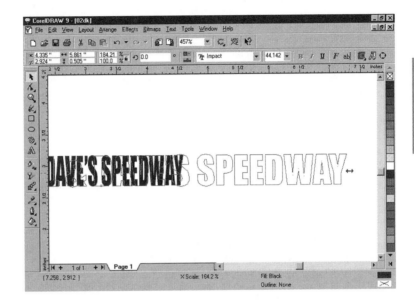

You can add (or remove) boldface, italics, or underlining to text using the Bold, Italic, or Underline button in the Text Property Bar. These attributes are not available for all fonts, because some fonts are designed to be specifically boldface or to have a light face.

The Format Text dialog box offers more detailed text formatting features. With your text object selected, click on the Format Text tool in the Property Bar or choose Text, Format Text from the menu bar. The Format Text dialog box has three tabs. The Font tab enables you to assign fonts and font sizes, as well as other font attributes, such as strikethrough, overscore, uppercase (including small caps), and superscript or subscript (available in the Position drop-down list). In Figure 2.6, I'm assigning small caps and a thin line overscore to my selected text.

FIGURE 2.6

Adding text formatting in the Format Text dialog box.

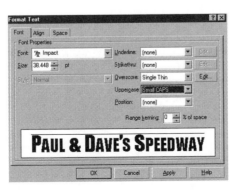

There are two other tabs in the Format Text dialog box. The Align tab provides the same options as the alignment buttons in the dialog box toolbar: None, Left, Center, Right, Full Justify (both margins, if you have enough text to look good, stretched margin to margin), and Force Justify. The Space tab enables you to define spacing between characters (letters), words, and lines in your text. You will often use these tabs to tweak paragraph text where you have many lines of text.

As you experiment with text formatting, you will see the font previewed in the small window at the bottom of the dialog box. When you are satisfied with the appearance of your text, click on the OK button.

Editing and Formatting Text Characters

You can edit text by clicking on the Text tool and then clicking in a text object. The vertical bar cursor represents the insertion point. You can press Delete or Backspace to delete text, or you can type new text at the insertion point.

For more heavy-duty text editing, you'll find the Edit Text dialog box more helpful. Open this dialog box for a selected text object by clicking on the Edit Text button in the Property Bar, or by selecting Text, Edit Text from the CorelDRAW 9 menu bar.

> Normally, when you edit images in CorelDRAW, you have your finger on your mouse, and it's rare that you'll take advantage of keyboard shortcuts. However, when editing text, keyboard shortcuts sometimes come in handy. We old-timers still use Ctrl+Shift+T to open this dialog box.

The Edit Text dialog box is a mini[nd]word processor in a window. You can insert or delete text here. Like many of the latest word processors, the Edit Text dialog box will even underline words not found in the dictionary with a wavy red line. You can instantly look up correct spellings by right-clicking a word, as shown in Figure 2.7.

Formatting Text Characters

You can apply text formatting by selecting all or part of the text in a text frame with the Text tool. An easy place to make text formatting changes is the Edit Text dialog box.

To apply formatting to selected characters within a text object, select those characters in the Edit Text dialog box, and then apply formatting. In Figure 2.8, I am changing the font size for selected characters only.

FIGURE 2.7

Editing and fixing spelling in the Edit Text dialog box.

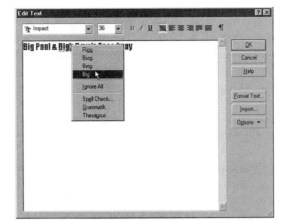

FIGURE 2.8

Selected text characters can be formatted in the Edit Text dialog box—my favorite shortcut to get there is Ctrl+Shift+T.

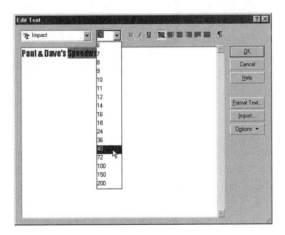

The Edit Text dialog box is not fully WYSIWYG (what you see is what you get). You have to click OK and view the results in the CorelDRAW window to see the exact effect of font attributes assigned to selected text.

If you want more power to assign detailed formatting to selected text, click on the Format Text button in the Edit Text dialog box. Font attributes assigned in this way will apply only to the selected text. When you have edited and assigned formatting to any text, click on OK in the Edit Text dialog box. The results will be visible in the CorelDRAW window.

Rotating, Sizing, and Locating Text

Earlier in this hour, you learned to size text by dragging object handles. That works. You can also move a selected object by dragging the X that appears in the middle of a selected object. In Figure 2.9, I'm dragging the selected text up the page. The cross-shaped cursor indicates the new location for the object.

FIGURE 2.9

Moving text.

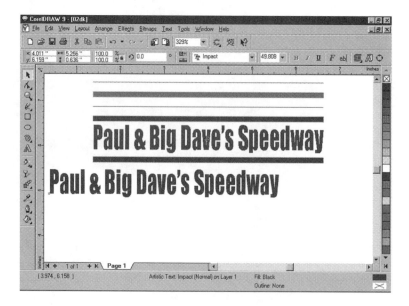

To rotate text, choose the Pick tool (the one at the top of the Toolbox) and click on an object twice. As you do, the handles change from small black squares to curved arrows, as shown in Figure 2.10.

Drag the rotation handles in a clockwise or counterclockwise direction to rotate the selected object.

You can also precisely define the size, location, and rotation using the Property Bar. To flip text to the left, enter 90 in the Rotation Angle box in the Property Bar. The results are illustrated in Figure 2.11. To flip text to the right, enter 270 in the Rotation Angle box.

FIGURE 2.10

Rotation handles indicate the text is ready to rotate.

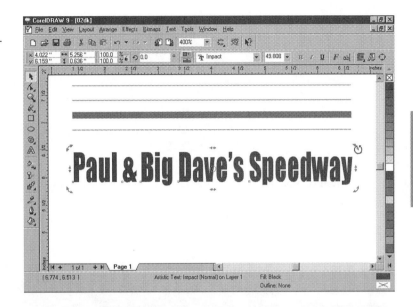

FIGURE 2.11

Text copied and rotated 90 degrees.

To create a copy of text, like that in Figure 2.11, simply select a text frame and press Ctrl+D to duplicate the selected object.

When you rotate text, you can edit or reformat it. It can get a little tricky to edit rotated text in the Drawing window, because the text editing cursor does not rotate with the text. You might find it easier to edit rotated text in the Format Text or Edit Text dialog boxes.

To precisely locate or size a text object, you can enter coordinates or dimensions in the Position or Size boxes in the Property Bar. In Figure 2.12, I have assigned a size of exactly 1 inch by 7 inches, and located the text object about 1 inch from the left side of the page, and 7 inches from the bottom. The location coordinates are defined from the center of the object.

FIGURE 2.12

Precisely sized, rotated, and located text.

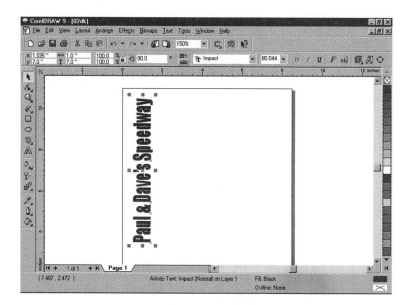

For quick, rough sizing and locating, use your mouse. For extremely precise sizing and locating, use the Property Bar.

Assigning Text Fill and Outline Color

Outline and fill colors can be assigned to an entire frame of artistic text, or to selected letters. To assign a fill color to text, either select an entire text frame or click and drag to choose characters. Then, click on a color in the color palette on the right side of the screen.

In Figure 2.13, I am assigning a 10% black fill to selected text.

FIGURE 2.13

Assigning a fill color to selected text.

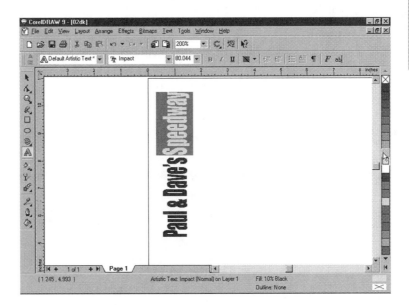

Outline colors are assigned to selected text by right-clicking a color in the color palette. You can create quick text effects by combining light-colored text fill colors with dark outline colors. Figure 2.14 shows text with a yellow fill and a black outline.

FIGURE 2.14

Combining light text fill colors with dark outline colors adds impact to text.

Managing Fonts with the Font Navigator

CorelDRAW 9 comes with a vast assortment of available fonts. These fonts are on the CorelDRAW 9 CD and can be added to your system using a utility provided by Corel called the Font Manager.

To add a font from the CorelDRAW 9 CD to your system, run the Bitstream Font Navigator program. You can find this program in the Productivity Tools group under the CorelDRAW 9 group.

As soon as you launch Bitsteam Font Navigator, the Font Navigator Wizard appears. Click the Next button in the wizard, and the second window allows you to navigate to the drive with your CD. Select the Fonts folder and then the Ttf (True Type fonts) folder. The Ttf folder has a series of folders named with the letters that begin the fonts they contain. So, for instance, if you want the Eras Bk BT font, open the E folder.

FIGURE 2.15

Finding fonts on the CorelDRAW 9 CD.

After you select a folder from which to install fonts, click the Finish button. The Font Manager opens an Installed Fonts window that shows how many fonts you currently have installed on your system. You can add fonts by dragging them from the Contents window (on the left) to the Installed Fonts window on the right.

> To preview what a font looks like, simply open the Font Navigator dialog box and in the Contents window, click on the name of the font you want to preview. The preview appears in the Font Sample window.

In Figure 2.16, I'm adding the Eras Contour font to my system.

FIGURE 2.16

Adding a font.

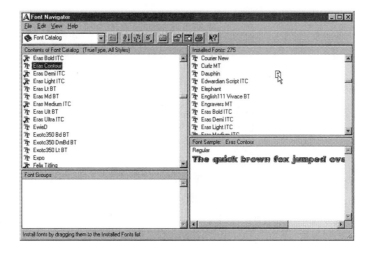

After you install additional fonts to your system, you can close the Font Navigator window.

Inserting Symbols

Fonts aren't just good for words. Many fonts come with a nice selection of symbols that you can use as quick and easy clip art. In fact, the large array of symbol characters provides the easiest way to add artwork to your illustration.

2.2: Inserting Symbols As Clip Art

1. To choose from selections of symbols, select Tools, Symbols and Special Characters from the menu bar.

2. Pull down the list of fonts in the Symbols window and select one. You'll have to experiment to find one with the symbol you want, but the Webdings and Wingdings character sets have dozens of useful images.

3. When you find the symbol you want, drag the symbol into the Desktop (see Figure 2.17).

FIGURE 2.17

Dragging a symbol onto the Desktop.

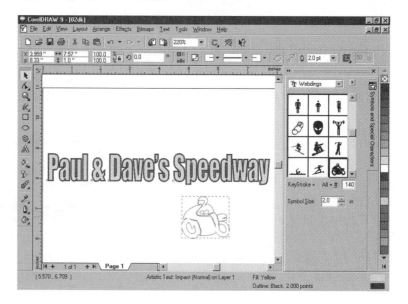

4. When you finish dragging symbols into the Dekstop, you can close the Symbols docking window by clicking on the Close Docker Group (X) button.

The Close buttons in docking windows are a bit different in appearance than conventional windows Close buttons. Why? Just to be unique! But they are the small X in the upper-right corner of the window.

As you have seen so far, artistic text can be sized, formatted, edited, and rotated. You can add fonts from CorelDRAW's large collection and use text characters as symbols.

Next, you will see what can be done when artistic text is combined with shapes.

Summary

Artistic text is easy to enter and can be edited at any time. Artistic text can have many of its attributes edited using the Text property bar. Property bars can be used to edit the size, location, rotation, and other features of artistic text.

Workshop

With this workshop, you'll begin re-creating a racetrack logo that Paul Mikulecky designed for us. To begin, open a new document and enter some artistic text naming a racetrack, as I have done in Figure 2.18. This text will be located at the bottom of the logo.

1. Select your text frame and press Ctrl+D to create a duplicate of the text frame. Rotate that text 90 degrees, and move the rotated text so that the two text frames meet in the lower-left corner of the logo, like the text you see in Figure 2.18. Refer to "Rotating, Sizing, and Locating Text" earlier in this hour for more information.

FIGURE 2.18

Rotating and moving copied text.

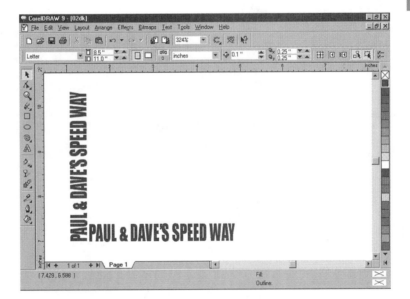

2. Assign a light color fill and a dark color outline to the rotated text. Stretch the original (unrotated) text so that it is about twice the height and width of the rotated text. Your drawing will look something like the one in Figure 2.19.

3. Review your line drawing skills by adding several parallel lines, and assign outline colors to each line by first selecting the line, then right-clicking on a color in the color palette. Your figure should look something like the one in Figure 2.20.

FIGURE **2.19**

FIGURE **2.19**

Text with a dark out-line color and a light-colored fill.

FIGURE **2.20**

Parallel lines added to the logo.

4. Select Tools, Symbols and Special Characters to open the Symbols Docker win-dow. Choose the Webdings set of fonts. Drag the hot motorcycle symbol (number 140) onto the Drawing page over the parallel lines and assign a light colored fill to the symbol(see Figure 2.21).

FIGURE 2.21

Dragging a symbol into the logo.

5. Save your file.

Be sure to save your file when you finish. You'll need it again in Hour 3, "Working with Shapes."

Quiz

The answers to the quiz are in Appendix A, "Quiz Answers."

1. How do you edit artistic text?
2. How do you rotate text?
3. What is a quick, easy way to access dozens of clip-art images?
4. What font attributes can you assign from the Font Property Bar?
5. How do you format individual text characters?

HOUR 3

Working with Shapes

CorelDRAW 9 has three different shape tools that you use to create ellipses (including circles), rectangles (including squares), polygons, and stars. Shapes have their own rules in CorelDRAW 9. In this hour, you'll learn to create and edit shapes, and you'll learn the basics of saving and printing files.

By combining artistic text with these shapes, you can create impressive designs. In Figure 3.1, our resident graphic designer Paul Mikulecky combined shapes with graphic text to complete the cover of *Window on the Arts* magazine. You'll be seeing more of Paul's work in the course of this book. Paul's cover combines techniques you've already learned (lines and artistic text) with shape techniques that you will learn in this hour.

FIGURE 3.1

*Our goal—create a
cover something like
Paul's.*

Although CorelDRAW 9 has a gazillion effects and combinations of effects, most
graphic designs boil down to combinations of shapes and text. The sizing, locating, and
rotation techniques you learned to apply to artistic text can be applied to shapes as well.
So, you've already learned much of what you need to know to work with shapes! All that
remains is to explore the specific shape tools and then experiment with line and fill
coloring.

Shapes are an underrated design tool. Figure 3.2 shows how Paul composed a magazine
cover relying on a few basic shapes, with a twist. The star, the arc, the grid, and the two
spirals were created with shape tools, as was the basic rectangle.

FIGURE 3.2

*Simple shapes are
powerful layout
elements, as are
complex shapes such
as stars and spirals.*

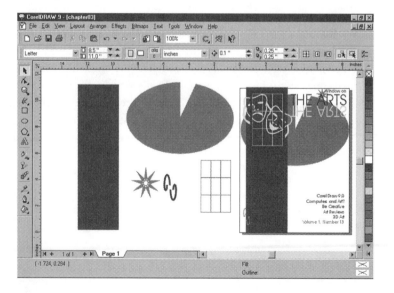

Working with Rectangles

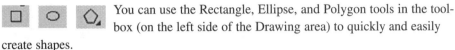 You can use the Rectangle, Ellipse, and Polygon tools in the tool-box (on the left side of the Drawing area) to quickly and easily create shapes.

To draw a rectangle, select the Rectangle tool, and then simply click and draw anywhere in the Drawing area. In Figure 3.3, I'm drawing a large rectangle on the Drawing page.

FIGURE 3.3

Drawing a rectangle.

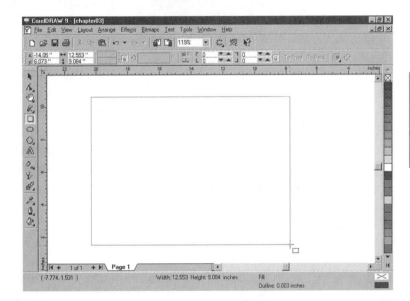

To draw a square, select the Rectangle tool in the toolbox but then hold down Ctrl as you drag. To draw a rectangle from the inside out that increases symmetrically as you draw, hold down the Shift key as you drag. You can draw a square from the inside by holding down both the Shift and Ctrl keys as you draw.

Creating Ellipses and Circles

To create an ellipse (also known as an oval), choose the Ellipse tool in the toolbox and drag. You can continue to refine the size and shape of your oval until you release the mouse button.

To draw a prefect circle, hold down Ctrl while you draw the ellipse. Figure 3.4 shows several rectangles and ellipses on the Drawing page.

FIGURE 3.4

Rectangles and
squares, ellipses, and
circles.

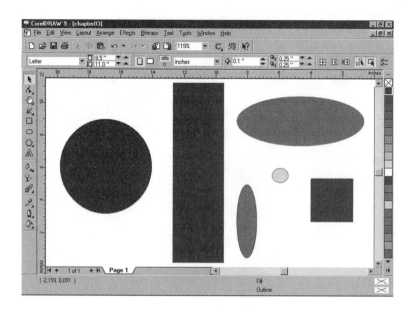

Drawing Polygons

The default shape for the Polygon tool is a pentagon: a five-sided object. To draw a pentagon, just click on the Polygon tool and drag to create the pentagon. In Figure 3.5 I'm drawing a pentagon in the Drawing page.

FIGURE 3.5

This is probably how
someone invented
baseball.

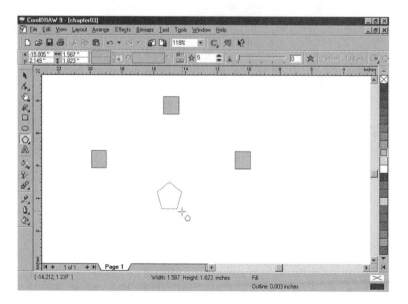

You can change the number of sides that you draw with the Polygon tool. If you define the polygon as a three-sided object, you'll draw triangles with it. The maximum number of sides a polygon can have assigned to it is 500, which is pretty much indistinguishable from an ellipse.

To change the number of sides assigned to the Polygon tool, right-click on the Polygon tool in the toolbox and choose Properties from the shortcut menu that appears. Then, in the Polygon tool area of the Options dialog box, enter a number of sides in the Number of Points/Sides spin box. In Figure 3.6, I'm defining an octagon by entering 8 in the spin box.

FIGURE 3.6

Octagons are useful for drawing stop signs and octopuses.

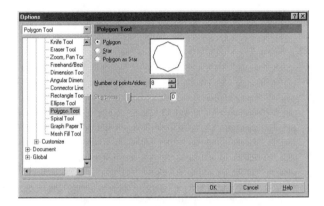

You can also use the Polygon tool to draw stars, or polygons as stars. The polygon-as-star feature is great for drawing five- or six-pointed stars, but you can also create amusing little objects. What do you suppose a 13-pointed polygon-as-star looks like? You can right-click on a polygon, select Properties from the context menu, and change a polygon into a Star (or vice versa) by using the option buttons in the Polygon tab of the Property dialog box.

3.1: Creating Stars

In this exercise, you will create a 13-point star.

1. Right-click on the Polygon tool in the toolbox and choose Properties from the shortcut menu.
2. Choose the Polygon as Star radio button in the Polygon tool area of the Options dialog box.
3. Enter 13 in the Number of Points/Sides spin box.
4. Experiment with the Sharpness slider. More sharpness means sharper points in stars. In Figure 3.7, I dragged the sharpness slider up to 85 to create a spindly, pointy-looking 13-point star.

FIGURE 3.7

Does anyone know the name of a 13-point star?

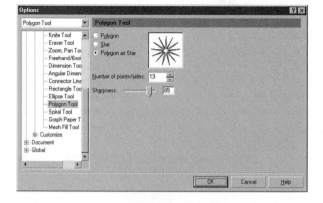

5. When you are through defining your polygon-as-star, select OK in the Options dialog box. Even though the Polygon tool still looks like a pentagon, don't be fooled. When you drag on the Drawing area, you will create the polygon or star you defined in the Options box.

In Figure 3.8, I'm drawing a 13-point polygon-as-star.

FIGURE 3.8

Drawing a 13-point polygon-as-star.

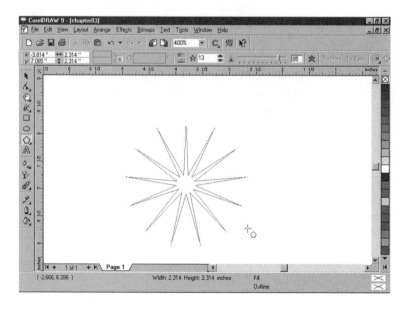

As with other shapes, you can constrain a polygon or star to an equal-sided shape by holding down the Ctrl key as you draw the shape. You can also draw the polygon or star symmetrically by holding down the Shift key as you draw.

Drawing Spirals

You may have noticed that the Polygon tool has a small arrow in the lower-right corner of the tool. That little arrow indicates that this tool is a *flyout,* meaning it can transform into other tools. The Polygon tool can be transformed into a tool that draws spirals or a tool that draws graph grids.

To activate the flyout, click on the Polygon tool and hold down the mouse key. As you do this, the flyout pops out revealing the other tools.

You will notice that *most* of the toolbox tools have flyout arrows. This is how CorelDRAW stashes dozens of tools in the toolbox.

Both the Spiral and the Graph tools can be adjusted by right-clicking on them and making changes in the Options dialog box.

You can define the number of spirals you want for your object in the Number of Revolutions spin box. You can also choose between symmetrical and logarithmic spirals by clicking on either of the two radio buttons. If you choose Logarithmic, each spiral increases its extension exponentially, as opposed to the smooth, even spirals created by symmetrical spirals. If you select the Logarithmic spiral radio button, you can use the Expansion slider to define just how far you want each spiral to extend. The default setting of 100 is the maximum expansion for each spiral. A minimum setting of 1 sets you back to a symmetrical spiral.

In Figure 3.9, I'm defining a Logarithmic spiral with 5 revolutions and a 50 setting on the Expansion slider.

When you use the Spiral tool, you can hold down Ctrl to force the spiral to conform to a circular shape, as shown in Figure 3.10. Circular spirals have evenly spaced spirals, whereas logarithmic spirals are more compressed inside and more expanded outside.

FIGURE 3.9

Defining a logarithmic spiral.

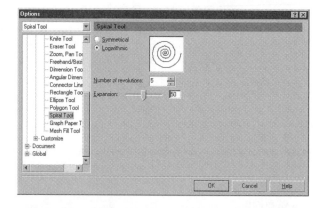

FIGURE 3.10

Drawing a circular logarithmic spiral.

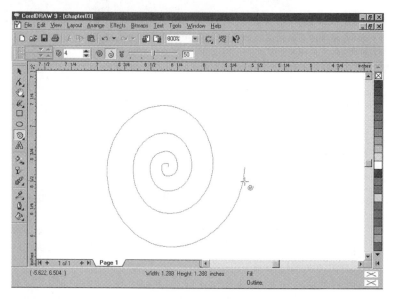

Drawing Graph Paper Grids

To draw graphic grids, select the Graph Paper tool from the flyout. Graph Paper options can be defined by right-clicking on the Graph Paper tool and choosing Properties from the shortcut menu. The Options dialog box enables you to define how many cells high and how many cells wide you want to draw with the Graph Paper tool. Figure 3.11 defines a 3-row-by-3-column Graph tool.

FIGURE 3.11

*Defining the Graph
Paper tool.*

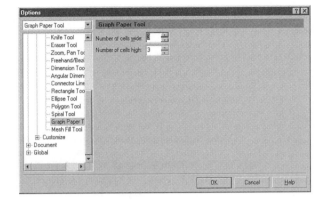

In Figure 3.12, I'm drawing a graph in the Drawing page.

3

FIGURE 3.12

Graphing.

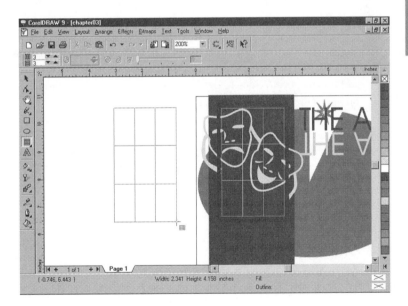

If you want to make your graph square, you can hold down Ctrl as you define the graph.

Editing Shapes

When you select a shape with the Pick tool, a corresponding Property Bar appears for the
shape. These Property Bars vary somewhat depending on which shape you select, but
most of the Property Bar options are the same for all shapes.

First, let's explore the common features that are in Property Bars for all shapes. Then we'll look at a few unique features that apply to either rectangles, ellipses, or polygons.

Figure 3.13 shows the Property Bar for a selected rectangle.

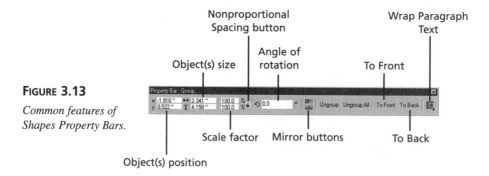

FIGURE 3.13

Common features of Shapes Property Bars.

The Object(s) position boxes enable you to define the exact location of the selected shape. You explored this same feature in Hour 2, "Creating Artistic Text," when you worked with artistic text. You can enter *x* values to define the distance from the left edge of the page, or *y* values to define the distance from the bottom of the page. Values correspond to the distances to the center of the selected object.

> The reason the ToolTip reads Object(s) instead of object is that Property Bar features can be applied to more than one object at a time if the objects are grouped. You can explore grouping in Hour 5, "Setting Up Page Layout," of this book.

Sizing Shapes

You can size a selected shape exactly by entering values in the x and y fields in the Object Size area of the Property Bar. This is similar to a feature you explored working with artistic text.

You can resize a selected shape by percent; just enter a value in the x or y boxes in the Property Bar's Scale Factor area. If the Nonproportional Spacing button is selected (pressed "in" on the Property Bar), changes that you make to one dimension will reflect in only that dimension. If the Nonproportional Spacing button is *not* selected, changes to one dimension will be reflected in the other dimension as well.

That can be a little confusing. Why didn't Corel just call it a Proportional Spacing button so we didn't have to try to sort out a bunch of double-negatives? Let's look at a couple of examples to make this more clear. In Figure 3.14, I have reduced the size of the middle circle 50% *without clicking on* the Nonproportional Spacing button in the Property Bar.

FIGURE 3.14

Reducing size proportionally and nonproportionally.

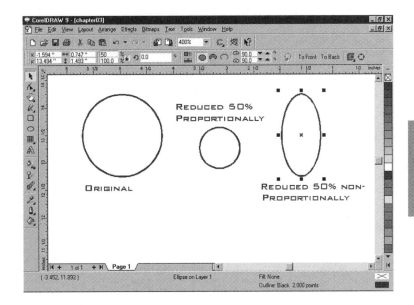

When you change size for the x axis in the Property Bar without clicking on the Nonproportional Spacing button, *both the x and y* sizing will shrink to 50% of the original. In other words, the change to the size of the selected object is proportional. The shape stays the same. Your circle becomes a smaller circle.

If you click on the Nonproportional Spacing button, only the x value (width) of your selected object changes, and you end up with an ellipse. Let's walk through an example using nonproportional spacing.

3.2: Resizing Shapes Without Maintaining Proportions

▼ To Do

In this exercise, you will change the size of shapes, distorting their proportions.

1. Select the object to be resized.

2. Make sure Nonproportional Spacing is selected (the button is pressed).

▲

3. Change the x scale value while leaving the y scale unchanged.

The object's width changes, but the height is the same.

Rotating Objects

You can rotate a single selected shape by clicking on it twice with the Pick tool and dragging on any of the six rotation handles. Or, you can rotate several selected shapes at once by using the Angle of Rotation area of the Property Bar. Just enter an angle of rotation and press Enter. The rotation angle will affect all selected shapes.

Mirroring rotates objects 180% horizontally or vertically. If you want to flip the selected shape horizontally, click on the top Mirror button. If you want to flip your shape vertically, flip on the bottom Mirror button. Mirroring is a useful tool for creating symmetrical designs. For example, Figure 3.15 shows a one-revolution, symmetric spiral that has been duplicated (Ctrl+D). The copy was mirrored both horizontally and vertically.

FIGURE 3.15

Creating a symbol using horizontal and vertical mirroring.

Moving Shapes from Front to Back

Shapes, like other objects, can be moved in front of or behind other objects. When you select a shape, the Shape Property Bar displays a To Front and To Back button.

The To Front and To Back buttons become essential as soon as you start to add fills to shapes and you move objects on top of each other. Figure 3.16 shows a Graph Paper shape being moved from behind a rectangle to a position in front of the rectangle.

You'll explore fills in the next section of this hour. For now, just note the To Front and To Back buttons. The Convert to Curves button transforms a shape into a curved line. You'll learn to work with curves in Hour 5, "Setting Up Page Layout," of this book.

Transforming Shapes

Rectangles, ellipses, and polygons can be transformed in unique ways. Rectangles can be rounded. Ellipses can be made into arcs. Polygons can be made into stars. These special transformations can be assigned by the different Property Bars that appear when you select a shape.

FIGURE 3.16

Moving a shape from back to front.

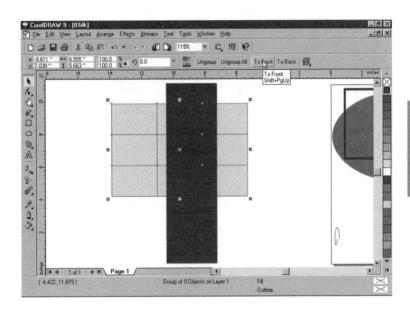

The Rectangle Corner Roundness sliders rounds off the corners on a selected rectangle. These rounded corners can have different radii defined for each corner.

If you select the Round Corners Together lock icon in the Property Bar, all corners will be rounded equally. If you deselect this icon, you can use the four corner roundness spin boxes to set different roundness specifications for different corners. In Figure 3.17, I've set the slider to 20 for the top- and bottom-left corners and 50 for the top- and bottom-right corners.

Upper-left corner roundness   Upper-right corner roundness

FIGURE 3.17

Rounding a square.

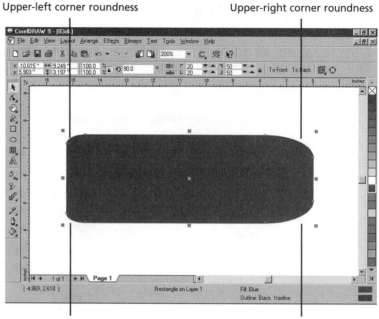

Lower-left corner roundness   Lower-right corner roundness

Ellipses, too, have a unique feature on their Property Bar. The Pie and Arc buttons transform ellipses to pies and arcs. These tools are visible only when an ellipse is selected and the Ellipse Property Bar is in view.

An arc is a pie, but not filled in, as shown in Figure 3.18.

You can define the radius of a pie or an arc using the Starting Angle spin box (the top one) and the Ending Angle spin box (the bottom one). In Figure 3.18, I defined a pie and an arc with a starting angle of 90 degrees and an ending angle of 75 degrees.

The unique Property Bar features for polygons enable you to change the number of points or sides and to transform a shape from a star to a polygon, or vice versa. In Figure 3.19, I used the Polygon/Star button to change my shape to a star.

FIGURE 3.18

Ellipses can be transformed into arcs or pies.

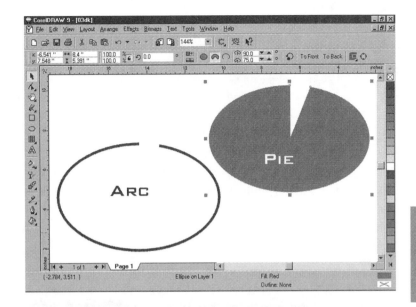

FIGURE 3.19

The Polygon Property Bar used to change a polygon into a filled star.

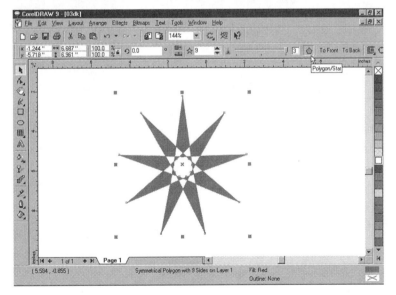

In this hour, you learned to create and edit one of the most useful and widely used objects in graphic design: shapes. Before ending this hour, let's take a look at how to assign color fills and outlines to these shapes.

Selecting Fill Colors from Palettes

The default CorelDRAW screen comes with a color palette on the right side of the Drawing area. This palette has a small down arrow at the bottom and an up arrow at the top. Clicking on the up and down arrows reveals more colors in your color palette. Or you can click on the small left-pointing arrow at the bottom of the palette to display the entire set of colors at once. You can shrink the color palette back to one column by clicking in the lower-right corner of the palette.

To apply a color from the color palette to the fill of a selected object, just click on the color. That's it! Experiment by filling your screen with some shapes and artistic text, and clicking on different fill colors. Figure 3.20 shows an expanded color palette.

FIGURE 3.20

An expanded color palette

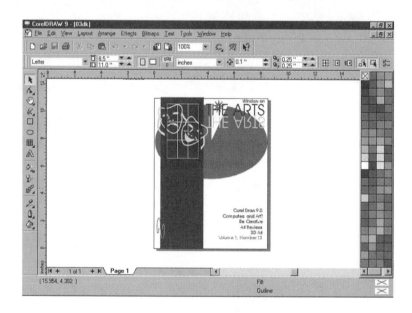

You'll explore different kinds of fills in detail in Hour 4, "Controlling the CorelDRAW 9 Environment," of this book, but you've already learned to apply color fills.

Selecting Outline Colors

Outline colors are assigned the same way you assign fill colors, except that you use your right mouse button. First, select the object to which you are assigning an outline color. Then, right-click on a color in the palette.

Experiment with different combinations of fills and outlines. Shapes can have both fill and outline colors assigned to it.

To assign *no* outline color to a selected object, right-click on the X in the color palette. To assign no fill color to a selected object, click on the X in the color palette. Of course, if you assign no fill and no outline color to an object, it will be invisible.

Were you wondering whether invisible text can be used for "reverse" white-on-black writing against a dark background? It's a good idea, but it doesn't work that way. Invisible text is really invisible, not white. So, if you want to place white text on top of a black shape, you need to assign a white line and/or fill to that text, not make it invisible.

Copying Shapes

You can copy a selected object (or objects) by choosing Edit, Duplicate from the menu bar or by pressing Ctrl+D. You can also use the Cut, Copy, and Paste tools on the Standard toolbar to cut, copy, or paste any selected object.

When you move (or copy) an object on top of another object, you can use the To Front or To Back buttons in the Property Bar to move the selected object on top of or behind other objects.

By adding fills and outlines to artistic text and shapes and layering one object on top of another, you can create sophisticated designs.

You might have noticed that next to Duplicate in the Edit menu is the menu command Edit, Clone. Cloning is different than duplicating, because the second (cloned) shape will reflect changes made to the original object.

Saving Your Drawing

CorelDRAW has powerful options for printing files and for saving them in various file formats. In fact, whole hours in this book are devoted to both printing and saving objects in other file formats. In Hour 10, "Working with Shapes and Curves," you'll explore exporting and printing options, and in Hour 19, "From CorelDRAW to the World Wide Web," you'll learn to convert CorelDRAW 9 objects into Web-compatible graphics.

Although converting CorelDRAW drawings to other file formats can be complex, and working with different printing environments can be tricky, it's easy to save files as CorelDRAW 9 files and print them on your printer. In the next sections , you'll learn to save files in the CorelDRAW format and to print them using your own printer.

Saving Files

You can save your entire workspace or just selected objects by selecting File, Save from the CorelDRAW 9 menu bar.

3.3: Save Your Entire Drawing

1. Select File, Save from the menu bar. If you are saving an already saved file under a new name, select File, Save As instead.

2. Use the Save In drop-down menu to navigate to the folder on your computer on network to which you want to save the file.

3. Enter a name for your file in the File Name area of the dialog box.

4. The Save As Type drop-down menu enables you to save your file in dozens of file formats. Saving your image to non–CorelDRAW 9 file formats may result in losing some of the attributes you assigned to images. If you need to save your drawing in another file format, it's safest to save it as a CorelDRAW 9 file as well.

5. If you click on the Selected Only check box, only the object(s) you selected with the Pick tool will be saved. You can explore selecting multiple objects with the Pick tool in Hour 2, "Creating Artistic Text," of this book.

6. If you click on Embed Fonts using TrueDoc, as shown in Figure 3.21, the fonts you used in your image will be saved along with your image. Choosing this option creates text that can be edited, even if the file is opened by a program or in a system without the included font.

FIGURE 3.21

Saving a CorelDRAW file with embedded fonts.

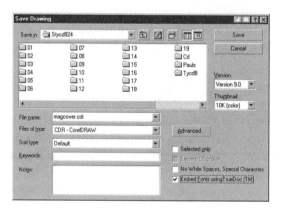

7. The Version drop-down menu enables you to save your file in older versions of CorelDRAW. The Thumbnail drop-down menu enables you to define what kind of thumbnail image you want to associate with your file. The thumbnail image is a

▼   small version of your file that will display in the File Open dialog box of many
           programs if you open the file applications other than CorelDRAW.

      8. After you define the name, location, and type of file, click on the Save button in
▲   the dialog box.

> You can ignore all the Save options and simply provide a filename. If you do
> that, your file will be saved as a CorelDRAW 9 file.

Printing Files

Printing a CorelDRAW file is as easy as clicking on the Print tool in the Standard
toolbar.

For more control over printing, choose File, Print from the menu. The General tab has all
the options you need to print your file on your installed printer. (You'll explore the other
options in Hour 18, "Printing.")

The radio buttons in the Print Range area of the Print dialog box enable you to choose
printing the entire file (the All radio button); the Current Page radio button prints only
the page on your screen. Use the Selection radio button if you selected an object with the
Pick button. You can use the Pages radio button to select which pages in a multipage file
you want to print.

When you have made these selections, click on OK in the Print dialog box to print
your file.

Summary

In the previous hour, you explored artistic text, and in this hour you explored using
shapes. Combining text and shapes creates unlimited options for illustrations, logos,
graphics, and publication design.

Fills and outline colors can be assigned from the color palette. Right-clicking on a color
assigns that color to the outline of a selected object. Clicking on a color assigns that
color to the fill of a selected object.

Each shape has an associated Property Bar. These Property Bars enable you to change
shapes and to move selected objects to the back of other objects.

Finally, in this Hour you learned to save your files, and to print them using your printer.

3

Workshop

The magazine cover Paul designed for us combines shapes, artistic text, fills, outlines, polygons, and symbols. Create a cover like Paul's.

1. Start with some artistic text; type THE ARTS. Duplicate the artistic text frame and mirror it vertically. Change the fill and outline colors for the duplicated text and align the two text frames as shown in Figure 3.22.

FIGURE 3.22

Mirrored text.

2. Add additional text above the text you just created for the magazine cover so that your design looks something like the text in Figure 3.23.

3. Draw a rectangle, place a graph paper grid on top of it, and add an arc to the page, as shown in Figure 3.24.

FIGURE 3.23

Text for the magazine cover.

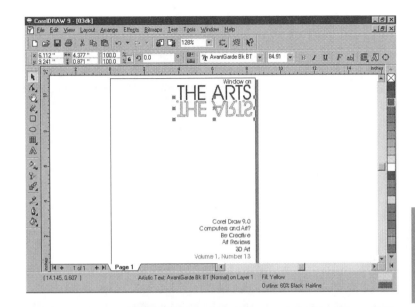

FIGURE 3.24

Using a rectangle, graph paper, and an arc as design objects.

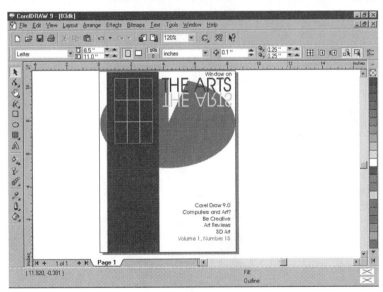

4. Create a nine-pointed star and two mirrored spirals to the page design, as shown in Figure 3.25. Move the star to near the top of the page and the mirrored spirals to the lower-left of the page, as shown in Figure 3.26.

FIGURE 3.25

Adding a nine-pointed star and mirrored spirals to the design.

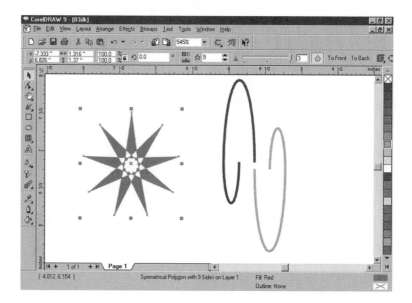

5. Use the Symbol Dockers to add the theater symbol, number 174 in the Webdings set.

6. Resize, experiment with fun fills, and move objects to the back as necessary, until your magazine cover looks something like Figure 3.26.

FIGURE 3.26

Magazine cover with rectangle, pie, graph paper, star, spiral, and artistic text.

This exercise gave you a chance to experiment with all kinds of shapes, including polygons and stars.

Quiz

The answers to the quiz are in Appendix A, "Quiz Answers."

1. The Shapes tool flyout enables you to create which additional shapes?
2. What shapes can you create with the Polygon tool?
3. What are the unique features of the Ellipse Property Bar?
4. How do you assign no outline to a selected shape?
5. How can you define different radii for the rounded corners in a single rectangle?

3

PART II

Orchestrating Your Illustration

Hour

Hour 4

Controlling the CorelDRAW 9 Environment

In Hour 1, "Dive In! Having Fun with CorelDRAW 9," of this book, you jumped right into CorelDRAW 9. You didn't need a detailed investigation into the program environment to create a wide array of text and shapes and combine them to make a fairly complex illustration.

As you continue to work with CorelDRAW, you'll find that the features that make CorelDRAW so powerful require you to customize and define the working environment. For example, if you create designs with dozens of objects, you might find working in Wireframe view faster and easier. If you create technical drawings, you'll want to use CorelDRAW's capability of attaching dimensions to objects. If you design graphics for a Web site, you might want to create a custom Drawing page the size of a typical monitor, defined in pixels, not inches. These are just a few examples of the wide-ranging changes you can make to CorelDRAW.

You can customize the basic look and feel of CorelDRAW 9 to serve your own specific design tasks. In this hour, you learn how to work with the Standard toolbar, place Docker windows, and work with the status bar and rollups.

Viewing Property Bars and Toolbars

CorelDRAW 9 has Property Bars, and toolbars, and a toolbox. The toolbar is directly under the menu bar, and it displays tools like New, Open, Save, Print, Copy, and Paste. You'll probably recognize most of these tools from other applications, and we'll introduce them as we need them. Property Bars appear under the toolbar, and they change depending on what you have selected I the Drawing window. Normally docked on the left side of the Drawing window is the toolbox, with it's own set of tools. The Pick tool is at the top of the toolbox. You've used the Shapes and Artistic Text tools as well. We'll explore additional tools in later hours.

The Standard toolbar is always available, but you can display additional toolbars as well.

Along with the Standard toolbar (and any other toolbar you elect to display), CorelDRAW 9 activates interactive Property Bars when you select different types of objects. For example, if you select a shape, the Shape Property Bar appears under the Standard toolbar. If you select a text frame, the Text Property Bar becomes active.

If you don't have any object selected, the No Selection Property Bar is displayed. This Property Bar controls page size and layout, and we will explore it in Hour 5, "Setting Up Page Layout."

In short, toolbars stay on the screen until you turn them off, and Property Bars appear or disappear depending on what object you select.

There will be times later in this book when you will view and move additional toolbars. In Hour 19, "From CorelDRAW to the World Wide Web," for example, you will use the Internet Objects toolbar. When that happens, I'll remind you how to view additional toolbars. But you can try it quickly right now just to familiarize yourself with the process of viewing and moving a toolbar.

Any toolbar can be displayed or hidden. And you can move toolbars onto the Drawing page, or dock them under the Standard toolbar. If you don't want the Property Bar to appear, right-click on it, and uncheck Property Bar from the context menu.

4.1: View, Dock, and Remove the Text Toolbar

1. Right-click in either the Standard toolbar or the current Property Bar. A list of toolbars appears.

2. Click on Text from the context menu, as shown in Figure 4.1.

FIGURE **4.1**

Opting to display the
Text toolbar in the
Options dialog box.

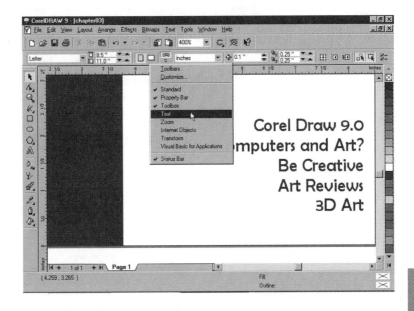

When you elect to display the Text toolbar, it appears on your screen whether or not you have selected any text. Use this configuration if you are planning to do a lot of text editing and want the Text toolbar (or Property Bar, which is basically the same thing) always available. Figure 4.2 shows the Text toolbar displayed on the screen, with some text selected.

3. You can dock the floating Text toolbar at the bottom of the screen by dragging it to the bottom of the CorelDRAW window and releasing the mouse button to dock the toolbar.

In Figure 4.3, I docked the Text toolbar below the Property Bar by moving it directly over the status bar. I'm using the Font Size List drop-down menu to choose a font size for selected text.

FIGURE 4.2

Formatting text with a floating Text toolbar.

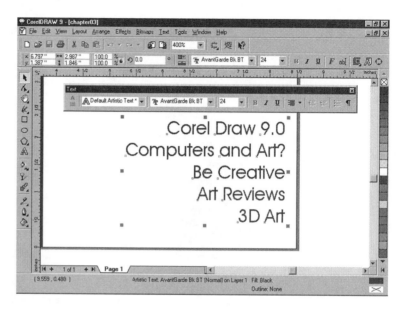

FIGURE 4.3

Formatting text with a docked Text toolbar.

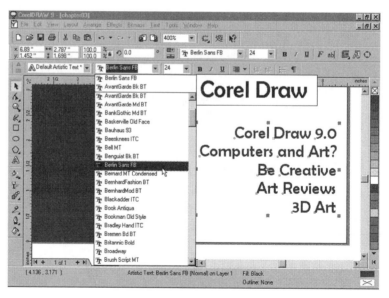

4. Remove the Text toolbar from your screen by right-clicking on the Property Bar and deselecting the Text from the list of open Property Bars.

If you display the Text toolbar and select some text on your screen, you might have astutely noticed that many of the features on the Text toolbar are already displayed on the Text Property Bar that displays automatically when you select a text object. And you might be asking yourself, "Isn't the Text toolbar a bit redundant?" I think so. In general, you will find that Property Bars provide easy access to the features you want to apply to a selected object, and that the default settings displaying the Standard toolbar, the Property Bar, and the status bar provide the cleanest environment in which to work.

To pull a docked toolbar onto the Drawing area, click on a section of the toolbar between tools (not on a tool) and drag the toolbar into the Drawing area. In Figure 4.4, I've dragged the Standard toolbar onto the Drawing area.

FIGURE 4.4

The Standard toolbar can float.

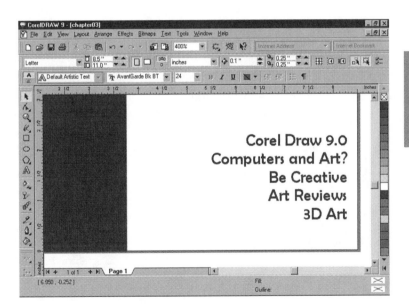

4

What's on the Standard Toolbar?

Many of the tools on the Standard toolbar are familiar to the user of any Windows program. Others are unique to CorelDRAW 9, and some activate features that will be explored later in this book. Table 4.1 identifies the tools on the Standard toolbar.

TABLE 4.1   THE STANDARD TOOLBAR

Tool	Tool Name	What It Does
	New	Opens a new file.
	Open	Activates the Open Drawing dialog box so you can open an existing file.
	Save	Resaves an already saved file, or opens the Save Drawing dialog box.
	Print	Opens the Print dialog box.
	Cut	Cuts selected objects and places them in the Clipboard, from which they can be pasted.
	Copy	Copies selected objects into the Clipboard.
	Paste	Pastes the contents of the Clipboard into the Drawing area.
	Undo	The icon undoes your last action; the drop-down list enables you to undo a series of actions.
	Redo	The icon redoes the last undone action; the drop-down list enables you to redo multiple undo actions.
	Import	Opens the Import dialog box from which you can import non-CorelDRAW files.

TABLE 4.1 CONTINUED

Tool	Tool Name	What It Does
	Export	Opens the Export dialog box, enabling you to export objects or files to other file formats.
100%	Zoom levels out on your drawing.	The drop-down list enables you to zoom in or
	Application Launcher	Enables you to start other Corel applications.
	Corel Graphics Community	Opens your default Web browser and connects to Corel's online graphics Web site.
	What's This?	Click and then point at components of the screen to get quick explanations of what the component does.

Working with Docker Windows

Docker windows provide another way to access features in CorelDRAW 9. In Hour 1, you used the Symbol Docker window to drag symbols from font lists onto the Drawing area. The Scrapbook, Script, and Present Docker windows are also useful. Before we examine them, let's explore how you can control Docker windows in general.

Managing Docker Windows

The Symbol Docker window you used in Hour 1 is great for pulling symbols onto your Drawing area. (To open the Symbol Docker window, select Tools, Symbols and Special Characters.) The problem is, it takes up about a third of your screen, reducing your work area. You can solve that problem by simply closing the Docker window. You do that by clicking on the small X in the upper-right corner of the window. In Figure 4.5, I am closing the Symbol Docker window.

FIGURE 4.5

Click on the X in the upper-right corner of the rollout to close the Symbol Docker window.

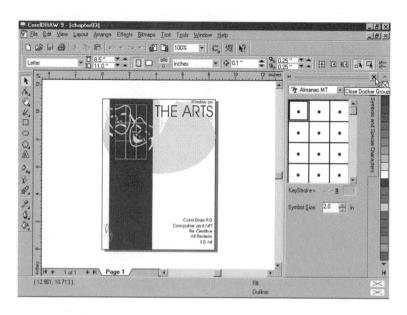

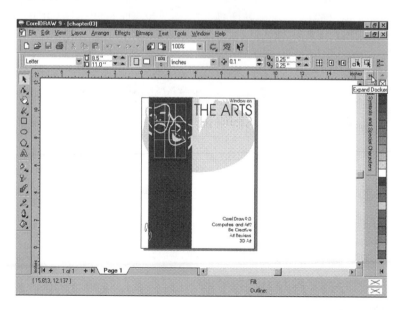

A less extreme solution is to shrink the Docker window by clicking on the two right arrows on the left side of the top of the Docker window.

When you shrink a Docker window, the window zips itself up into a vertical bar that you can reopen by clicking on the two left-pointing arrows at the top of the compacted window. In Figure 4.6, I am expanding a Docker window.

FIGURE 4.6

Expanding a compacted Docker window.

Using the Script and Preset Docker Window

The Script and Preset Docker window makes available a number of predefined wizards that, among other things, apply sets of effects to selected objects.

4.2: Apply Scripts

1. Draw or select an object in the Drawing window. In Figure 4.7, I'm working with the Webding character we used to create a logo in Hour 2, "Creating Artistic Text." (In the Webding character set, it is #140.)

2. Select Tools, Corel Script, Script and Present Manager from the toolbar.

In Figure 4.7, I've selected a symbol, and I am about to use a script to apply some effects to the symbol. Make sure your symbol (or other object) is selected before you run a script.

FIGURE 4.7

Getting ready to zap a symbol with a script.

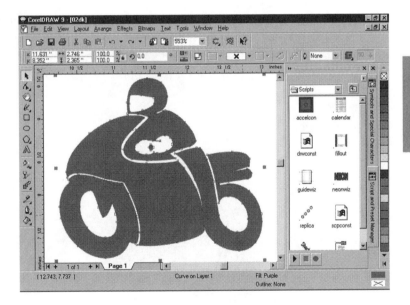

3. Double-click on the Scripts folder to see a selection of scripts. Scroll down the list and double-click on the Neonwiz icon in the Scripts Docker window. The Neon Effect Wizard dialog box appears. Click on Next.

4. In the first Wizard dialog box, just click on the Next button to keep the same color for your selected object.

▼   5. In the next Wizard dialog box, click on the Just the outline radio button to apply
        the effects to just the object outline, as shown in Figure 4.8. Then, click on Next
        again.

FIGURE 4.8

*Defining a wizard
effect.*

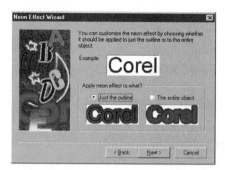

    6. In the final wizard dialog box, crank the Narrow-Wide slider all the way to the
        Narrow (left) end of the slidebar. When you have defined your Neon effect, click
        on the Finish button in the dialog box. Figure 4.9 shows the Neon effect applied to
        the symbol.

FIGURE 4.9

Neon effect in effect.

▲

Using the Scrapbook Docker Window

The CorelDRAW Scrapbook is something like a visual version of the Windows Explorer.
It enables you to pull objects off your system drives and into an open drawing. It also
enables you to drag objects off your drawing and into the Scrapbook.

To open the Scrapbook Docker window, select Tools, Scrapbook, Browse. In Figure 4.10, I am dragging a symbol off the Drawing page and into the Scrapbook, so I can find it and use it easily in other illustrations.

FIGURE 4.10

Placing a graphic object in the Scrapbook.

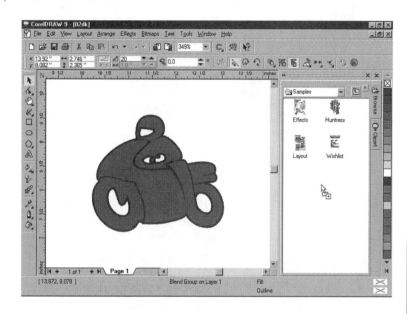

If you drag an object off the Drawing page into the Desktop, that object will save as part of your CorelDRAW file, and it will be available whenever you open and work in that file. However, objects saved in the Desktop (or on the Drawing page) are not available for use in *other* CorelDRAW files. If you place an object in the Scrapbook, it will be available there to drag back into *any* open CorelDRAW file.

The drop-down list at the top of the Scrapbook Docker window enables you to navigate your system drives and folders to find files. The tabs on the right side of the window help you sift through objects.

You rename files in the Scrapbook by right-clicking on the icon and choosing Rename from the shortcut menu. In Figure 4.11, I'm renaming the camera symbol I dragged into the Scrapbook and assigning the filename wildbug.cdr to that image.

Objects stored in the Scrapbook are easy to find and place in CorelDRAW designs. You can also import files, but the graphical interface of the Scrapbook makes it a handy way to manage files.

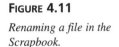

FIGURE **4.11**

Renaming a file in the Scrapbook.

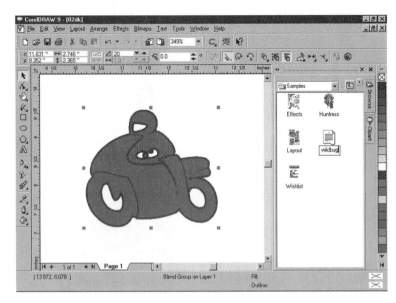

Interpreting the Status Bar

The status bar located underneath the Drawing area tells you a couple of important things about a selected object. The status bar tells you the type of object you have selected and the type of fill. In Figure 4.12, the status bar is advising me that the object I selected is a rectangle and that the fill color is yellow. That's not such big news if a yellow triangle is the only object in your illustration, but when your illustration involves hundreds of objects, the status bar is a handy way to tell exactly what object is selected.

The status bar also identifies the location of the cursor in x and y coordinates on the left side of the screen. The x value (the first one) represents the distance from the left edge of the Drawing page. The y value (the second one) represents the distance your cursor is from the bottom of the Drawing page.

Finally, the status bar tells you what layer you are working with. Complex CorelDRAW files can have more than one layer. Layers are explored in detail in Hour 16, "Managing Layers and Pages," of this book.

FIGURE 4.12

Selecting a yellow rectangle.

Defining Default Outline and Fill Settings

You can define default settings for outlines and fills by choosing attributes from the outline or fill flyouts. We'll explore those specific attributes in more detail in the Hour 6, "Defining Outlines," and Hour 6, "Mixing Up Fills." But you should understand how outline and fill defaults are defined.

The trick is to select an outline or fill attribute with *no object selected.* For example, with no object selected, click on a color in the color palette. You'll see a dialog box like the one in Figure 4.13. This dialog box enables you to set the selected fill as the default color for graphics, artistic text, paragraph text, or any combination of these.

You can assign a default outline color the same way. With no objects selected in the desktop, right-click on a color in the color palette and define which kinds of objects for which this color will be applied by default.

FIGURE **4.13**

Assigning a default fill color for graphics.

Finally, you can define a default outline thickness by selecting a thickness from the Outline tool flyout, as shown in Figure 4.14. Here, again, if you have not selected any object when you choose an outline thickness, you can define that thickness to serve as the default for graphics, artistic text, or paragraph text.

FIGURE **4.14**

Defining outline thickness.

Summary

With CorelDRAW 9, the folks at Corel have begun to streamline the interface. Even so, the DRAW environment can be somewhat overwhelming. There are at least three ways to apply many effects to objects: the menu bar, the toolbar, and the Property Bar. As you experiment with CorelDRAW, you will settle on ways you like to assign properties to objects. You'll find the Property Bar is a useful jack-of-all-trades that enables you to define the properties you use most frequently to edit objects.

Other powerful features of CoreDRAW are stored in various docker windows, including the Scripts docker, with its built-in array of effects.

Finally, in this hour you learned to define default fill colors, outline colors, and outline widths.

Workshop

In this workshop, you will use your new environment-control skills to look at a drawing in different ways.

1. Open the logo you designed in Hour 1. View your project with no toolbars or Property Bars displayed.

2. View both the Standard toolbar and the Property Bar.

3. Drag the toolbox to the right side of the Drawing area and dock it there.

4. Organize your workspace with the toolbox, toolbar, and Property Bar set in a way you want to work with them.

5. Apply a script effect (such as shadow or Neonwiz) to the symbol used for the logo.

6. Save the juiced-up symbol to the Scrapbook.

Quiz

Answers to the quiz are in Appendix A, "Quiz Answers."

1. Where can you save objects that you want to be able to quickly get to in any publication?

2. What button on the toolbar cancels your most recent action(s)?

3. How do you close those Docker windows?

4. What does the x value in the status bar represent?

4

Hour 5

Setting Up Page Layout

CorelDRAW can be all things to all folks. Laying out a tabloid newspaper? a magazine? a fanfold brochure? a business card? a Web page? The page area can be all these things and more. CorelDRAW predefines many popular page sizes, and you can easily assign them to your project. You can custom-define others.

After you have defined your page, other layout tools help you work on it. Grids, guidelines, and the capability of snapping objects to grids or guide-lines are very handy features for laying out your design. In this hour, you learn how to define different sizes of page layout. You also learn to use guidelines, grids, and alignment features to place objects on your page. And, you learn to work more quickly by using less-detailed views when possible.

Defining Page Size

The easiest way to define your page size is to click on a blank part of the Drawing area. When you do, the Page Layout Property Bar becomes active. This Property Bar is also referred to as the No Selection Property Bar (because it is active when you don't select any object). You can use this Property Bar to define the size and orientation of your page, as well as many other attributes.

5.1: Define a Page Size

In this exercise, you'll define the size of a page.

1. Click anywhere except on an object.
2. Pull down the Paper Type/Size drop-down list from the Property Bar. In Figure 5.1, I am selecting a Photo Card–sized Drawing page.

FIGURE 5.1

Defining a Photo Card–sized page.

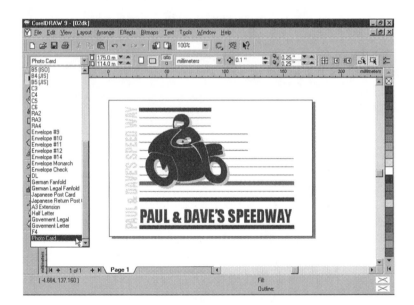

 You can manually define custom page sizes using the Paper Width and Height spin boxes in the Property Bar.

If you plan to use a custom page size quite a bit, you can define that page and include it in the list of predefined page sizes. Because I create many Web graphic images, I often define a custom page size fitted to a 640-by-480-pixel monitor screen.

5.2: Define a Custom Page Size to Fit a 640-Pixel–Wide Monitor Screen

In this exercise, you'll define a custom page sized to fit a VGA standard monitor screen.

1. Select Layout, Page Setup from the menu bar.
2. Double-click on Size in the left side of the Options dialog box.

▼   3. When the Size section of the Options dialog box becomes active, pull down the
       Paper list and select Custom.

    4. Select Pixels from the drop-down list of measurement options. In the Resolution
       drop-down list, select 72 as the resolution. This is the pixel/inch resolution of most
       monitors.

    5. Enter 640 (pixels) in the width spin box, and 1000 (pixels) in the height spin box.
       The 1000-pixel height is an arbitrary decision on how long you want your Web
       page to be, but allows for a page that can be scrolled vertically. The small preview
       screen in the right half of the Size area of the dialog box displays a thumbnail of
       your page size. Figure 5.2 shows a Web screen being defined.

FIGURE 5.2

*Defining acustom page
size.*

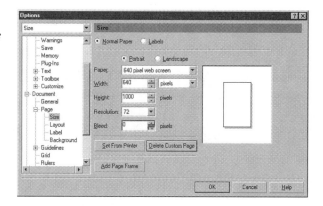

Another popular monitor resolution is 800 pixels wide. You can also create a
predefined page size for that screen resolution.

    6. After you define your custom page size, you can save that definition by clicking on
       the Save Custom Page button in the dialog box. Name your page definition. Then,
       click on OK in the Custom Page Type dialog box. In Figure 5.3, I have named my
       custom page 640 pixel web screen.

    In Figure 5.4, I'm selecting a custom-defined page size from the Paper Type/Size drop-
▼   down list.

FIGURE 5.3

Naming a custom page definition.

FIGURE 5.4

Applying a custom page size in the No Selection Property Bar.

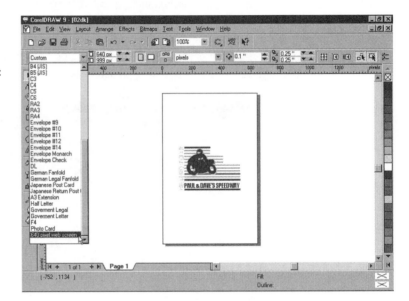

Defining Page Properties for More Than One Page

You can add pages to a publication by selecting Layout, Insert Page. The Insert Page dialog box opens, and you can define how many pages to insert and where you want them to appear. The Insert Page dialog box is shown in Figure 5.5.

FIGURE 5.5

Adding pages.

After you insert pages, you can move from page to page by clicking on the page tabs at the bottom of the CorelDRAW window. When you work with a publication with more than one page, you can either define properties such as page size for a selected page or for all pages.

The No Selection Property Bar in CorelDRAW 9 includes a button that enables you to define page size for *all* default pages or just the selected page. This button is relevant if you are working with a publication with many pages. If the button is depressed, DRAW will apply changes you make in the Property Bar to all pages that have not had specific formatting changes applied to them. If the button is not depressed, changes you make in the No Selection Property Bar apply only to the current page.

Customizing Your CorelDRAW 9 Page Layout

The Portrait and Landscape buttons in the Property Bar enable you to transform many page layouts from portrait (pages that are taller than they are wide) to landscape (pages that are wider than they are tall).

You can also select any unit of measurement for your page by pulling down the Drawing Units list (see Figure 5.6).

FIGURE 5.6

Selecting pixels as the unit of measurement.

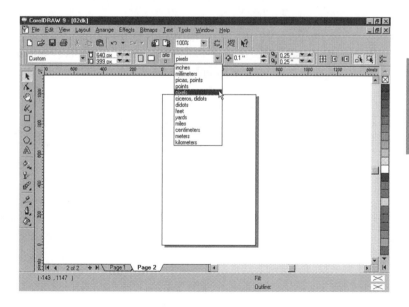

Defining Nudge and Duplicate Distance Properties

Nudging an object is a way to move it ever so slightly in one direction or another. You nudge objects by selecting them, and then using the up, down, right, or left cursor keys to move them.

The Nudge Offset box is found in the No Selection Property Bar that is active when no object is selected. The Nudge Offset defines how far a selected object moves when you nudge it by clicking on the right, left, up, or down arrows on your keyboard. If you set the distance to 1 inch, for example, you can choose any object with the Pick tool and press the down arrow on your keyboard, and that object moves 1 inch down. Exactly. Custom-defined nudge offsets can be a big time-saver. One scenario is that you have four rectangles sitting on top of each other and you want to space them 1 inch apart. A custom-defined nudge value makes this as easy as hitting the right arrow one, two, three, or four times.

The Duplicate Distance value boxes are also found on the No Selection Property Bar. These boxes define how much offset will be applied to a selected object when you duplicate it by pressing Ctrl+D, or by choosing Edit, Duplicate from the menu bar.

Setting duplication distance is handy when, for example, you want to create a bunch of duplicated squares, exactly an inch from each other. Once you set the duplication distance at an inch, you can simply press Ctrl+D to generate precisely placed duplicates.

Using Guidelines and Grids

Grids and guidelines work like invisible magnets on your screen and enable you to easily locate a selected object to a horizontal or vertical location, or both.

When you select View, Grid from the menu bar, dots appear on your screen. They won't print; they're only there as location points. When you click on the Snap to Grid button in the Page Property Bar, the grid coordinates act like magnets that attract the object you are moving. If you want to move an object to a location not on a grid coordinate, you'll find that difficult with Snap to Grid turned on.

The hotkey for toggling Snap to Grid on and off is Ctrl+Y.

Snap to Objects works in a similar way, but instead of grid coordinates, other objects act like magnets. When you click on the Snap to Objects button in the Page Property Bar, objects on your page attract the object you are moving.

Finally, you can place custom-defined guidelines on your page and use them as snap-to objects. To place a horizontal guideline, drag on the ruler on the top of the screen and drag down to a location on your page. In Figure 5.7, I am dragging the top ruler to the 10.5 inch mark on the vertical ruler to create a guideline there.

FIGURE 5.7

Defining a horizontal guideline.

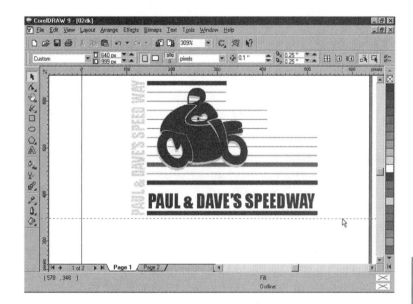

Vertical guidelines are created pretty much the same way horizontal ones are, except that you drag from the vertical ruler on the left side of the Drawing window to create them. Guidelines can be deleted just like other (printing) objects, simply select them, and press the Delete key.

5.3: Define a Vertical Guideline at Six Inches and Align a Rectangle at the Guideline

▼ To Do

In this exercise, you'll place a vertical guideline, and use it to align an object.

1. Drag on the ruler on the left side of the Drawing window, and pull it until the top of the ruler is aligned with the six-inch mark on the horizontal ruler on the top of the page.

2. Click on the Snap to Guidelines button in the Page Property Bar. This guideline acts as a magnetic border.

▼

5

▼   3. Draw a rectangle. Select that rectangle and drag it near the guideline you defined. Let the magnetic attraction of the guideline pull the right side of your rectangle right to the 6-inch point.

    4. Click on a blank part of the page to make the Page Property Bar active. Click again on the Snap to Guidelines button in the Page Property Bar.

You can remove guidelines from the Drawing area by selecting them with the Pick tool
▲   and pressing the Delete button.

Working with Views

You can zoom in and out in CorelDRAW, and you can use the Pan tool to drag parts of your drawing into the viewable window. The Zoom tool works as an interactive magnifying (or telescoping lens), enabling you to focus on a small part of your page or zoom out to see the entire Drawing area.

You can also control how you see and work with your page by selecting from five view quality options. CorelDRAW objects take quite a bit of system resources, and when you fill a screen with them, editing can slow to a crawl. Lower quality views can speed up that process. View quality settings from lowest to highest are Simple Wireframe, Wireframe, Draft, Normal, and Enhanced.

With CorelDRAW 9, Enhanced view has become the default view setting. Enhanced view does provide a cleaner, less grainier picture of your illustration, but it is also slower to reflect drawing changes than Normal view. Depending on your system resources and your demands, you can experiment with using Normal view. When you are working with illustrations that slow your screen resolution down to a crawl, work in Draft view, and even Wireframe view when possible. Fills are not visible in Wireframe view. Figure 5.8 shows an illustration in basic Wireframe view, revealing only outlines.

Zooming and Panning

You can select different zoom magnifications from the Zoom Levels drop-down list in the Standard toolbar. Or you can zoom in and out interactively by clicking on the Zoom tool in the toolbox and then clicking on a portion of your drawing that you want to magnify. You can zoom back out by pressing the F3 function key on your keyboard.

You can also define zoom level by choosing the Zoom tool and right-clicking on the Drawing area. The shortcut menu that appears provides a list of zoom options. In Figure 5.9, I am using the Zoom tool to zero in on my symbol.

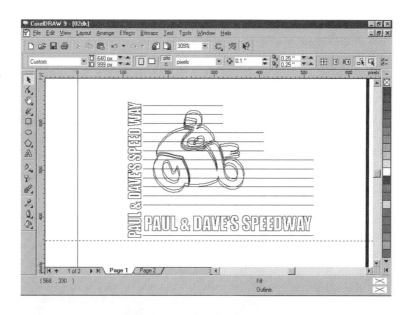

FIGURE 5.8

*Saving system
resources by viewing
an illustration in wire-
frame view.*

FIGURE 5.9

Zooming in.

The Zoom tool is a flyout, and when you click on it and hold down the mouse button,
you can choose between the Zoom tool and the Pan tool.

The Pan tool enables you to click on a section of an image and drag that section of the
image into view. The Pan and Zoom tools have no effect on the actual appearance of

your finished image; they simply enable you to view your image from different perspectives. The Pan tool cursor looks like a hand, and the Zoom tool cursor looks like a magnifying glass.

In Figure 5.10, I'm using the Pan tool to drag the symbol into the center of my screen.

FIGURE 5.10

Using the Pan tool to drag a symbol into the center of the screen.

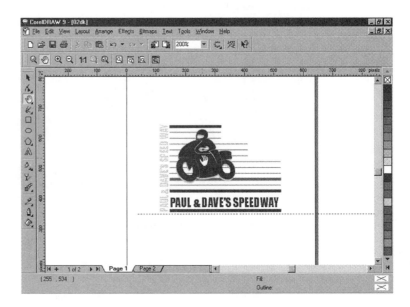

Controlling Objects

You learned to control many properties of a selected object: size, fill, outline, location, rotation, and more. Now it's time to learn to control the attributes of more than one object at a time.

With CorelDRAW, you can select and edit many objects at once. You can temporarily bind objects together as a Group and edit them collectively. CorelDRAW also makes it easy to define the relationships between objects; they can be aligned with each other in a variety of ways.

Selecting Multiple Objects

The first step in editing many objects at once is to select more than one object. In Hour 1, "Dive In! Having Fun with CorelDRAW 9," you learned to select a single object by choosing the Pick tool from the toolbox and clicking on an object you want to select.

To select more than one object, you can click on the Pick tool and then draw a marquee around a number of objects you want to select. Or you can hold down Shift while you click on more than one object. In Figure 5.11, I am selecting two symbols at once.

FIGURE **5.11**

Selecting two objects with the Pick tool.

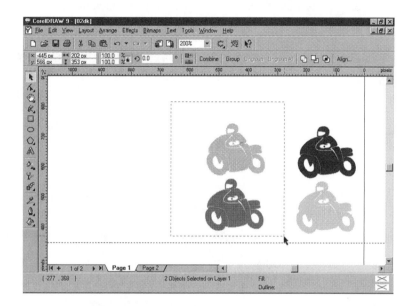

You can move, cut, copy, paste, and resize selected objects the same way you edit a single selected object. You can also select noncontiguous objects—objects that aren't touching each other. By selecting the Pick tool and holding down Shift, you can select any number of objects. In Figure 5.12, I selected the symbols in my illustration, and I'm dragging them to the right.

Grouping Objects

You can edit grouped objects the same way you edit groups of selected objects. But the advantage of grouping is that the objects appear as one, and you don't need to select them each time you want to edit them as a group.

To group objects, first select them. Then choose Arrange, Group from the menu bar. You can ungroup objects by clicking on the grouped objects with the Pick tool and choosing Arrange, Ungroup.

Grouped objects can be rotated, resized, and moved like a single object. Earlier in this hour, you examined the Mirror buttons in the Standard toolbar that are available to any

selected object(s). You can also flip objects vertically and horizontally by dragging a
side or top handle past the opposite side. This is easier to show than explain. In Figure
5.13, I dragged the left handle of the middle grouped object to the right, past the right
edge of the object. The result, displayed as a dotted line while I drag, is an object that is
not only resized but horizontally flipped.

FIGURE 5.12

*Moving two selected
objects.*

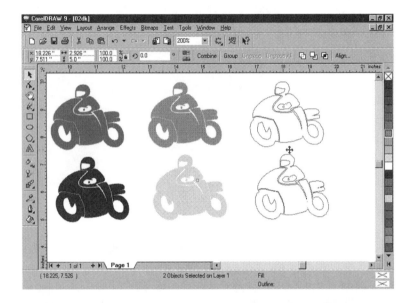

FIGURE 5.13

*Flipping while resizing
grouped objects.*

Combining Objects

Combining objects is different from grouping them, even though the terms sound similar. Grouping enables you to work with several objects at once. But the simple act of grouping objects does not change them. That's not true when you combine objects.

Combining objects actually transforms the objects that are combined, as you can see in Figure 5.14. You combine objects by selecting them with the Pick tool and choosing Arrange, Combine from the menu bar. Combined objects can be broken apart (Arrange, Break Apart). However, the objects do not revert to their original shape and fill but retain changes made when they were combined. Use combining for effect, but not to temporarily join objects.

Figure 5.14 shows two objects grouped, combined, and welded.

FIGURE 5.14

Grouping versus combining versus welding.

Grouped   Combined   Welded

Welding

Welding is the most drastic way to join objects. The welded objects take on the outline and fill of the object that was selected last. Welded objects can revert to their original individual objects only by using the Undo button (or selecting Edit, Undo).

Aligning Objects

CorelDRAW 9 offers an almost unlimited array of alignment options for selected objects. How about aligning objects on their centers? No problem, as you can see in Figure 5.15.

To align objects to their centers, select all the objects with the Pick tool, and then choose Arrange, Align and Distribute from the menu bar. In the Align and Distribute dialog box, choose both Center check boxes, as shown in Figure 5.16. By selecting the Center of Page check box, you can align all selected objects in the middle of the page. The Distribute option evenly spreads out the selected objects, either within the total space occupied by the objects, or to fill the entire page.

5

FIGURE **5.15**

Aligned centers.

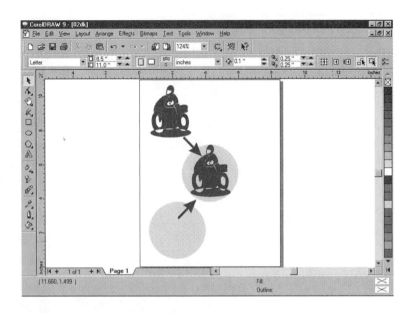

FIGURE **5.16**

Centering horizontally and vertically, and in the middle of a page.

Click OK in the Align and Distribute dialog box to apply the alignment to your selected objects.

You can also align objects by their tops, bottoms, right, or left edges. And you can have CorelDRAW automatically create equal spacing between selected objects. To align objects by their tops, space them evenly, and place them in the center of your page, follow these steps:

1. Select all the objects with the Pick tool.

2. Choose Arrange, Align and Distribute from the menu bar.

3. Click on the Center of Page check box.

4. Click on the Top check box on the left side of the Align tab of the Align and Distribute dialog box.

5. Click on the Distribute tab and click on the Spacing check box in the right/top section of the tab. Click on the Extent of Page radio button in the Distribute section of the dialog box to distribute the objects across the page.

6. When you have defined alignment and distribution settings, click on OK . All your selected objects should now be aligned by their tops, spaced evenly, and placed in the center of your page.

Summary

In this hour, you learned to control both the page layout settings for CorelDRAW, and also to control objects on your page.

Page layout settings can range from envelopes to Web sites. If CorelDRAW does not have a setting for your publication, you can define a custom setting.

All of DRAW's toolbars can be displayed or hidden. Property Bars appear on cue when you select objects on your page. When no object is selected, the No Selection Property Bar enables you to define page layout.

You can edit and work with multiple objects by grouping, combining, or welding them. And you can use DRAW's Align and Distribute dialog box to arrange objects in relation to each other.

Workshop

In this workshop, you open the logo you have been working on in previous hours. You zoom in on, and edit, different objects within the illustration.

1. Open the CorelDRAW file with the logo you have worked on in earlier hours.

2. Switch to Wireframe view. Try Normal view. Continue to work in Normal view.

3. Zoom in on the center of your drawing. Use the Pan tool to move the drawing around on the screen so that you can see the lion in the middle of your illustration.

4. Create a circle, about the size of the symbol in your illustration.

5. Select both the symbol and the circle.

6. Align both the symbol and the circle in the center of your page.

7. Save your file.

You just practiced viewing your drawing using both Wireframe and Draft views, and you used Align tools to arrange objects on your page.

5

Quiz

Answers to the quiz questions are in Appendix A, "Quiz Answers."

1. How do you select more than one object if you cannot draw a marquee around them?

2. How do you select a page size?

3. How do you delete a guideline?

4. Name two ways to align the tops of objects.

HOUR 6

Defining Outlines

In Hour 1, "Dive In! Having Fun with CorelDRAW 9," you discovered the quick and easy way to assign or change the color of the outline of any selected object(s). Just choose the Pick tool to select the object(s) and then right-click on the color palette to assign an outline color.

Ah, but there's so much more! CorelDRAW 9 provides a nice supply of outline styles, such as thick and thin, dashed and dotted. In Figure 6.1, our resident artist Paul Mikulecky from Electronic Design Studio has taken an eye created from an arc and altered it with four different outlines. Each outline gives the eye a different look, and the outlined eyes combine for their own composite effect.

FIGURE **6.1**

Applying outlines.

Figure 6.2 zooms in on the eyes to show off a couple of the techniques Paul applied. You can see that one eye has a thick unbroken line, contrasting with a thin dashed outline on the other eye.

FIGURE **6.2**

The eye outfitted with contrasting outlines.

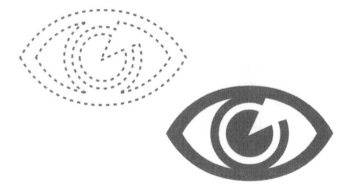

Now that you have a taste of what outlines can do, it's time to dive in and examine how to apply these effects. This hour shows you how to create various outlines as well as to set default outline styles.

Creating Outlines

You can assign outline styles in several ways in CorelDRAW 9. You can define outlines quickly from a flyout or in more detail from the Property Bar.

The most detailed control over your outline thickness and style is available in the Outline Pen dialog box, which is available from the Outline Tool flyout.

Defining Outline Width from the Outline Flyout

The quickest way to assign an outline width to a selected object (or objects) is to click on the Outline tool in the toolbox and choose from one of the preset widths. The options are hairline, 2 points, 8 points, 16 points, or 24 points (the widest).

◄ To Do 6.1: Assign an 8-Point Outline to a Rectangle

In this exercise, you assign a medium thickness outline to a selected object.

1. Draw a rectangle.
2. Click on the Pick tool. The rectangle is still selected.
3. Click on the Outline tool and click on the 8-point line—the one I'm selecting in Figure 6.3.

FIGURE 6.3

When you assign line widths from the Outline flyout, the line width is indicated in the status bar.

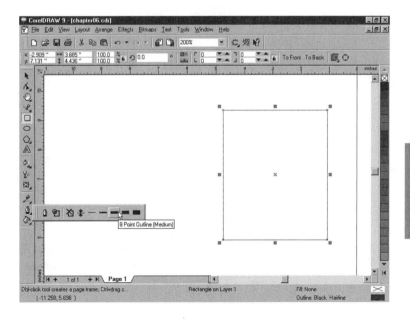

▲

6

Defining Outline Options with the Property Bar

The Property Bar that appears when you select a curve enables you to define several attributes of that object's outline. The Property Bar tools that define an outline are shown in Figure 6.4. They are

- The Start Arrowhead Selector drop-down palette defines the look of the arrow (if any) at the start of the curve.
- The Outline Style Selector drop-down palette defines the look of the outline, ranging from dashes and dots to solid lines.
- The End Arrowhead Selector drop-down palette defines the look of the arrow (again, if any) at the *end* of a curve.
- The Outline Width drop-down menu enables you to pick from a larger set of outline widths similar to those available in the Outline flyout.

FIGURE 6.4

Four tools in the Curve Property Bar enable you to fine-tune outlines.

Outline Width Selector
End Arrowhead Selector
Outline Style Selector

Start Arrowhead Selector

Using the Outline Pen Dialog Box

To micromanage outline details you never dreamed existed, use the Outline Pen dialog box. You can open the Outline Pen dialog box by choosing the dialog box from the Outline tool flyout (it is the first tool in the flyout). In Figure 6.5, I am selecting the Outline Pen dialog box

As an alternative to opening up the Outline Pen dialog box, you can right-click on an object and choose Properties from the shortcut menu. When you do, an Object Properties dialog box appears. Select the Outline tab.

This dialog box is a stripped-down version of the Outline Pen dialog box—kind of like "Outline Light." The advantage of the Object Properties dialog box is that it can sit on the Drawing window while you work, as shown in Figure 6.6. Combined with the Outline flyout, the outline features in the Curve Property Bar, and the Outline Properties dialog box, I think CorelDRAW has provided *at least enough* ways to define outline properties!

FIGURE 6.5

*Choosing the Outline
Pen dialog box from
the Pen flyout.*

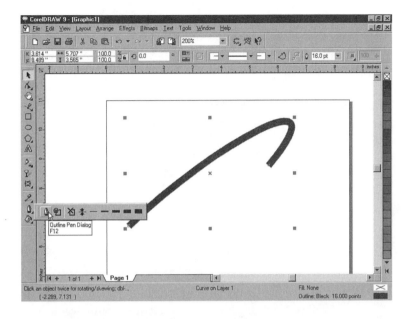

FIGURE 6.6

*Consider the Outline
tab in the Object
Properties dialog box
a stripped-down ver-
sion of the Outline Pen
dialog box.*

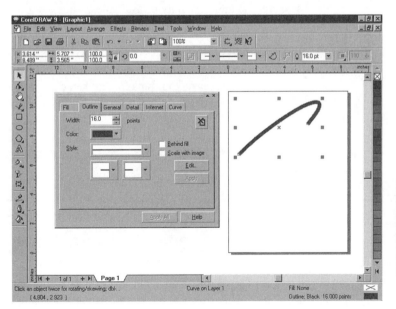

The larger Outline Pen Property Box is shown in Figure 6.7. It has all the features in the Outline tab of the Object Properties dialog box. After you explore the features in the larger Outline Pen dialog box, you can select some of those same features in the Object Properties dialog box.

FIGURE 6.7

The Outline Pen dialog box.

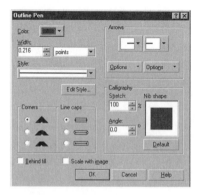

The Outline Pen dialog box provides minute control over line width (to 1/1000 of an inch!). There are also a wide variety of available dashed and dotted lines in the Outline Pen dialog box.

By clicking on the Edit Style button, beneath the Style drop-down menu in the dialog box, you open the Edit Line Style dialog box. Here, you pull on the I-beam cursor to define the number of squares in your pattern and then click on white squares to color them. In Figure 6.8, I have defined a dashed line style with eight squares, five of them darkened.

FIGURE 6.8

Defining a customized dashed line.

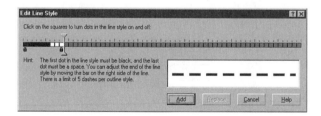

After you define a custom line style, click on the Add button in the Edit Line Style dialog box to add that custom style to the list of available line styles. You can then use that style at any time, in any CorelDRAW project, even if you don't save your image.

If you click on the Replace button in the Edit Line Style dialog, you'll immediately exit the dialog box and apply the defined line style to any selected object(s).

The Arrows section of the Outline Pen dialog box defines arrows assigned to the beginning or end of a curve. In Figure 6.9, I'm assigning an airplane as my arrow.

FIGURE 6.9

Assigning an arrow.

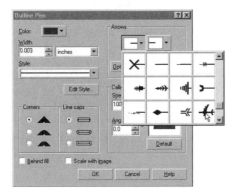

Not impressed? How about the fact that you can *edit* the look of these arrows? In Figure 6.10, I'm fine-tuning the airplane arrow by clicking on the Options button in the Outline Pen dialog box, and choosing Edit.

FIGURE 6.10

Editing an arrow.

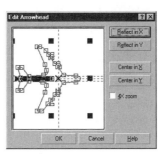

6

To demonstrate my custom-defined dotted line and arrow, I've proposed a new logo for the Fargo International Airport, in Figure 6.11.

FIGURE 6.11

Combining a customized outline with a customized arrow.

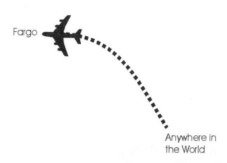

The Corners area of the Outline Pen dialog box enables you to assign a couple of variations of rounded corners. The Line Caps section of the dialog box defines the appearance of the ends of lines. The options are

- Square Line Caps
- Rounded Line caps
- Extended Square Line Caps

In Figure 6.12, I assigned (from top to bottom) square, rounded, and extended square line caps to the three arc ends, and rounded corners to the rectangle.

FIGURE 6.12

The three Line Cap options provide subtle control to the appearance of the ends of lines.

Square Line Caps

Rounded Line caps

Extended Square Line Caps

Adding line caps extends the length of lines. If you attach Line Cap options to dashed lines, you extend those lines and might ruin your dashes by filling in the spaces between them.

The Outline Pen dialog box also enables you to define three types of corners in the Corners area. The options are square, rounded, or beveled corners. I've illustrated all three in Figure 6.13.

FIGURE 6.13

Beveled, rounded, and square corners.

Other outline options include

- Calligraphy settings simulate the effect of tilting a marker at an angle to produce a thinner line.
- The Behind Fill checkbox moves an outline behind the filling in a filled shape.
- The Scale with Image checkbox causes an outline to get thicker or thinner as an object is resized to maintain a consistent relationship to the object.

Defining Default Outlines

You can set default outline attributes by defining outline properties in the Outline Pen dialog box with no object selected. When you do, the Outline Pen dialog box (like the one shown in Figure 6.14) presents you with three check boxes. These check boxes define what kinds of objects will be subjected to the outline you define. If you choose all three, the outline attributes you assign in the dialog box will apply to the outlines of every object you draw.

FIGURE 6.14

Choosing objects to which you will apply custom-defined default outline attributes.

6

One potential source of chaos is if you accidentally redefine outline defaults. It's easy to do. If you open the Outline Pen dialog box and define line attributes with no line selected, those attributes become the default settings for lines.

Summary

Outlines can be any thickness or color. You can define outline properties for any object in CorelDRAW 9. Outlines can be assigned from defined styles or created by customizing an outline style.

Workshop

In this workshop, you enhance the magazine cover you created in previous hours by adding outlines to the objects. To begin, open the document you worked on in the previous three hours.

1. Drag the Eye symbol out of the Webdings set (use Ctrl+F11 as a shortcut to view the Symbols Docker window), as shown in Figure 6.15.

FIGURE 6.15

Start the illustration with an eye symbol.

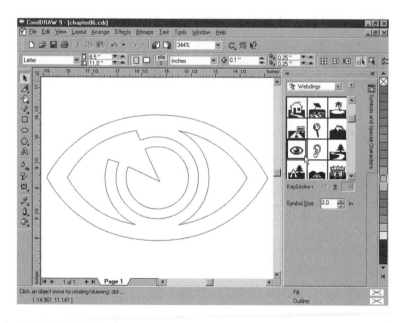

2. Duplicate the eye three times (Ctrl+D is the shortcut for duplicating a selected object).

3. Assign a dashed line outline style to the first symbol, a thin outline to the second copy of the eye, a thick line to the third eye, and a thin outline with a color fill to the last eye. Arrange the eyes something like the ones in Figure 6.16.

FIGURE 6.16

Eye outliners.

4. Draw a segmented line using the Freehand draw tool, double-clicking at each corner, to almost completely surround the eyes, as shown in Figure 6.17. (You learned to draw segmented lines in Hour 1.)

5. Tweak the outline by applying a thick outline, rounding the corners, and adding an arrow line ending.

FIGURE 6.17

The framing line has rounded corners, a thick outline, and an ending arrow.

6

6. Finish the illustration with some text and save the changes to your illustration.

Feel free to experiment with additional outline properties.

Quiz

Answers to the quiz questions are in Appendix A, "Quiz Answers."

1. How do you define a default outline?

2. How do you define an outline width to four decimal places?

3. Name five attributes that you can assign to an outline.

4. Does an object need an outline to be visible?

HOUR 7

Mixing Up Fills

CorelDRAW 9 enables you to assign five basic types of fills to any selected closed object:

- Uniform fills—Single color fills, although that single color can be applied
- Fountain fills—Fills that fade from one color to another, sometimes referred to as gradient fills
- Pattern fills—Fills made from bitmap or vector files
- Texture fills—Fills (that can be edited) made from bitmap image files
- PostScript fills—Fills that use the PostScript programming language to generate patterns

Pattern fills, Texture fills, and PostScript fills are used to create special, even spectacular effects. Most of the time, you will use Uniform fills to assign a single color or Fountain fills to assign colors that merge into each other.

I mentioned that you can apply fills to *closed* objects. What does that mean? A closed object is a shape—such as the ones you have worked with in the previous two hours (a rectangle, an oval, or a polygon)—or a free-form drawing with a continuous (connected) outline. You'll explore freehand drawing in the next hour in this book.

> One way to tell whether or not a curve is closed is by whether the Auto-Close Curve button is active in the Curve Property Bar. If the button is grayed out, that means the curve is already closed.

A Uniform color fill is Corel's way of describing a fill that consists of just one solid color, such as the one I applied to the world map in Figure 7.1.

FIGURE 7.1

A uniformly filled world.

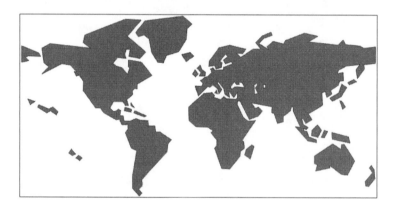

> I'm using another symbol from the Webdings set (#251) for the world map.

Fountain fills combine two colors that fade into each other within an object. There are different types of fountain fills, including linear fills that start with one color, and transform into another along a straight line, and radical fills that "radiate" out from one color to another. In Figure 7.2, the world is being filled with a Fountain fill that fades from a dark color in the upper-left corner of the object to a light color in the lower-right corner.

Figure 7.2

A Fountain-filled world.

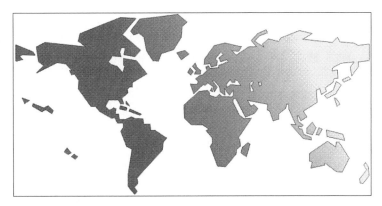

You can insert Pattern fills into an object from either bitmap graphic images or from vector images. Figure 7.3 shows both our Pattern-filled world and the graphic file that provided the fill.

Figure 7.3

A bitmap image used as a fill pattern.

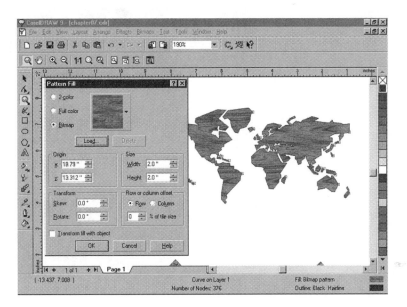

Texture fills are bitmap based fill patterns that can be selected from several lists of wild and trendy designs.

7

PostScript fills are fills-created patterns defined using the PostScript page-description language. These patterns can be viewed if the default Enhanced view is selected from the View drop-down menu in the Standard toolbar. Lower-quality views (such as Normal) allow CorelDRAW to work faster, but will not display PS fills.

Okay, you have a taste of what CorelDRAW fills can do; now you'll learn to apply them.

Uniform Color Fills

You already know how to assign a color to a selected object. You just click on the color in the color palette to the right of your Drawing area. If you work with a printer that requires you to select colors from a fixed-color palette, such as Pantone Matching System colors, you can assign those colors to your color palette by choosing Window, Color Palettes from the menu bar, and then choosing from the options for preset colors. Figure 7.4 shows the Color Palettes list.

FIGURE 7.4

The Color Palettes list.

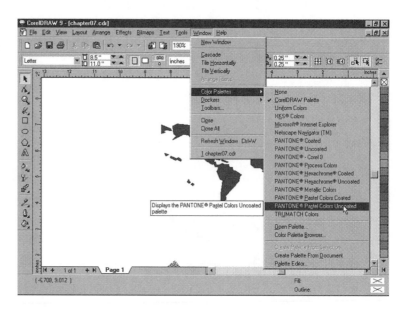

If you are not constrained to a fixed color palette, you can mix custom colors from the Uniform Fill dialog box.

I'll explain the distinction between *fixed* and *mixed* color palettes at the end of this hour, in the section "More on Color Palettes."

Mixing Colors for Uniform Fills

The process of mixing colors is similar in the Uniform Fill dialog box and the Color Docker window, except that the dialog box has more features, and the Docker window stays on the Drawing area while you work.

Figure 7.5 shows the Color Docker window being selected from the Color flyout, and displayed on the screen as well.

FIGURE 7.5

The Color Docker Window.

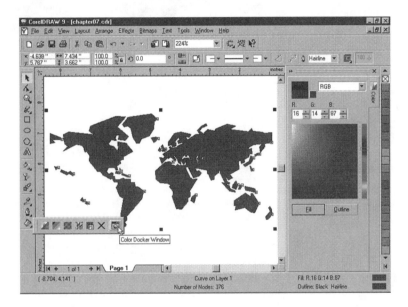

Figure 7.6 shows the Uniform Fill dialog box being selected from the Color flyout.

The four tabs on top of the Uniform Fill dialog box switch between four different ways of defining colors. The first two buttons (Models and Mixers) enable you to mix custom colors. Use the other two tabs to select colors from fixed color palettes.

Of the four tabs, the Models and Mixers tabs enable you to mix colors using the three widely used methods for defining custom colors: CMYK, RGB, and HSB. CMYK stands for Cyan, Magenta, Yellow and Black, and is widely used for printed output. RGB stands for Red, Green, Blue. HSB stands for Hue, Saturation, and Brightness.

7

FIGURE **7.6**

Selecting the Uniform
Fill dialog box.

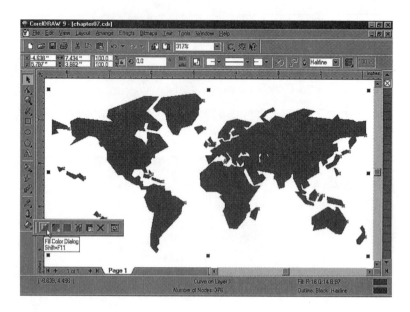

The Models and Mixers tabs provide similar options for mixing up colors. The Models tab allows you to define colors by clicking in the large palette that fills most of the left side of the dialog box. The Mixers tab allows you to define a color grid based on an adjustable wheel for defining four base colors.

The Model drop-down menu in both the Models and Mixers tabs provides more choices than CMYK, RGB, and HSB. CMY is similar to CMYK, but is used for mixing print colors for presses that cannot add black to the color mix. HLS stands for Hue, Lightness, and Saturation, and is similar to HSB. Lab and YIQ are very specialized color palettes.

You can also select color models from the drop-down menu at the top of the Color Docker window.

Mixing Colors Using CMYK Definitions

Use the Model drop-down menu in the Models Mixers view of the Uniform Fill dialog box, or the drop-down menu at the top of the Color Docker Window to choose between the different methods of defining colors.

In Figure 7.7, I'm choosing the CMYK method for defining pure yellow, using the Color Docker Window. This method defines colors as a mix of Cyan (a shade of green), Magenta (a bluish purple), Yellow, and blacK (represented with a K in the CMYK

acronym so as not to be confused with Blue). In Figure 7.7, I'm mixing 100% yellow
with no other colors by entering values of 0 (zero) in the C, M and K spinners, and a
value of 100 in the Y spinner.

FIGURE 7.7

Mixing pure yellow, CMYK style.

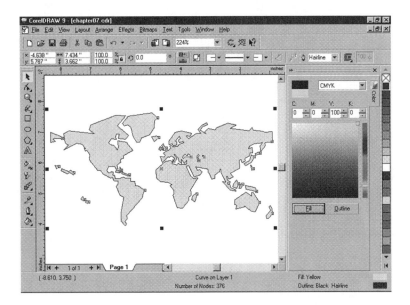

You can use the CMYK method of mixing colors for four-color printing. You can separate colors defined using CMYK into four different masters—a technique you'll explore
in Hour 10, "Working with Shapes and Curves."

Defining Colors with RGB or HSB Definitions

The RGB and HSB color definition systems are useful for defining Web graphic image
colors. RGB defines colors as a mix of red, green, and blue. For example, say you are
designing a Web image and getting coloring advice from Lynda Weinman and Bruce
Heavin's *Coloring Web Graphics* book. If Lynda advises you to use a background tile
color of R 204, G 204, and B 0, you can define that color using the RGB model. I'm
doing just that in Figure 7.8.

The HSB model defines colors in terms of Hue, Saturation, and Brightness. Hue is the
location of a color on a color wheel or ramp, with 0 and 359 representing red and 240
representing blue. Saturation controls the amount of hue, and Value defines brightness. A
Saturation setting of 50 mixes white pixels into your color at a ratio of 50/50. A
Saturation value of 0 mixes no color pixels with 100 white pixels to produce white, no
matter what value you enter for Hue. A Brightness setting of 0 produces black, no matter
what hue you define, and a Brightness of 100 produces the brightest possible color for
your Hue.

7

FIGURE 7.8

Defining colors using RGB model.

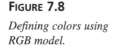

Assigning Colors Without Worrying About Definitions

At this point, you might be saying to yourself, "Do I really need to know all these color definition systems?" The answer is maybe not. If you create images that you want to view on a color monitor, just rely on your visual good sense and click on colors in the color grid in the Uniform Fill dialog box.

When you select custom colors by clicking on the color grid on the left side of the Uniform Fill dialog box, you automatically generate CMYK, RGB, and HSB values on the right side of the dialog box.

This becomes more relevant when you decide to send your CorelDRAW illustration to a printer or to a Web site. Both of those forms of output have different limitations as to which color definition systems they accept. You'll return to color definition issues in Hour 18, "Printing," and Hour 19, "From CorelDRAW to the World Wide Web."

After you select a color in the Uniform Fill dialog box, click on OK to assign that color to all selected objects.

Fountain Fills

Fountain fills, which fade one color into another, are one of the most interesting effects you will apply to an object—and one of the most fun to do.

You can define Fountain fills using the Fountain Fill dialog box (the second tool in the Fill tool flyout). Or you can use the Interactive Fill tool. In Figure 7.9, I have selected the map, and I'm choosing the Interactive Fill tool from the toolbox.

From the Fill Property Bar, pull down the Fill Type drop-down menu and select Fountain Fill. When you do, the Property Bar displays two different color drop-down menus: the First Fill Picker and the Last Fill Picker. These two drop-down menus define the starting and ending color for your Fountain fill.

Choose a starting and ending color and then drag from one part of your selected object to another to define the Fountain fill pattern. In Figure 7.9, I chose a dark color for my first color and a light color for my end color. I used the Interactive Fill tool to drag from the west to the east on my map, directing the flow of the fill pattern.

FIGURE 7.9

Defining a Fountain fill interactively.

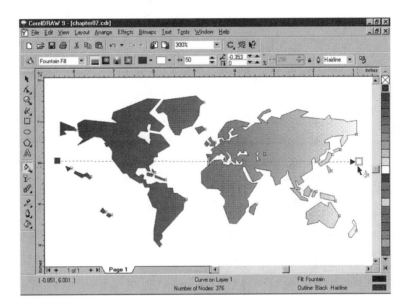

The Fountain Fill Midpoint slider in the Property Bar enables you to shift the transition point between your two colors. In Figure 7.10, I've dragged the midpoint far to the left (or west) creating an effect where the light, ending color fills more of the world. You can adjust the slider while you have the fill selected, or you can use the Interactive Fill tool again to select the object later to change the slider settings.

7

FIGURE 7.10

*Adjusting the Fountain
fill midpoint.*

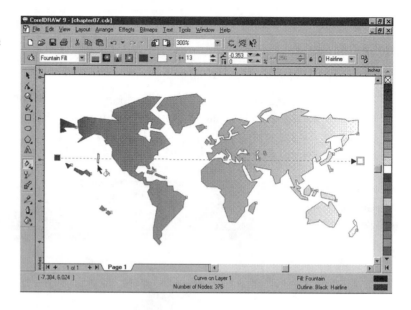

The Fountain Fill Property Bar also includes buttons to transform Fountain fills from
Linear to (from left to right) Radial, Conical, or Square fills.

In Figure 7.11, I applied each of the four types of gradient fills to the map.

FIGURE 7.11

*Four types of Fountain
fills.*

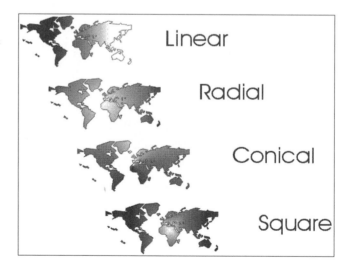

In Figure 7.12, I've zoomed in on adjusted the radius midpoint of a conical fill by dragging the interactive Midpoint Fill slider right in the Drawing window. There's really no way to describe the fun of applying and tweaking Fountain fills. Experiment with different colors, using the Linear, Conical, Radial and Square Fountain fills.

FIGURE 7.12

*Tweaking a conical
Fountain fill.*

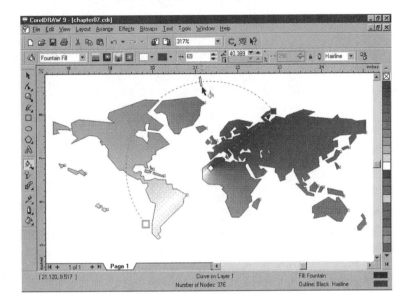

Pattern and Texture Fills

The Pattern Fill, Texture Fill, and PostScript Fill flyout tools open up different galleries of fill patterns that you can apply to selected objects. If you choose the Pattern Fill tool in the Pattern Fill dialog box, you can select from galleries of Two Color, Full Color, or Bitmap images from the drop-down menu.

Each type of fill has a gallery of images that you can choose from the respective dialog box In Figure 7.13, I applied one of the Full Color patterns from the gallery of images.

The Pattern fill options are two-color fills, full-color fills, and bitmap fills. Two-color fills create images composed from two different colors that you select in the dialog box. Full-color patterns have the advantage of using CorelDRAW's vector-based graphics logic and are based on lines and curves. The third option, bitmaps, are composed of pixels, not lines and curves. Be aware that when you use bitmap images, they tend to increase your file size quite drastically.

7

FIGURE 7.13

Assigning a Pattern fill.

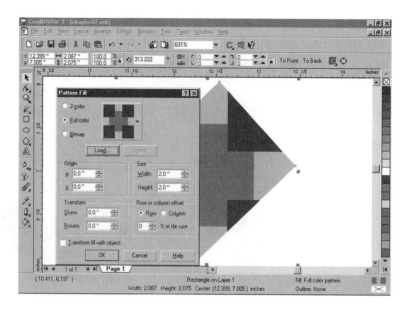

The Texture Fill dialog box (to open it, use the fourth tool in the Fill flyout) enables you to define bitmap fills using a set of designs generated by complex mathematical equations called *fractals*. Because texture fills are bitmaps, like all bitmap images they increase file size quite a bit.

CorelDRAW 9 comes with a graphic utility called Corel Texture that enables you to generate your own fractal designs. But you'll find that by manipulating the long list the textures built into CorelDRAW, you can create an almost infinite series of designs without leaving CorelDRAW.

Corel TEXTURE 9 enables you to generate textures by combining patterns and lighting. The program is found in CorelDRAW 9's graphics utilities set, and includes a foolproof wizard that appears when you select File, New from the TEXTURE 9 menu bar.

After you define a pattern in TEXTURE 9, select Texture, Render to File from the menu to save your pattern to one of several available bitmap file formats. Importing bitmaps into CorelDRAW is discussed in detail in Hour 11, "Working with Bitmap Images in CorelDRAW 9."

Experiment with TEXTURE 9 only if you need almost infinite control over patterns and shading. For most pattern needs, the mixes available in the Texture Fill dialog box provide plenty of options.

Each Texture fill comes with a set of variables like Texture #, Softness %, Brightness, and so on. You can experiment with the different variables to alter the fills. In Figure 7.14, I'm applying a texture fill to a selected shape.

FIGURE 7.14

Applying a texture fill.

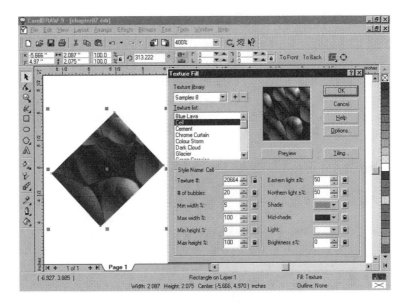

The final technique for applying fills is found in the PostScript fill dialog box. PostScript fills are defined by lines of PostScript code that is interpreted by printers. PostScript fills are not as easy to display or manipulate as bitmap and vector fills, and in general are not appropriate for images destined for display on monitors, such as Web graphics. However, they have the advantage of being interpreted very reliably by printers.

Each of the three different fill dialog boxes enables you to fine-tune each specific fill pattern. Each of these dialog boxes has a Preview button that enables you to test the effects you apply to a fill.

After you define a fill, click on the OK button in the dialog box to apply that fill to selected objects.

Fill Defaults

You can define a default fill for your drawing by using any of the techniques you learned in this hour to define a fill. Just define the fill without selecting any objects. This process is similar to defining a default outline that you learned in Hour 6, "Defining Outlines."

7

For example, if you want to create shapes, text, and lines, and have them all appear immediately with a custom-designed fill, you can define a default fill that will be applied as you create each object.

7.1: Assign a Default Fill

1. With *no object selected,* click on the Fill flyout and select any of the tools (except the Color Docker Window).

2. As soon as you select a flyout tool (such as the Texture tool, for example), a dialog box will appear for that type of fill, with three check boxes. Select Graphic, Artistic Text, and/or Paragraph Text to define what kinds of objects to apply the default fill. In Figure 7.15, I'm applying the default fill to all three types of objects.

FIGURE 7.15

Selecting a default fill.

3. Click on OK in the dialog box and define your fill. As soon as you OK the Fill dialog box, the defined fill becomes the default fill for the objects you selected in step 2.

4. You can test your fill by drawing a shape or entering text, and observing the effect of the default fill. To change the default fill back to a solid color, simply click on a color in the color palette and select the objects for which the selected color will become the new default fill.

Spot Colors Versus Process Colors

In this hour, we have touched on the two basic ways CorelDRAW defines colors. Each method of defining colors produces its own color palette that appears on your screen. You can define color palettes in two basic ways:

- Fixed palettes (also referred to as color matching systems or spot colors)
- Process color (also referred to as color models or mixed colors)

If you are simply designing an illustration to appear on your monitor, you don't have to worry about which method you use to define colors. However, if want to print or display your illustration on a Web page, you need to figure out a way to tell those output destinations how you want your colors defined.

Fixed palettes (also known as spot colors) are used in printing and to define colors on Web sites. Mixed color is also used in color printing. These options are discussed more in the hours on printing (Hour 18) and Web sites (Hour 19). But as you work in CorelDRAW, you do have the option of deciding which way you want to define your colors.

Fixed Palettes

Fixed palettes have a number of preset colors. You can create custom color by mixing these preset colors. When your file is reproduced by a printing process that uses the same fixed color palette you used when you created your image, the final output will match the colors you assign. An example of using a color matching system is a situation where you are designing a two-color brochure. Your printer might tell you that he or she can handle any spot color you select from the Pantone color palette. In that case, select your colors from the Pantone color palette. If your printer allows you to save money by creating your own color separations, explore this process in Hour 10.

Process Color

Process, or mixed, color models enable you to define colors by combining primary colors, or by using systems that attach values to colors. The most popular mixed color model is CMYK, which enables you to mix percentages of four primary colors (Cyan, Magenta, Yellow, and Black). An example of using the CMYK palette is one where you prepare illustrations for four-color printing processes. Again, you can provide your printer with a CorelDRAW file, or you can produce your own color separations for each of the four colors. (You'll learn to create your own color separations in Hour 18.)

> For more information about working with color palettes for Web site design, see Hour 19.

When you know which color palette you need to match your output, you can replace the default CorelDRAW 9 palette with one that matches the colors available to you.

7

Summary

You can define outline and fill properties for any closed object in CorelDRAW 9. Closed objects include shapes.

You can mix any color imaginable and apply it to a color fill. You can also fill objects with Fountain fills that fade from one color to another, or with patterns from a large selection of Pattern, Texture, or PostScript fill files. You can edit these Pattern fills to create unique fills for objects.

Workshop

For our sample project this hour, Paul whipped up the cover of an imaginary (we think!) magazine called *Geophysical Quarterly,* shown in Figure 7.16.

FIGURE 7.16

Paul's magazine cover includes fountain fills, bitmap fills, and texture fills.

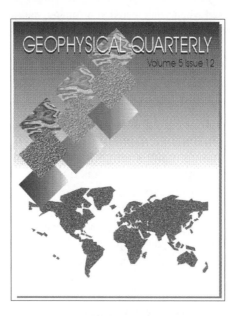

1. Start by opening a new page (letter size) and creating a background rectangle that fills the whole page. You can use the Objects Size boxes in the rectangle Property Bar to assign a size of 8 1/2-by-11-inches. Use the Interactive Fill tool to assign a Fountain fill with a darker color on top and a light color on the bottom. Move the Interactive Fill slider to the top quarter of the fill, as shown in Figure 7.17.

FIGURE 7.17

Using a Fountain fill as a page background.

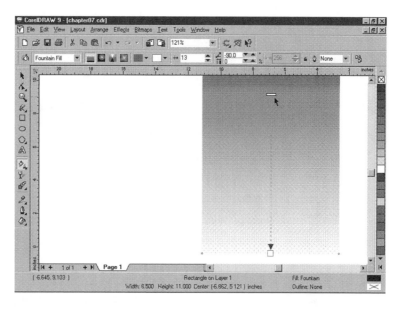

2. Next, use the Symbol docker (select Window, Dockers, Symbols and Special Characters) to drag the world map from the Webdings symbol set (it's near the very bottom of the symbol set). Enlarge the map to fill the width of the page.

3. Create a rectangle (about 2 inches square, but anything close to that is fine) and rotate it about 45 degrees. Duplicate the rectangle nine times, and arrange the rectangles on the page. Then, add a masthead for *Geophysical Quarterly,* so that your magazine cover looks something like the display in Figure 7.18.

FIGURE 7.18

Arranging shapes for a magazine cover.

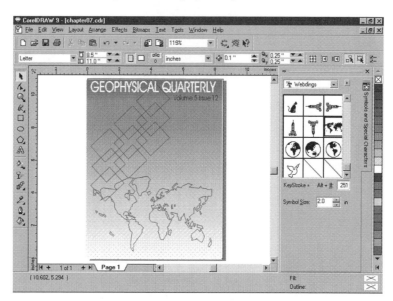

4. Now comes the fun. Experiment by assigning different types of fills to the shapes and to the world symbol. Use Paul's model for inspiration (you can see it in color at `www.ppinet.com`), but add your own fills.

Quiz

The answers to the quiz are in Appendix A, "Quiz Answers."

1. How do you define a default fill?

2. How do you define a Fountain fill path?

3. Can a pattern be used for a fill?

4. What are three popular methods for defining mixed colors in CorelDRAW 9?

5. How do you select a color palette?

PART III
Working with Curves

Hour

HOUR 8

Drawing and Editing Freehand Curves

In this hour, we'll explore most of the tools in the Freehand tool flyout. The main tool is the Freehand tool itself. In addition, we'll have some fun with DRAW's new Artistic media tool. And finally, to keep the technical illustrators in the audience happy, we'll take a quick look at the Dimension Connector tool and the Flow Lines tool.

You can use freehand curves to draw designs on your screen in CorelDRAW 9. Even skilled artists find it difficult to draw complex designs with their mouse, but the ability to add to or enhance a design with freehand curves is a powerful tool in creating illustrations.

Every once in a while, you'll find a freehand curve, even crudely drawn, can be an effective design element. In Figure 8.1, the waves in the logo were drawn with a simple freehand curve.

FIGURE 8.1

*You can use freehand
curves many ways in
illustrations.*

The tools in the curves are drawn with the Freehand Drawing tool. This tool is part of a flyout that also includes the Bézier tool, the Natural Pen tool, and the Dimension tool, and they are shown in Figure 8.2. In addition to the tools covered in this hour, the Freehand flyout includes the Bézier Curve tool. Bézier curves are powerful and fun, and deserve a whole hour of their own, which is what they get in Hour 9, "Bézier Curves."

FIGURE 8.2

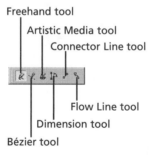

Freehand tool

Artistic Media tool

Connector Line tool

Flow Line tool

Dimension tool

Bézier tool

In this hour, you focus on the Freehand Line tool. To be honest, nobody draws great-looking shapes with a mouse, or even a more sophisticated computer drawing device. The trick is to sketch out a crude drawing that is close to what you want, and then touch it up by editing the resulting nodes.

Because nodes are very powerful, you will explore different aspects of them in this hour, and in the next two hours as well.

New curve algorithms (math formulas) in DRAW 9 go a long way to helping even the shakiest of hands draw pretty smooth curves. But don't get frustrated if your curves aren't quite what you hoped for. Your shapes will turn out nicely as you learn to edit nodes.

Draw Freehand Curves

In Hour 1, "Dive In! Having Fun with CorelDRAW 9," you learned to draw straight lines by clicking once, holding down the Ctrl key, and clicking again. With that technique, you can draw horizontal or vertical lines, or lines at 15-degree increment angles (such as 45 degrees or 30 degrees). You also learned to create objects composed of several line segments by double-clicking to add new nodes to your object.

The process of drawing freehand curves is more freestyle. You simply click on the Freehand tool and then click and draw on the Drawing area. By draw, I mean hold down the mouse button, and move your mouse. As previously mentioned, your first, and even 100th, attempts are not likely to produce smooth and elegant curves. That's okay. Try drawing a curved line such as the one in Figure 8.3 for practice.

FIGURE 8.3

Freehand curves never look like much until you touch them up.

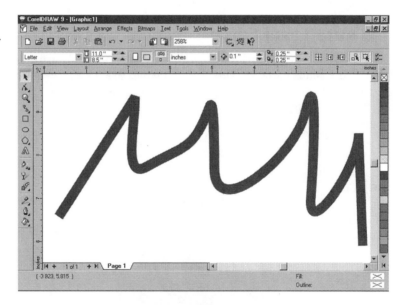

After you draw a curved line, you can apply any outline attribute to that curve. Refer to Hour 6, "Defining Outlines," to refresh your outline skills.

Closed Curves

You can transform curves into closed curves. These closed curve objects can have fills assigned to them. Sometimes, it is difficult to tell whether an object is a closed curve. One way to tell is to look at the Property Bar and see whether the Auto-Close button is grayed out. If the button is grayed out, your curve is already closed.

You can also tell whether a curve is closed by selecting it and checking the Curve Property Bar. If the Auto-Close button is available, the curve is not closed.

Manually Close Curved Objects

You can create a closed curved object by having the curve end where it started. For example, if you try your best to draw a circle, it might not look too round, but if you end at the point where you started to draw, your circle will be a closed object.

CorelDRAW assists you a bit in creating closed objects. If you come pretty close to ending your curve at the starting point, CorelDRAW will assume you wanted to end exactly where you started and close your object.

Later in this hour, when you start to use the Shape tool, you'll learn to convert closed curves to curves that are not closed objects.

Auto-Close Curves

If you have a curve that you want to convert to a closed object, you can use the Auto-Close button in the Property Bar. To do this, select a curved object and click on Auto-Close in the Property Bar. That's it! The first and last point (or *node*) in the curve automatically connects with a straight line.

Figure 8.4 shows the same curved line that I drew in Figure 8.3, but this time it has been transformed into a closed curve, and I've applied a fill.

FIGURE 8.4

Any curve can be closed using Auto-Close.

Edit Curve Nodes

You have already seen how every selected object displays eight handles. These black squares on the corners and sides of a selected object enable you to resize the object by pulling on them.

Selected objects also display much smaller control points called *nodes*. These nodes enable you to edit the shape of a selected object with tremendous detail. In this hour, you learn to use nodes to edit the shape of curves and to edit text in micro-detail.

Some node editing is possible using the Pick tool. More complex node editing requires the Shape tool. In this next section, you start by editing nodes using the Pick tool.

Examine Nodes

When you select a single object and examine it closely, you see tiny nodes. These nodes are smaller than the handles around the selected object, and nodes are visible only when you select one object.

Another difference between nodes and handles is that nodes actually appear on the outline of the actual shape or curve, whereas handles appear on the corners and sides of a rectangle around the object.

Nodes do different things under different conditions. They behave differently in artistic text, shapes, and curves. Here, you learn to edit nodes on curves and artistic text. For now, you need to know that every shape has nodes. When you draw a shape, CorelDRAW automatically generates nodes and curves that, together, compose your object.

In Figure 8.5, you can see that my crudely drawn curve is composed of many nodes that separate curves. Together, these curves and nodes make up the curved object.

FIGURE 8.5

Every curve is defined by nodes.

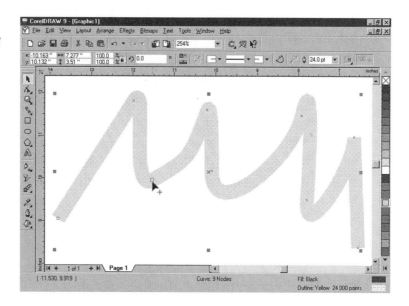

If you click on the Curve tab in the Object Properties dialog box, you can see whether your curve is closed, as you can see in Figure 8.6.

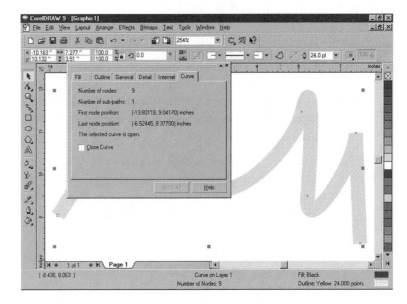

Edit Nodes

The first step in editing a node is to select it. You can select a single node in a curve by clicking on it with the Pick tool.

You can move a selected node by dragging on it. In Figure 8.7, I drag one of my curve's nodes and, in the process, reshape the curve.

FIGURE 8.7

Reshaping a curve by dragging a node.

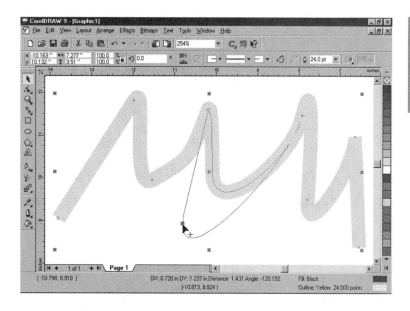

Add and Delete Nodes

You can add and delete nodes by right-clicking on a node with the Pick tool and choosing Add or Delete from the shortcut menu that appears. In Figure 8.8, I add a node to my curve.

FIGURE 8.8

Adding a node to a curve.

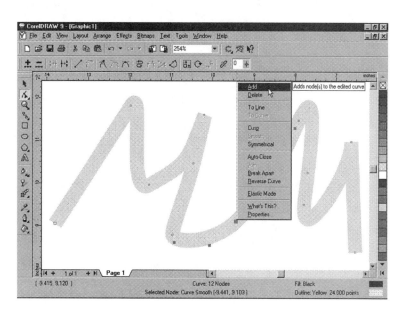

By adding or deleting nodes and moving them around, you can tweak the shape of your
freehand drawing.

Edit Artistic Text Nodes

While we're exploring editing curve nodes, let's take a look at how nodes can be used to
edit the look of artistic text. Text nodes behave differently than curve nodes; for example,
you cannot edit them using the Pick tool. However, if you select an artistic text object
with the Shape tool, you can edit individual text nodes, and you can control spacing
between characters.

The individual nodes that appear with each letter (after you select Artistic Text with the
Shape tool) enable you to move individual letters. To move a letter, click and drag on the
node to the left of the letter, as shown in Figure 8.9.

FIGURE 8.9

*Editing individual
Artistic Text nodes.*

Edit Text Spacing

Selecting Artistic Text with the Shape tool also displays the vertical and horizontal
shape-sizing handles. The vertical shape-sizing handle appears on the left edge of the
selected text, and the horizontal shape-sizing handle appears on the right of the selected
text (see Figure 8.10).

FIGURE 8.10

Shape-sizing handles.

Vertical shape-
sizing handle

Horizontal shape-
sizing handle

8

The vertical shape-sizing handle is useful only if you have more than one line of text. If you do, the vertical sizing handle increases line spacing when it is pulled down and compresses spacing when it is pushed up.

You can expand the spacing between letters by dragging the horizontal shape-sizing handle to the right. Or compress letter spacing by dragging it to the left. In Figure 8.11, I compressed the letter spacing.

FIGURE 8.11

Compressing spacing between characters.

You can achieve some interesting effects by combining expanding or compressing letter spacing with changing the location of individual characters with the Shape tool. In Figure 8.12, I rearranged my text to create a wavelike effect.

FIGURE 8.12

Compressed or expanded artistic text can be combined with individually located letters.

Convert Text to Curves

You can edit the shape of individual text characters in extreme detail by transforming text to curves. After you do that, you can no longer edit the content of the text in the Text Edit dialog box. But you can reshape individual characters. Figure 8.13 shows my original text with individual character shapes changed.

FIGURE 8.13

Reshaped text.

8.1: Editing the Shape of Text Characters

▼ To Do

1. Type artistic text. I like to use a very solid, thick font such as Impact if I am going to edit the shape of characters.

2. Select the Pick tool, then right-click on the text, and choose Convert to Curves from the shortcut menu.

3. If you want to edit each character as a separate object (useful if you want to move them in relation to each other), select Arrange | Break Apart from the menu bar.

4. Click on one of your characters, if you have broken your text object apart.

5. After you convert text to curves, you can use the Pick tool to reshape the text by dragging the nodes. In Figure 8.14, I am reshaping the letter *F*.

FIGURE 8.14

Reshaping text.

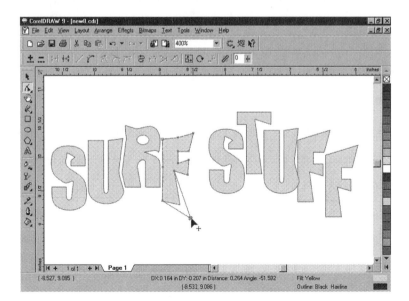

▲

Drawing with the Artistic Media Tool

The Artistic Media tool is similar to the Freehand tool, except that it's nothing like it! It's similar because it draws lines as you click and drag with your mouse. It's completely different because the line that gets produced is "filled in" with a media of your choice.

The Artistic Media tool is actually a collection of tools. When you choose the Artistic Media tool from the Freehand flyout, the Artistic Media Property Bar displays tools for several different types of effects, as well as associated tools for each effect.

The Preset tool displays a set of fountain pen–like effects that can be selected from the Preset drop-down menu. Figure 8.15 shows a line drawn with one of the Presets, after a fill has been applied.

FIGURE 8.15

Drawing a line with a Preset effect.

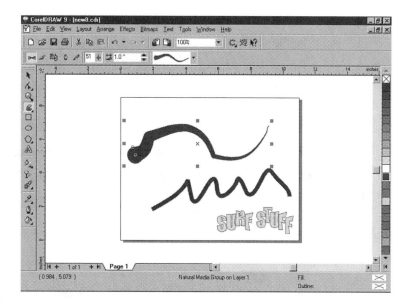

The Brush tool enables you to draw lines using effects available from the Brush Stroke List drop-down menu in the Property Bar. Figure 8.16 shows a Brush tool line drawn using one of the shapes available from Brush Stroke List.

FIGURE **8.16**

*Drawing an arrow
with the Brush Artistic
Media effect.*

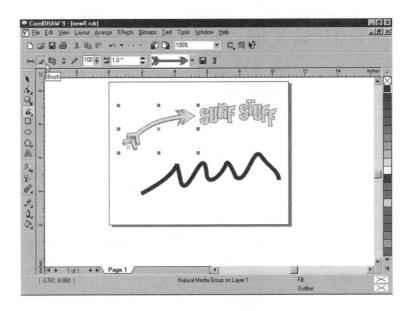

The Sprayer provides a really wild set of effects that look nothing at all like the line you
draw. Figure 8.17 shows one of these effects applied while I drew a wavy line.

FIGURE **8.17**

*One of the arsenal of
Sprayer effects avail-
able from the Artistic
Medial tool Property
Bar.*

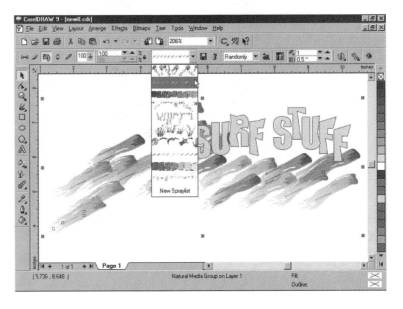

The Calligraphic tool simulates pen calligraphy. It's a tricky tool to use, but it's a lot easier than real calligraphy. Figure 8.18 shows my name, quickly etched using one of the Calligraphic effects.

FIGURE 8.18

Drawing a Artistic media tool line with a Calligraphic effect.

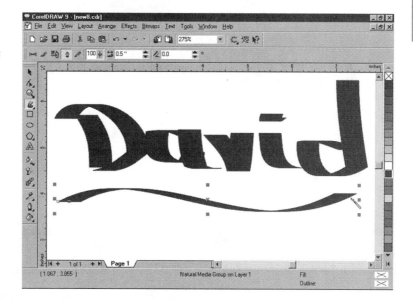

Finally, the Pressure tool enables you to increase line thickness by slowing down as you draw. Or to decrease line thickness by drawing faster.

You can also apply Artistic Media effects to already existing lines.

8.2: Applying Artistic Media Effects

1. Draw a wavy line using the Freehand drawing tool.

2. With the line still selected, choose Window, Dockers, Artistic Media from the menu. The Artistic Media Docker window appears. In the top half of the window is a list of Artistic Media tools you recently used (if any). In the bottom window, you can select effects.

3. Use the Menu flyout to select which types of Artistic Media effects you want to choose from, as shown in Figure 8.19.

4. Use the scrollbar in the lower Docker window to find an effect to apply to your line. Click on the effect and click on the Apply button.

FIGURE 8.19

Choosing Artistic Media Effects from the Artistic Media Docker window.

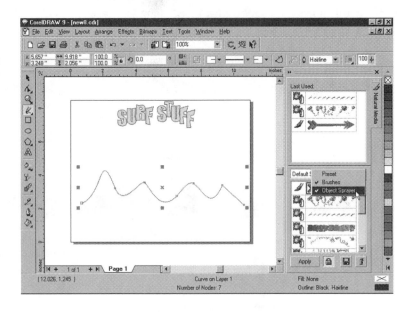

If you select the AutoApply button at the bottom of the Docker window (it looks like a padlock), effects are automatically applied when selected, and you don't need to click on the Apply button.

The Save tool in the docker window enables you to save Artistic Media effects as files for future use. The Delete button deletes effects from the list, so use it with caution!

A Quick Look at Dimension, Connector, and Flow Lines

The Dimension tool can be used to mark dimensions on a drawing. The Connector tool is used to draw interactive connecting lines between objects. The Flow Lines tool is used to create flowcharts. You can choose any of these tools from the Freehand flyout.

The Dimension tool can display linear measurements or angles. A set of tools in the Property Bar that appears with the Dimension tool enables you to choose the type of measurement you want to display. In general, the routine is to first click on one location, then a second, and finally a point at which you want to display the measurement. Figure 8.20 displays a drawing that employs vertical, diagonal, and angle dimension lines.

The Dimension Property bar that becomes active when you create dimension
lines includes several drop-down menus and boxes in which you can define
units of measurement, fractional display or decimal numbers. The Property
bar also allows you to define the prefix or suffix, such as " or ' to display
before or after the dimension values.

8

FIGURE 8.20

Displaying dimensions.

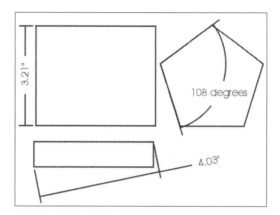

Connector lines connect two objects. If either of the objects is moved, the connector line
reacts by redrawing itself to maintain the same connection.

The Flow Line tool is similar to the Connector Line tool, except that lines can be jointed.
Here, too, when you move an object to which a Flow Line is connected, the line itself
adjusts, as you can see in Figure 8.21.

FIGURE 8.21

Connecting Lines adjust when a connected object is moved.

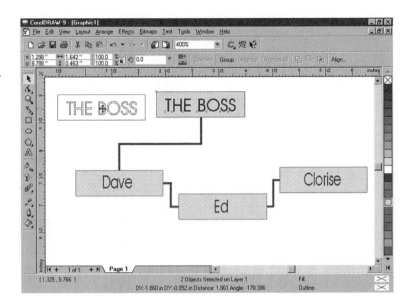

Summary

By combining freehand curves and editing nodes, you can create infinite variations on drawn curves and even text. Your first try to draw a freehand line will be crude, but CorelDRAW offers many options for editing your drawing.

Selected objects have handles, which you explored in earlier hours. They also have nodes. You can move curve nodes using the Pick tool to edit the shape of a selected object.

Artistic Text nodes move the location of individual characters. Use the shape-sizing handles to edit text spacing. The new Artistic media tool allows you to draw curves using images to create flowing lines of graphic patterns and pictures.

Workshop

In this workshop, you can develop your curve drawing skills by creating a logo something like the one in Figure 8.22.

FIGURE 8.22

Try creating this logo with Freehand tools.

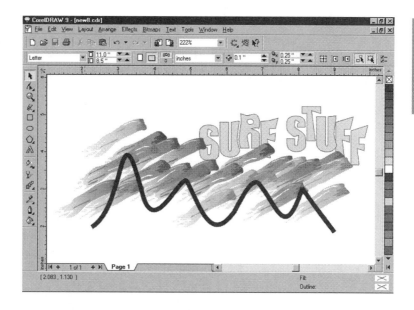

1. Draw a wavy line using the Freehand drawing tool.
2. Assign a medium line thickness to the line, then duplicate it (press Ctrl+D).
3. Use the Artistic Media Docker window to assign one of the Object Sprayer Artistic Media effects to the second (duplicate) line.
4. Add some text, as shown in Figure 8.22.
5. Change the text into shapes, and move and edit the individual characters.
6. Move the objects around, and arrange them front to back so the logo looks something like the one in Figure 8.22.

Quiz

Answers to the quiz can be found in Appendix A, "Quiz Answers."

1. How do you expand the spacing between letters?
2. How can you tell whether a curve is closed?
3. How do you create a closed curved object while you are drawing it with the Freehand tool?
4. How do you add and delete nodes to an object?
5. How do you convert Artistic Text to curves? And why would you want to? What's the drawback in converting text to curves?

HOUR 9

Bézier Curves

There are two main drawing tools in CorelDRAW: the Freehand tool and the Bézier tool. The Freehand tool intuitively (more or less) follows your mouse when you click and draw on the screen. The Bézier tool is a more powerful weapon for creating curves, but not so intuitive.

Bézier curves are named after a French engineer who developed a system of mathematically generated curves.

The real power of the Bézier tool comes from drawing smooth curves. Just like your experience with the Freehand tool in Hour 8, "Drawing and Editing Freehand Curves," you'll find that wielding the Bézier tool to draw curves is awkward and challenging. However, just like designs drawn with the Freehand tool, you can easily move nodes around to adjust the curves you draw.

One thing that is fun to do with the generated curves is use them as paths for text. In Figure 9.1, I fit text to a curve and then delete the curve.

FIGURE 9.1

You can fit text to a curve and then delete the curve.

In Figure 9.2, you can see how parallel Bézier curves are used in the background of the illustration, combined with text fit to a curve.

FIGURE 9.2

This logo combines parallel Bézier curves and text fit to a curve.

Trace with the Bézier Tool

Even with dramatic improvements in the smoothness of curves generated by the Freehand tool, it is difficult to draw nice, smooth curves with the Freehand tool. As you have already seen, the goal is to create a rough sketch and then enhance that by editing node location.

The Bézier tool makes it easier to draw more detailed sketches. You can draw straight lines with the Bézier tool by clicking once and then clicking a second time. The result is a straight line between the two nodes.

9.1: Use the Bézier Curve Tool to Trace the House Symbol

In this exercise, you'll practice using the Bézier Curve tool by outlining a symbol.

1. Open the Symbols Docker window (select Window, Dockers, Symbols and Special Characters). Select the Webdings font and drag the house with a sun and a cactus (it matches the letter E in the symbol set) onto the Drawing window.

2. Select the Bézier tool from the Freehand flyout; it's the second tool in the flyout.

3. With the Bézier tool, you can continue to click and add nodes as long as you want. There's no need to double-click. If you want to finish drawing a Bézier curve and start a new one, you can press the spacebar twice.

> Pressing the spacebar once deselects the Bézier tool, and selects the Pick tool. Pressing the spacebar a second time reselects the Bézier tool, and begins a new curve.

4. When you finish creating your shape, press the spacebar on your keyboard. That ends your Bézier drawing and selects the Pick tool. Use the AutoClose Curve button to turn the outline into a closed object, and fill it with a light color fill. Move the fill to the back, so the original symbol is on top of the fill.

In Figure 9.3, I used the Bézier tool to trace the house with a sun and a cactus.

FIGURE 9.3

The Bézier tool is useful for tracing because it's easy to add nodes to curves.

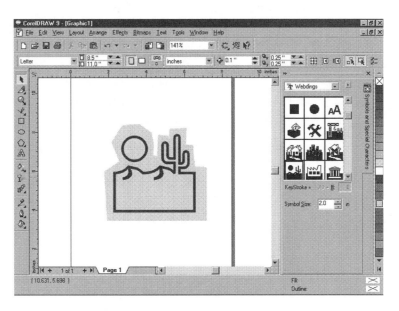

You can edit nodes while you add line segments with the Bézier tool. Just hold down the Alt key and edit existing nodes. In Figure 9.4, I'm moving a node.

FIGURE 9.4

Hold down Alt to edit nodes while drawing Bézier curves.

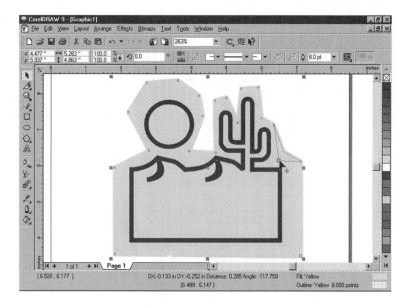

Draw Curves with the Bézier Tool

You generate curves with the Bézier tool by selecting nodal points and directions for the curve. The key to having fun with Bézier curves is to remember that they can be edited. In this section, I'll show you how to draw waves with the Bézier tool. Those waves can be resized and rotated, so don't worry about the size or height of your wave when you generate it.

Bézier curves are also not the way to draw a complex shape. To do that, define the rough outline for the shape or curve and then edit nodes. In Hour 10, "Working with Shapes and Curves," you'll learn to edit the curve nodes themselves, so that is also something you don't need to worry about when you generate Bézier curves.

The most commonly used Bézier curve is a basic wave. Waves are easy to edit, but it's helpful when you create them to make them symmetrical. One way to do that is to utilize the Snap to Object feature to locate wave nodes that are evenly spaced.

9.2: Draw a Wave

1. Draw a rectangle (using the Rectangle tool).

2. Select the Bézier tool from the toolbox.

3. From the View menu, turn on Snap to Objects.

4. Draw with the Bézier tool from the top-left corner of the rectangle to the bottom-left corner, as I'm doing in Figure 9.5.

FIGURE 9.5

Step one in drawing a symmetrical Bézier curve.

5. Drag from the top-right corner of the rectangle to the bottom. I'm doing that in Figure 9.6, to finish the curve.

6. After you finish the curve, press the spacebar once to select the Pick tool.

7. Because the whole point of the rectangle was to provide a fixture to keep the curve symmetrical, delete it.

FIGURE 9.6

Finishing a wave-like curve.

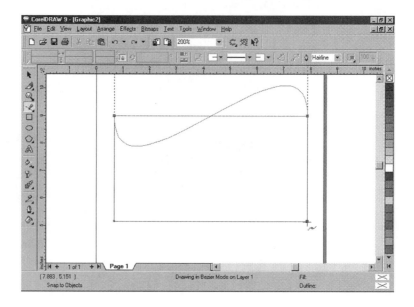

After you create a wave-like curve, you can rotate it 45 degrees or 90 degrees. You can compress it to make the curves steeper or stretch it to make the curves smoother. You can flip the curves horizontally or vertically and match them next to each other.

Curves are rotated just like any object. You can select them twice to view the rotation handles. Or click and drag on handles to resize or reshape them. I've done all this in Figure 9.7.

FIGURE 9.7

Many ways to use a wave.

Editing Bézier Curves

You can edit an existing Bézier curve with either the Shape tool or the Pick tool. Resizing a curve with the Pick tool has a different effect than moving nodes with the Shape tool. Experiment with both. Resizing with the Pick tool creates less radical changes in the curve structure. Moving nodes with the Shape tool radically reforms the curve. However, if you create a symmetrical curve (using my in-a-rectangle trick), that symmetry will be maintained as you reshape your curve with either the Pick or the Shape tool.

In Figure 9.8, I'm using the Pick tool to compress the curve.

FIGURE 9.8

You can preview the changes you make to a curve before you release the mouse button.

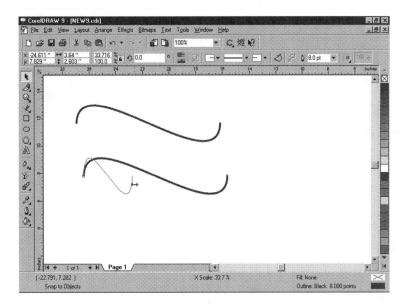

Figure 9.9 shows the more radical change produced by using the Shape tool to compress the curve by dragging in on a node.

You can further expand your wave options by copying waves and organizing them into parallel lines or by placing them next to each other to create continuous waves.

FIGURE **9.9**

*Use the Shape tool to
radically revise your
curve.*

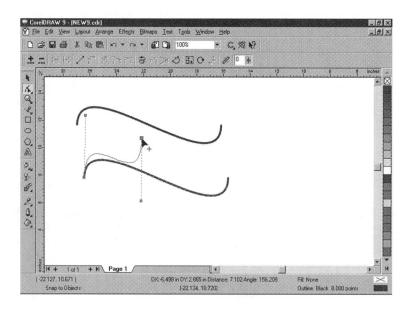

Fit Text to Paths

You can use a shape or path that you create as a baseline for text. In Figure 9.10, I fit text
to a path.

FIGURE **9.10**

*Text fitted to a Bézier
curve.*

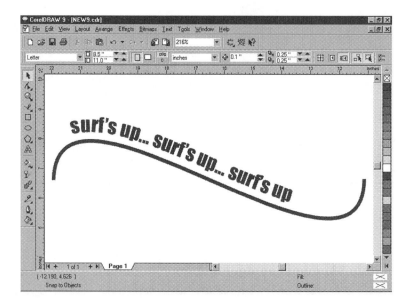

There are two options for fitting text to a path. You can type the text directly on a shape or curve, or you can take existing text and apply it to a curve.

Type Text on a Path

To type text on a path, the first step is to create the shape or curve to which you will be fitting the text. The path can be any shape, but you should size and edit the shape or curve before you apply text to it.

Then, with the shape or curve selected, choose Text, Fit Text To Path from the menu bar. When you do that, the Text Property Bar becomes active. Select a text font and size (and other text attributes) from the Text Property Bar.

After you assign text properties, simply start typing. Your cursor automatically attaches itself to the shape or curve you selected. The text appears, on top of the shape or curve you selected, as you see in Figure 9.11.

FIGURE 9.11

Typing text on a shape.

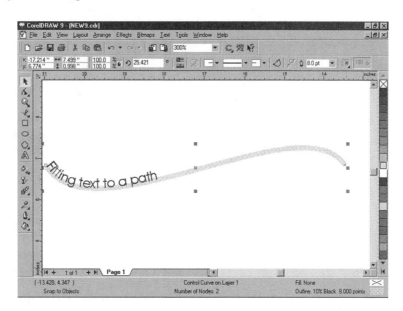

Your text might not end up exactly the way you want it to look in relation to the curve or shape. You have many options for changing the position of your text. You'll learn them in the section "Align Text on Paths," later in this hour.

Attach Text to a Path

You can type text directly on a shape or curve, but you can also attach existing text to a path. All you need is text and a curve or shape.

9.3: Attach Text to a Curve

1. Type some text (a couple of words) and draw a curve.

2. Select the text object. Then, hold down Shift so you can select two objects at once, and click to select the curve or shape to which you will be fitting the text. In Figure 9.12, I selected a multisegmented line curve and a text object.

FIGURE 9.12

With text and curve objects selected, I am ready to fit the text to the curve.

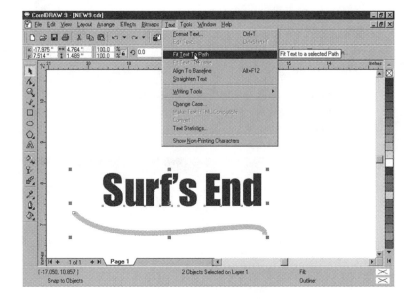

3. With both the text and path object selected, choose Text, Fit Text To Path in the menu bar.

4. When you attach existing text to a path, you're likely to find an uncomfortable match. The text might not display on the part of the path you want. The text might be too close to the path. You can correct this and other options with the Fit Text To Path Property Bar that becomes active after you attach text to a shape or curve.

In Figure 9.13, my text does not fit on the path well, but the Property Bar has appeared that will let me fix it. When you select text fitted to a curve, a Property Bar appears with buttons that help you adjust the text. In the next section of this hour, I show you how to use those tools to adjust your text so it fits better on your curve.

FIGURE **9.13**

This text needs to be realigned on the path using the Property Bar.

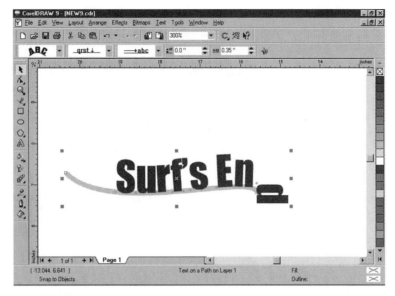

Align Text on Paths

The Property Bar that appears when you select text fitted to a path provides several options—such as centering your text on the curve—for controlling the relationship between your text and the path.

When you attach text to shapes or curves, the text sometimes appears upside down or on the wrong side of the path.

You can move text from one side of a path to the other by selecting the fitted text and then clicking on the Place Text on Other Side button in the Property Bar.

After you place the text on the proper side of the path, you can choose from one of four Text Orientation options from the first pull-down menu in the Property Bar.

Select an Orientation option before you start worrying about the placement and alignment of your text. Different orientation styles will sit differently on your path, and you can determine how you want the text to display before you align it.

The four Orientation options display when you select your fitted text and pull down the first menu in the Property Bar. You can see these options in Figure 9.14.

FIGURE 9.14

Text Orientation options require experimenting; you can't tell what they will look like from the drop-down menu.

With your fitted text selected, choose one of the Orientation options. These options have different effects, depending on the text size and font you select, and the path to which you apply text. Experiment with all of them until you see which one works best for your text.

After you decide on a Text Orientation, you can define the vertical and horizontal alignment of your text in relation to the path. The Vertical Placement drop-down list offers different options, depending on the Text Orientation you selected. For simple Text Orientation (the first option in the Text Orientation list), you can align text above or below the path, and use "in between" options as well. Other Text Orientation options enable you to place text only on top of a curve. In Figure 9.15, I'm moving text below my curve.

With Text Orientation and Vertical Placement selected, you can use the Text Placement drop-down menu to left-align, center, or right-align your text. In Figure 9.16, I'm centering text on a path.

FIGURE 9.15

*Some text works
beneath a path.*

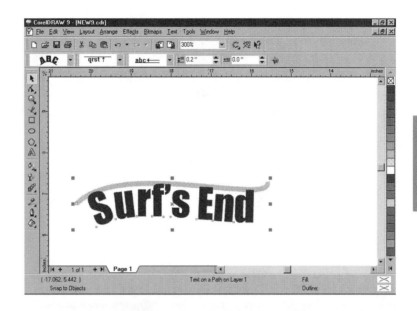

FIGURE 9.16

Text centered on a path.

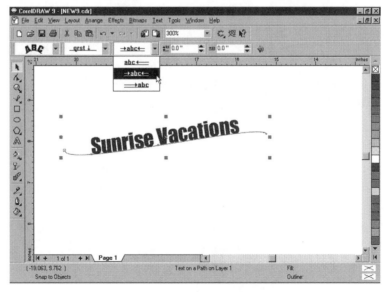

The Distance from Path and Horizontal Offset spin boxes enable you to fine-tune the
relationship between your text and the path, to achieve just the effect you want. The
Distance from Path defines vertical spacing between the text and the path. You can move
your text above (with positive values in the box) or below your path.

The Horizontal Offset spin boxes enable you to shift text right or left along your path. In Figure 9.17, I increased the space between the text and the path by entering a positive value in the Distance from Path box.

FIGURE 9.17

You gain more control over fitted text when you fine-tune the relationship between text and its path.

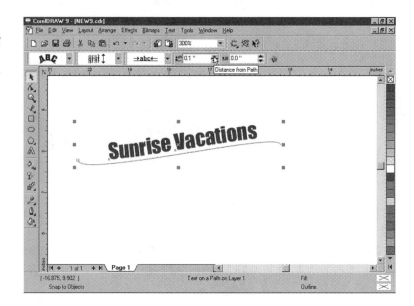

Stretching and Shaping Curved Text

As if the Property Bar didn't offer options enough for fitted text, you can transform the look of your fitted text by editing the resulting objects. For starters, you can delete the path, leaving just the text.

You can select the text with the Shape tool, and use the shape-sizing handle to adjust the spacing of the text. In Figure 9.18, I'm compressing the spacing between characters using the horizontal shape-sizing Handle.

You can also use the Shape tool to select the node for single characters and move them on or off the path to which you have fixed the text.

FIGURE 9.18

Just because you have fitted text to a path doesn't mean you can't apply the shaping techniques you learned in Hour 8.

Summary

You can use the Bézier tool for drawings that the Freehand tool doesn't handle well—including outlining objects and drawing waves. Drawing curves with the Bézier tool is not intuitive. Instead of drawing the curve itself, you generate calculated curves by placing nodes and drawing control lines that determine the height of the curve.

You can fit text to curves you design with the Bézier tool, or to any shape. Fine-tune fitted text to create interesting effects.

Workshop

In this workshop, you create the logo in Figure 9.19.

FIGURE 9.19

This logo combines text fitted to a shape with waves made from Bézier curves.

1. Create the wave using the Bézier tool. You can edit the curve if necessary using the Shape tool. Use the Auto-Close Curve button to make the wave into a closed shape, and assign a dark fill color.

2. Draw a circle. Fill it with yellow. Attach text, as shown in Figure 9.19.

3. Arrange the sun with text, and the wave to create the logo, something like the one shown in Figure 9.19.

Quiz

Answers to the quiz questions can be found in Appendix A, "Quiz Answers."

1. Where do you find the Bézier tool?
2. What are two main drawing tools in CorelDRAW?
3. How do you complete a Bézier curve?
4. How do you move text from one side of a path to the other?
5. How do you center text on a path? Or right- or left-align it?

Hour 10

Working with Shapes and Curves

One technique CorelDRAW illustrators use is to start with rough sketches of their drawings created by shapes. They then refine them to create the exact image they want to produce. For example, the sailboat and sails in Figure 10.1 were created by starting with simple triangles.

You can edit shapes. You've already seen that you can resize shapes using sizing handles. But you can also edit shapes by moving nodes, adding or deleting them, or by using the Knife or Erase tools.

You can do much more with shapes by converting them into curves. You can edit curve nodes in minute detail and define different types of curves to produce any shape you want.

FIGURE **10.1**

A shape and two curves, all created from two triangles.

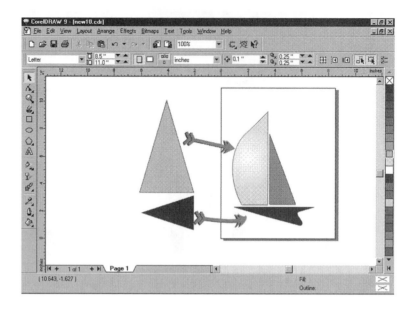

Editing Shapes

When you click on a shape (an ellipse, a rectangle, or a polygon) with the Shape tool, nodes appear. Rectangles have four nodes, one for each corner. Polygons have a node for each side and one for each point, as you can see in Figure 10.2.

FIGURE **10.2**

Pentagons have ten nodes.

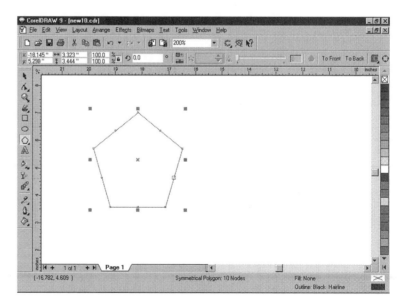

Nodes vs. handles: Nodes are smaller than handles, and control a single end of a line or curve segment, while handles are large, and are used to resize or reshape an entire object.

Editing Ellipse Nodes

You started to explore editing shape nodes in Hour 3, "Working with Shapes." Rectangle and polygon nodes are used to edit the ending of a line. Ellipses, however, are a special case. Ellipses have an infinite number of sides. Ellipses have just one node. You can move this node to create an arc or pie. To do that, drag clockwise or counterclockwise on the node, as shown in Figure 10.3.

FIGURE 10.3

Drag the single node on an ellipse to create a pie-slice shape.

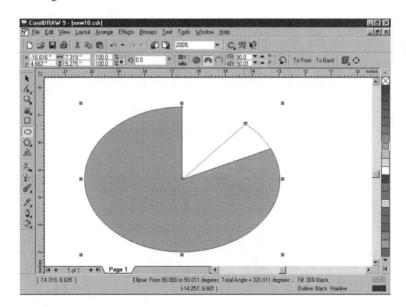

Moving Shape Nodes

You can move the nodes on rectangles and polygons to change the shape of the polygon. Dragging down on the corner handles of a rectangle rounds the corners, as you can see in Figure 10.4. Or you can drag up on a bottom corner node to round a rectangle.

Of course, if you can settle for the amount of rounding that comes automatically with a rounded rectangle shape, that's quicker. But by moving corner nodes, you can assign the exact amount of rounding you want to a corner. If clicking and dragging on a corner node is not accurate enough for you, the top and bottom Left Rectangle Corner, and Right Rectangle Corner Roundness spinners in the Property bar enable you to define roundness digitally using a scale of 0 (no roundness) to 100 (the maximum).

FIGURE 10.4

Use the Shape tool to drag down and round nodes on the corners of a rectangle.

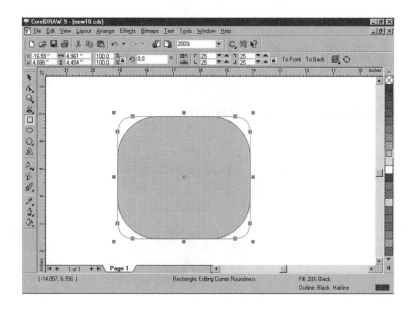

You can custom-transform polygons into stars by dragging on the side or corner nodes. In Figure 10.5, I'm transforming a pentagon into a kind of warped star by dragging on one of the side nodes.

FIGURE 10.5

When you drag on a side node in a shape, all side nodes move symmetrically—this is true for point nodes as well.

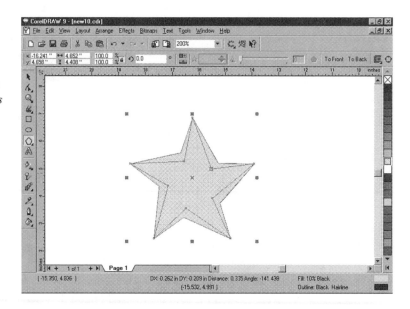

Editing with the Knife Tool

The Knife tool is one of the more descriptively named weapons in the toolbar. It can cut objects in two! The basic routine is that you click twice on an object to make incision points, and those points become a line that divides your object into two new objects.

The Knife and Eraser tools are on the Shape tool flyout. You select them by clicking on the Shape tool and holding down the mouse button while you click on either the Knife (the second tool) or the Eraser (the third tool).

As usual with CorelDRAW, you can accomplish a task in many ways. Any shape you create with the Knife tool can also be designed by editing a shape, but sometimes the Knife tool is easier to use. For example, cutting off the top of a triangle is an easy way to create a trapezoid. Or if you want two shapes to fit together and be complementary, you can use the Knife tool to cut one shape in half.

10.1: Cut Shapes with the Knife Tool

▼ To Do

To use the Knife tool to cut a shape into two or more parts:

1. Select Knife tool from the Shape tool flyout.
2. Click once at a point on a shape that you want to cut.
3. Click a second time at the endpoint of the cut. In Figure 10.6, I am cutting a triangle in half vertically.
4. After you cut your shape, use the Pick tool to select either of the two new shapes you created. You can drag to move either of the two objects, or delete one of them.

FIGURE 10.6

Dissecting a triangle with the Knife tool.

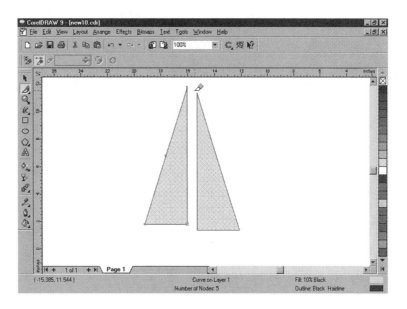

When you select the Knife tool, the Auto-Close on Cut button is automatically selected in the Property Bar. This is the button you want if you are cutting up shapes. The (also available) Leave as One Object button is not that useful if you want to cut up objects with the Knife tool. With the Auto-Close on Cut button selected, you create two shapes from one with the Knife tool. Turning this button off changes the Knife tool so that it cuts the object but creates a nonclosed curve (a line) instead of a new shape.

Erasing Pixels

The Eraser tool is also located on the Shape flyout and works like an eraser on a pencil. You can erase any pixel within an object, down to the smallest dot. The Eraser Property Bar has a spin box that you can use to change the width of the eraser.

After you select the Eraser tool, you can delete pixels you don't want. In Figure 10.7, I'm using the Eraser tool to "erase" clouds into a blue sky.

FIGURE 10.7

The Eraser is not a subtle tool, but it creates a unique effect.

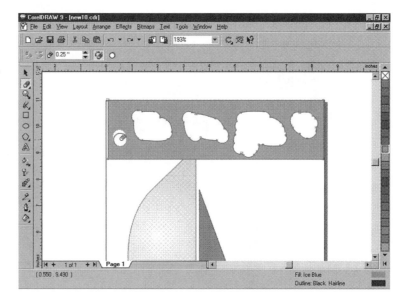

If you accidentally erase more than you want to, click on the Undo button in the toolbar.

Using Free Transforms

Free transformations rotate, mirror, resize, and skew selected shapes around a selected pivot point on the shape. Free transform tools do not work on artistic text, but they do work on shapes and curves. If you want to apply free transform effects to text, you must first convert the text to a curve (using the Convert To Curve button in the Text Property Bar).

There's really no substitute for experimenting with free transforms. If you need a verbal description of how they work, imagine a table with four legs that can be rotated or have its shape mirrored or distorted, using any of the four legs as the focal point for the rotation or distortion.

To apply a free transform, first select the object with the Pick tool and then choose the Free Transform tool from the Shape tool flyout (Free Transform is the last tool in the flyout).

You can choose from four Free Transform options in the Free Transform Property Bar: Free Rotation, Free Angle Reflection, Free Scaling, and Free Skewing.

Free Rotation pivots an object on a node. Figure 10.8 shows Free Rotation applied to a side node.

10

FIGURE **10.8**

Rotating a pentagon on a side node.

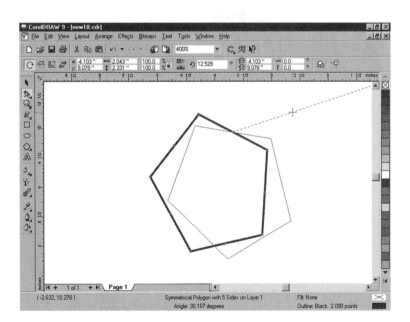

Free Angle Reflection is similar to Free Rotation, but it mirrors objects on the angle you define. Free Scaling changes both vertical and horizontal dimensions anchored on a selected node. Figure 10.9 shows a pentagon being scaled in relation to a point to the right of the shape.

FIGURE **10.9**

Free Scaling a pentagon.

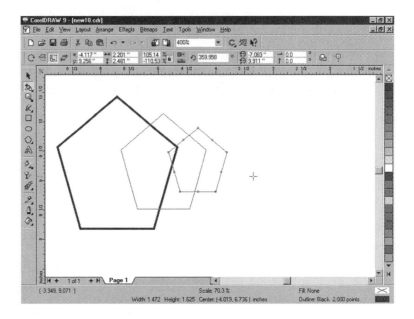

Free Skewing distorts the horizontal and vertical dimensions of a selected shape at the same time, again dependent on an anchor point you define by clicking anywhere in the Drawing window.

Transforming Shapes to Curves

As you have seen, you can edit shapes by moving shape nodes, by using the Knife tool, or by erasing with the Eraser tool. To have total control over a shape, however, you need to convert it into a curve.

When you select a shape node with the Shape tool, a To Curve button appears on the Property Bar. Click on that button to transform your shape into a curve. You can convert all the nodes in a shape to a curve by selecting the shape with the Pick tool and then choosing Arrange, Convert to Curves from the menu bar.

Why convert shape nodes to curves? You have seen that when you edit a node in a shape, you also affect other nodes in the shape. That can be handy when you convert a pentagon into a starfish. But what if you want to edit a single node and have your editing affect only that one node? For this, you need to convert the shape into a curve.

Curve nodes can also be edited much more powerfully than Shape nodes. Curve nodes can be of different types and can be fine-tuned to create complex shapes, as you will see in the next section of this hour.

Editing Curves

With the Shape tool selected, you can click on individual nodes to select them. If you hold down Shift while you click, you can select more than one node at a time.

You can also select all nodes in an object. This is handy when you want to convert every node in a shape to a curve.

▼ To Do ▲

10.2: Convert Object Nodes to Curves

In this exercise, you will covert a shape into a curve.

1. Draw a shape (a rectangle will do nicely).

2. Select the shape using the Shape tool (not the Pick tool).

3. Click on the To Curve button in the Property Bar.

> If you created your object as a shape, you don't have to convert it to a curve; the nodes are already all set to edit.

Add and Delete Nodes

When you select an object with the Shape tool, you can add nodes by clicking anywhere on the shape and then clicking on the + (plus) symbol in the Property Bar. You can delete nodes by clicking on a node and then clicking on the – (minus) symbol in the Property Bar. You can also add and delete nodes by pressing the plus and minus keys on the keyboard.

Defining Node Types

CorelDRAW offers three types of curve nodes: Cusp nodes, Smooth nodes, and Symmetrical nodes, which are illustrated in Figure 10.10.

10

FIGURE **10.10**

*Cusp and Smooth
nodes enable you to
edit line segments on
either side indepen-
dently. Symmetrical
nodes synchronize line
segment editing.*

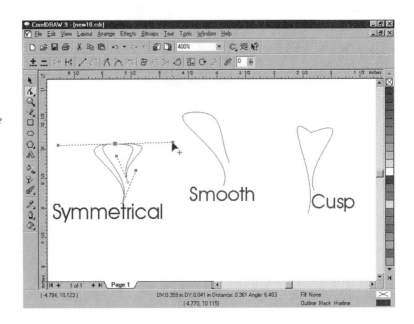

Use Symmetrical nodes to create curves that are equal on each side. Smooth nodes are best for creating rounded curves that are not symmetrical, and Cusp nodes are best for creating pointed curves. All this will make more sense as you experiment with curves and learn to edit control points.

Bending Curves with Control Points

When you select a single curve node with the Shape tool, you see two control points. Node curves are determined by the type of curve (Cusp, Smooth, or Symmetrical) and by the distance and location of the control points. When you pull away from a node on a control point, you increase the effect of the curve. In Figure 10.11, I'm stretching one of the two control points on a Cusp node to increase the intensity or sharpness of the curve.

Similarly, dragging in on a control point lessens the impact of a defined curve.

FIGURE **10.11**

Pulling out on a control point increases the sharpness of a curve.

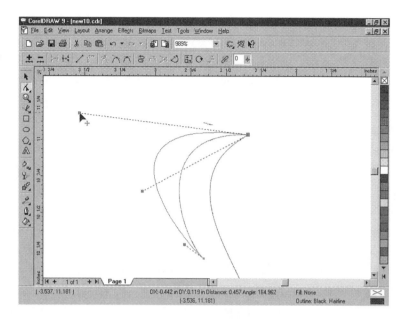

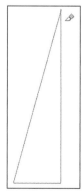

10.3: Transform a Triangle into a Sail

1. Draw a triangle.

2. Cut the triangle in half vertically using the Knife tool. Do this by selecting the Knife tool from the Shape flyout and clicking first at the top of the triangle. Then click on the center of the bottom leg of the triangle. Use the Pick tool to select the right half of the triangle and delete it. Make the triangle about three times as high as it is wide, so you end up with a triangle like the one in Figure 10.12.

FIGURE **10.12**

A couple of clicks with the Knife tool and an isosceles triangle becomes a right-angle triangle.

3. Use the Shape tool to select the lower-left node on the triangle. Convert the line above the node into a curve by clicking on the Convert Line To Curve button in the Property Bar. Use the control handles to shape the sail, as shown in Figure 10.13.

4. Manipulate the control handles at either end of the curve to create something like a billowing sail.

FIGURE 10.13

Control handles become active on either end of a line when you convert the line into a curve.

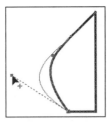

Sculpting Curves with Advanced Node Properties

You need to experiment with node editing. The sail exercise you just completed introduced you to curving lines. You can edit any line on any curve by manipulating nodes and control points.

Don't start with editing control points. Normally, you create a rough shape for your object using the Shape tool or the Freehand Drawing tool. Next, you can further edit the curve by moving nodes with the Shape tool. Finally, fine-tune your illustration by manipulating control points to shape your curves.

Some buttons on the Node Property Bar are features you can investigate on your own, but here is a brief description of them:

- The Stretch and Scale Nodes button enables you to resize only those curves in an object attached to selected nodes.

- The Rotate and Skew nodes enables you to rotate only selected nodes in an object. Nodes that are not selected will not rotate.

- The Align Nodes button enables you to align selected nodes horizontally or vertically.

- The Elastic Mode button changes the way selected nodes behave when one of the nodes is moved. With Elastic Mode on (the button pressed in), all selected nodes will move when you drag on any one of them.

Summary

CorelDRAW provides almost unlimited control over the appearance of a curve through manipulating nodes. However, manipulating nodes is used to fine tune a drawing, not to create a rough sketch. So don't start with the most detailed tools; start by drawing rough shapes and curves.

If you create a rough drawing using Shape tools (for example, a 12-pointed star), you can convert that shape to a curve by selecting the shape and choosing Arrange, Convert to Curves from the menu bar.

After you rough out your drawing with shapes or freehand tools, touch up your illustration by selecting a type of curve (Cusp, Smooth, or Symmetrical) and adjusting control points to shape those curves.

Workshop

Use your newly acquired ability to edit shapes, as well as some techniques you picked up in previous hours, to create the travel company logo shown in Figure 10.14, but feel free to modify it to fit your own skill level.

FIGURE 10.14

This logo is created from basic shapes transformed into curves.

10

Here are the basic steps to create the illustration:

1. Open a new document and create a five-pointed star (double-click on the Polygon tool to define a five-pointed star). Use the Shape tool to contort the shape into a star like the one in Figure 10.15.

FIGURE 10.15

Using the Shape tool to transform a star.

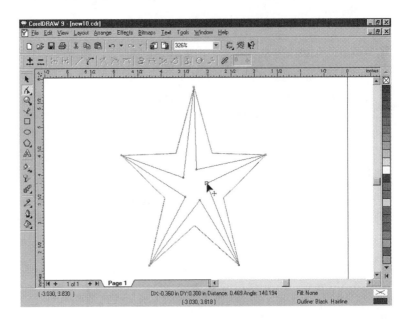

2. Duplicate the star (select it and press Ctrl+D) and rotate the second star. Place one on top of the other and assign the same fill color and outline color to both distorted stars to create a shape something like the star displayed back in Figure 10.14.

3. Begin to create the sailboat by creating one triangle and cutting it in half vertically with the Knife tool. Create a triangle for the bottom of the boat by rotating a triangle, cutting it in half, and deleting half the triangle so your illustration looks something like the one in Figure 10.16.

4. Add the following text: Star Tours.

5. The basic shape of the boat and sails are already created by the three triangles. Edit the nodes to produce the three elements of the boat. You can experiment with interactive fills (we covered them in Hour 7, "Mixing Up Fills") to enhance the effect of a billowing sail, as shown in Figure 10.17.

FIGURE 10.16

Creating the basis for the boat from three triangles.

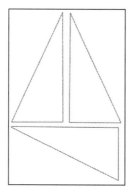

FIGURE 10.17

Two of the triangles are converted into curves to create sails. An interactive fill completes the effect.

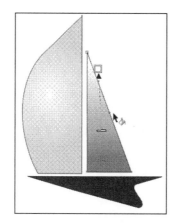

10

Quiz

Answers to the quiz questions can be found in Appendix A, "Quiz Answers."

1. How do you round the corners on a rectangle?

2. Which tool can cut a shape into two?

3. How do you transform a selected line or shape into a curve?

4. How do you add nodes to a curve?

5. How can you fine-tune the appearance of a curve?

PART IV
Adding Effects

Hour

Hour 11

Working with Bitmap Images in CorelDRAW 9

In Hour 1, "Dive In! Having Fun with CorelDRAW 9," you learned the difference between CorelDRAW's vector-based graphic images and bitmap images. Vector-based images consist of curves and nodes, which are stored on file as mathematical formulas, generated as you draw. Because of this, CorelDRAW gives you unmatched power to draw complex and smooth curves.

Furthermore, because objects in CorelDRAW are saved as formulas, these images can be reproduced at any size, from a postage stamp to a billboard. You will start to notice the difference between bitmap- and vector-based graphics when you attempt to edit them. Bitmaps cannot have outlines and fills defined with the same detail that vector-based images can. When vector-based images are enlarged, they maintain the same outline and fill characteristics. In Figure 11.1, the vector-based handicapped-accessible icon maintains the same resolution and quality even when enlarged five times, whereas its bitmap-based cousin does not maintain the same outline characteristics.

FIGURE **11.1**

The vector-based handicapped-accessible icon on the left keeps its outline width even when enlarged five times; the outline on the bitmap icon on the bottom gets blurrier when the object is enlarged.

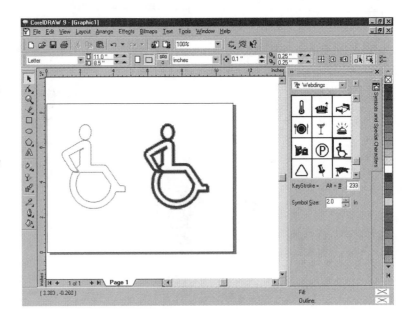

The advantages to using bitmap images include the following:

- For objects that will *not* be enlarged, bitmap files can be much more efficient than vector-based images. Because files are saved as bitmap dots, not curves, an object made up of a hundred curves is simpler to save if it is saved only as dots.
- Effects such as 3D effects, art strokes, and blurring effects are available for bitmap images and not available for vector-based objects.
- Graphic images used on most World Wide Web sites must be bitmapped in order to be recognized by Web browsers.

For these reasons, it is important that you become "bilingual" as far as graphic image formats are concerned, and that you learn to work with bitmap images as well as vector images. In this hour, you learn to incorporate bitmap images in your CorelDRAW illustrations.

What Are Bitmap Images?

When you start working with Corel PHOTO-PAINT 8, in Hour 20, "Diving into PHOTO-PAINT," you'll be introduced to bitmap images in detail. PHOTO-PAINT is exclusively a bitmap image editing program. But here's the "short course" on what bitmap images are and how they work.

Simply put, bitmaps are images that store a location and description of pixels. Pixels are nothing but dots. So, rather than defining images in terms of curves and lines, bitmap images are defined as dots.

Bitmap properties are defined mainly by the *resolution* of the image, expressed in dots per inch (dpi), and the *number of colors* that compose the image. These two properties determine the quality of the image and the size of the file. As you might guess, higher-quality images take up more disk space.

Frequently used bitmap resolutions include 300dpi (which is what older laser printers use to reproduce images), 600dpi (which is what newer laser printers support), and 72dpi (which is what most computer screens use). If, for example, you are creating an image for a Web site, don't assign a resolution higher than 72dpi because the final output (a computer screen) will not support the additional pixels. When you work with bitmap images in CorelDRAW, you assign resolutions to them.

Bitmap images can also have different numbers of colors. Those include black-and-white images, 8-bit grayscale (256 shades of gray), and 8-bit paletted (256 colors). Other color modes exist as well, but these are sufficient to use with most bitmap images that you will work with in CorelDRAW. When you explore PHOTO-PAINT 9, you'll learn to use bitmap color modes that support even larger numbers of colors.

11

Why Edit Bitmap Images in CorelDRAW?

CorelDRAW is not really a full-featured bitmap editor. PHOTO-PAINT is. And with every copy of CorelDRAW 9, you got PHOTO-PAINT 8 free. So what's the point of editing bitmaps in CorelDRAW 9? If you work *exclusively* with bitmap images, you should work in PHOTO-PAINT instead of CorelDRAW. But if you combine both vector and bitmap images, CorelDRAW supports this much better than PHOTO-PAINT or any bitmap editor.

At this point, you might be asking yourself, "Can't we all just get along? Why can't *somebody* come up with a program that will edit both bitmap- and vector-based graphics?" Well, somebody has, and you're using the program. CorelDRAW 9 includes a Bitmap menu that lets you create, edit, and save bitmap images in CorelDRAW. So, in effect, you can work in a mixed environment.

The one thing that you cannot do is transform bitmap images to vector-based images. Programs exist that attempt to trace the lines in bitmap images and convert them into vector-based curves, but these programs are basically trying to guess at which dots should be converted to which lines, and the results are usually not satisfactory.

Where to Get Bitmap Images

There are several ways to get bitmap images in CorelDRAW, including the following:

- Use a scanner or digital camera to bring images into CorelDRAW. The File menu has options that launch either your scanner or digital camera interface directly from DRAW.
- Import bitmap images created with other programs such as PHOTO-PAINT.
- Copy and paste bitmap images into CorelDRAW from the Web or from other sources.
- Convert objects created in CorelDRAW to bitmap images.

In this section, you learn to obtain bitmap images in CorelDRAW using importing, copying, and converting techniques.

Importing Bitmap Images

One way to place a bitmap image in the CorelDRAW Drawing window is to import an exiting image. This is a cinch. Simply select File, Import from the menu bar and use the Look In drop-down list to navigate to the folder on your system in which your graphic files are stored. Or, if you are opening one of the thousands of bitmap clip art images that come with CorelDRAW from your CD, navigate to your CD drive.

If you click on the Preview check box in the Import dialog box, you can see a thumbnail of your image before you elect to import it. In Figure 11.2, I've found the graphic image I want, and I'm looking at it in the Preview window.

FIGURE 11.2

The Preview check box turns the Import dialog box into a graphic index of your saved images.

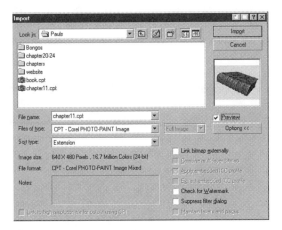

When you find your image, double-click on it to import it into your open CorelDRAW drawing.

Copy and Paste Bitmap Images

The easiest way to bring bitmap images into CorelDRAW is to copy and paste them. Any image that you can see on your computer screen can be copied and pasted into CorelDRAW as a bitmap object. That includes images that you see on the World Wide Web (provided of course that you have permission to copy them).

11.1: Copy a Bitmap Image into CorelDRAW

▼ To Do

1. Open a program in which you can view the bitmap image you want to import into CorelDRAW. This can be another graphics program or a Web browser.

2. Open the file or view the Web site containing the image you want to copy into CorelDRAW.

3. Right-click on the image you want to copy and select Copy from the shortcut menu. In Figure 11.3, I'm copying an image from a Web site.

FIGURE 11.3

I checked to make sure it was okay to copy images from this Web site before pulling a graphic into CorelDRAW 9.

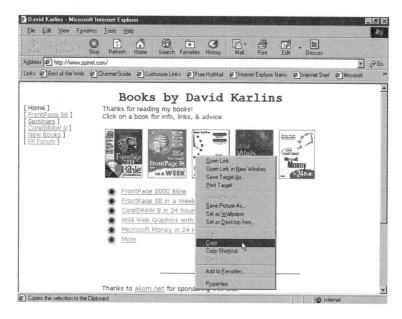

11

> If your program does not support this method of copying an image using the right-click shortcut menu, you can select the image and choose Edit, Copy from your menu bar. If neither of those options are available, click on the image and press Ctrl+C on the keyboard.

4. With your image copied to the Clipboard, close the program from which you copied it and return to, or open, a new CorelDRAW 9 drawing.

5. Right-click in the Drawing window and select Paste from the shortcut menu. The bitmap image will be copied into your drawing. In Figure 11.4, I'm pasting an imported bitmap onto the Drawing page.

FIGURE **11.4**

Pasting a bitmap image into CorelDRAW.

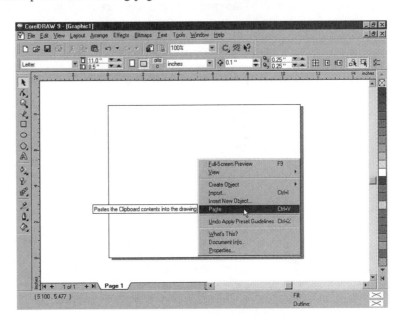

Most of the time that you work with bitmap objects within CorelDRAW, it will be because you brought a bitmap image from somewhere else into CorelDRAW. However, sometimes you'll want to convert a vector image into a bitmap so that you can apply effects that are available only in bitmap images. To learn how to do that, read on.

Converting Objects to Bitmaps

You can create bitmap images from CorelDRAW by first designing a drawing. To do that, just create a drawing in CorelDRAW. Select the objects that you want to convert into a single bitmap image and then choose Bitmaps, Convert to Bitmap from the menu bar.

The Convert to Bitmap dialog box is shown in Figure 11.5. The Color drop-down menu offers different color modes. Paletted is best for images that will be placed on Web sites. One color is best for black-and-white drawings. RGB or CMYK color is best for images that will appear on a high-resolution monitor or printed using a color printing process. For images destined for the Web, 256 colors is appropriate for GIF image format, and 24-bit color is best for images that will be saved to JPEG format.

FIGURE 11.5

The Convert to Bitmap dialog box.

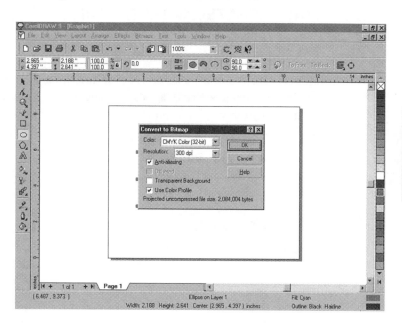

The Dithered check box enables a feature (*dithering*) that compensates for colors that are not on your color palette by mixing colored dots. The Transparent Background check box can eliminate a colored background from your image. The Resolution drop-down list enables you to choose how many dots per inch (dpi) you want to assign to your image. More dots make a higher quality image but take more disk space. The projected file size is shown on the bottom of the dialog box and changes as you select color and resolution settings.

Anti-aliasing is discussed in some detail in the hours in this book devoted to PHOTO-PAINT. The short explanation is that it eliminates jagged edges in bitmap objects, but the downside is that it makes the text blurrier. The Convert to Bitmap dialog box gives you three anti-aliasing options: None, Normal, or (the max) Super-sampling.

As you select properties for your bitmap conversion, the dialog box displays a projected file size at the bottom. Increasing colors and resolution increases file size, and stripping down to an 8-bit color palette and a 72dpi resolution (fine for most Web graphics) reduces file size dramatically compared to 300dpi, 24-bit color. After you define settings for your selected object(s), click on OK.

Applying Effects to Bitmaps

After you create a bitmap image in CorelDRAW 9, you can apply some useful effects that are not available for vector-based objects.

Those effects include using a color mask to strip any unwanted color out of an image, assigning transparency to bitmap images so that they appear to have no background when displayed on Web sites, and applying a range of distortion effects to your image that can be fun to use.

Other effects include transformations with names such as Solarize, Impressionist, Psychedelic, Glass Block, and Vignette. All bitmap effects are available from the Bitmap menu option in the menubar.

Using a Color Mask on Bitmap Images

You can use bitmap color masks to eliminate any color from any bitmap image. This is especially useful with scanned or imported photos. Color masking can be, in effect, a recoloring tool. Too much red or blue in a photo? You can correct that with color masking.

You can also use color masking to transform the fills of any bitmap images.

11.2: Strip a Color from a Bitmap Image

1. Create a bitmap image by scanning a photo, inserting a digital photo, converting a drawing, or importing or copying a bitmap image into CorelDRAW.
2. Select the bitmap image. Handles appear, just as they do when you select any object in CorelDRAW.
3. Select Bitmap, Bitmap Color Mask from the menu bar.
4. Click on the Hide Colors options button at the top of the Bitmap Color Mask Docker window.

▼   5. Click on the first bar in the Bitmap Color Mask Docker window. Then click on the
       Color Selector, as I am doing in Figure 11.6. (It looks like an eyedropper.)

FIGURE 11.6

*Use the color selector
to create a perfect
match for a color you
want to remove from a
bitmap image.*

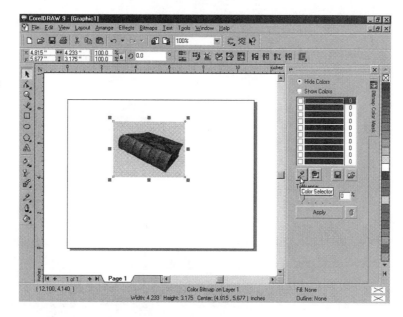

6. Move your cursor, in the bitmap image, over the color you want to remove. That
   color appears in the first bar of the Bitmap Color Mask rollup. When the color in
   the rollup matches the color you want to delete, click with the Color Selector cursor. In Figure 11.7, I'm selecting one color from my scanned image to delete.

7. To delete only the exact color you selected, leave the Tolerance slider set at or near
   0. To blast away at any color that even remotely resembles the one you chose, push
   the slider up to 100. Settings between 0 and 100 determine how close a color
   match you are defining.

8. If you need to delete additional colors from your bitmap image, use the remaining
   bars in the Bitmap Color Mask rollup and assign additional colors to as many of
   them as you need.

9. Before you apply the color mask, you can click on the check boxes next to any of
   the color bars to exclude that color from the list of those that will be removed.

10. When you've fine-tuned your Color Mask criteria, click on the Apply button to
    transform your bitmap. In Figure 11.8, I stripped the bright background color out
▼   of a copy of my book cover.

FIGURE 11.7

Moving your eyedropper cursor over even one pixel can change the selected color.

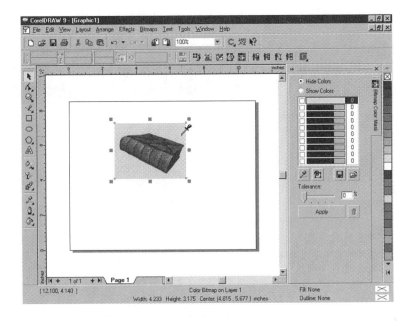

FIGURE 11.8

The Bitmap Color Mask rollup is basically a "decolorizer."

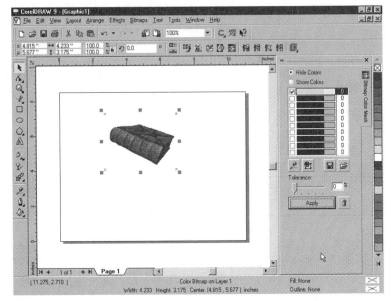

Assigning Transparency to Bitmap Images

Transparency is like color masking, but a bit simpler. When you assign transparency to a bitmap image, you strip away a single background color.

You can use the Convert to Bitmap dialog box to transform existing bitmap images. If you copy or import an image with a background that you want to remove, select it, choose Bitmap, Convert to Bitmap from the menu bar, and use the Transparent Background check box to strip the background from the image. The Transparent Background check box detects and strips the white background from behind an image.

In Figure 11.9, I selected an imported bitmap image, and I'm using the Convert to Bitmap dialog box to change the image to a 72dpi, 8-bit color, transparent image ready to be saved to a Web site.

FIGURE 11.9

Adding transparency to a bitmap image.

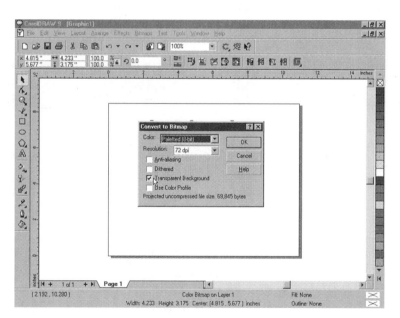

Assigning Effects to Bitmap Images

CorelDRAW's Bitmap menu includes a number of distortion effects that are fun to apply to bitmaps. These effects are culled from the arsenal of effects that you will learn to use in the hours in this book that you spend on Corel PHOTO-PAINT. You'll investigate these effects more in Hours 20–22. But you can try 3D effects now.

Not all Bitmap effects can be applied to every bitmap. The available effects depend on the color mode and type of the bitmap image.

When you select a bitmap image and choose an effect from the Bitmap menu, you can see the changes you are applying in two different ways. In the effect dialog box, shown in Figure 11.10, you can click on the Preview button to display changes you make with the sliders before they are applied to the image in the Drawing window.

FIGURE 11.10

You can preview bitmap effects in a dialog box.

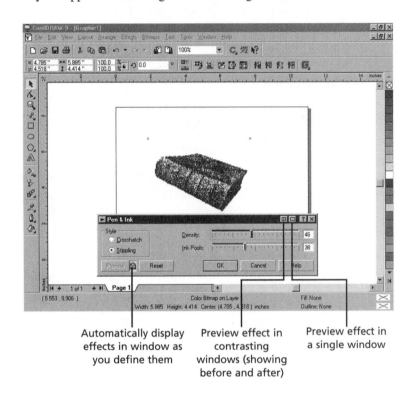

Automatically display effects in window as you define them

Preview effect in contrasting windows (showing before and after)

Preview effect in a single window

The buttons in the effect dialog box enable you to preview your effect in different ways. The first button displays the effect in contrasting (before and after) windows. The second button displays effects in a single preview window, or automatically transforms the image in the Preview window as you experiment with changes in effect settings.

The default setting for bitmap effect dialog boxes enables you to see your changes in the Drawing Window when you click on the Preview button.

You can moderate and change the impact of bitmap effects by experimenting with the sliders in each box. Figure 11.11 shows a bitmap effect being applied using the contrasting windows preview option, so the original can be compared to the new bitmap.

FIGURE 11.11

Previewing bitmap effects in contrasting (before and after windows).

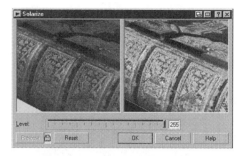

When you toggle to the effect dialog box without a Preview screen, the button on the left toggles back to the Preview dialog box, and the button on the right displays the effect you are defining in the Drawing area.

When you have defined and previewed a bitmap effect, click on OK in the dialog box to apply that effect to the selected bitmap object.

Summary

You have many reasons to work with objects as bitmap images. You might want to import images in bitmap file formats. Many effects and distortion tools are available for bitmap images and not available for vector-based objects.

You can edit bitmap images in CorelDRAW, but many of the editing techniques you've learned so far do not apply to bitmaps. You cannot edit nodes or curves in bitmap images, but you can apply a sample selection of bitmap effects to these images.

Workshop

In this workshop, you create a bitmap from a symbol. You also apply bitmap effects to the bitmap.

1. Drag a symbol of your choice (from the Symbols docker) into the Drawing window. Assign a thick black outline and a bright color fill to the symbol.

2. Enlarge the symbol so it is about 3 inches square.

3. With the symbol selected, convert it to a 72dpi, 8-bit color, transparent bitmap with anti-aliasing, as shown in Figure 11.12. As you learned earlier in this hour, these settings are found in the Convert to Bitmap dialog box (use the Bitmap, Convert to Bitmap menu selection).

11

FIGURE **11.12**

Converting a symbol to a bitmap.

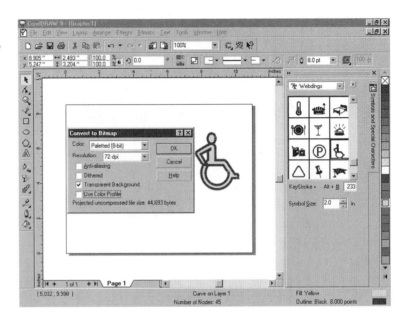

4. Select the bitmap object and choose Bitmap, 3D Effects, 3D Rotate from the menu bar; set the vertical effect slider at about 20 and the horizontal slider at about –20. Click on the Preview button to see the impact of your rotation in the Drawing window, as shown in Figure 11.13.

FIGURE **11.13**

Rotating a bitmap.

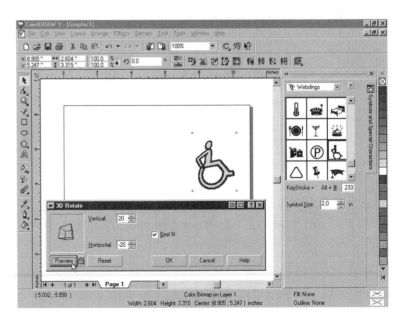

5. Change the settings for horizontal rotation at 18 and vertical rotation at –18, and preview the image again. Click on OK to assign the effect to your bitmap image.

6. Save your illustration.

7. Now that you've saved your bitmap image, experiment with other effects, such as Swirl or Find Edges.

Nice work! Even if you didn't exactly follow my steps, you experimented with combining bitmap and vector objects.

Quiz

Answers to the quiz questions can be found in Appendix A, "Quiz Answers."

1. What are bitmaps?

2. How do you remove a background from an imported bitmap?

3. How do you bring bitmaps into CorelDRAW?

4. How do you strip several undesired colors from a scanned photo?

11

Hour 12

Lenses and PowerClips

For the first 11 hours of this book, you've put in some hard work learning how CorelDRAW works. You've explored the process of generating curves, editing curve nodes, and working with bitmap images within CorelDRAW. Congratulations! Now it's show time!

Starting with this hour, you begin to explore some of the fun you can have with the effects that are available in CorelDRAW. This is where you get to play with the almost magical array of special effects, such as fisheye lenses, magnifying lenses, and filling objects with other objects. These effects are built into CorelDRAW's Lens and PowerClip tools.

In this hour, you learn to create lenses, like the one in Figure 12.1, where I'm using the Interactive Transparency tool to turn the magnifying glass into a lens with gradated transparency. Lenses can apply many different effects; the one in Figure 12.1 has a magnifying effect attached to it.

FIGURE **12.1**

Looking at artistic text through a lens effect.

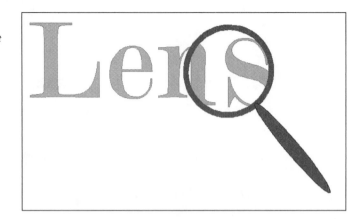

Here, you will also explore using PowerClips to insert bitmap fills into objects. In Figure 12.2, I've taken a fill and "injected" it into some artistic text.

FIGURE **12.2**

Filling artistic text with a bitmap PowerClip.

In this hour, you will also explore the Interactive Transparency tool. Transparent objects can be seen through, whereas opaque objects cover other objects completely. The Interactive Transparency tool enables you to assign varying degrees of transparency to different parts of a single object. In Figure 12.3, I'm tweaking the transparency assigned to the eyeball covering some of my artistic text.

So if you're ready to have some fun, read on.

FIGURE **12.3**

Interactive Transparency enables you to assign varying degrees of transparency to an object.

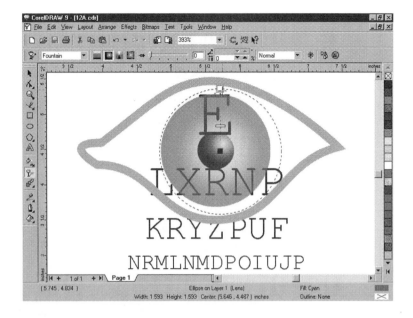

Creating Lenses

CorelDRAW's lens effect works just like a glass lens. But just as a glass lens can have many different effects, so can a CorelDRAW lens. For example, a glass lens can be dark like sunglasses, magnify like my glasses, or even warp an image. In the same way, lenses in CorelDRAW 9 can have different attributes (effects).

Applying a lens effect to an object (often a circle) enables that object to act like a lens—darkening, magnifying, or in some other way distorting any object it is placed over.

Lens effects are used in connection with an object below the lens. That object can be artistic text, a drawn object, or even a bitmap object in the Drawing window. The only objects that are not affected by placing lenses over them are objects that have extrude, contour, or blend effects applied to them.

The key thing to keep in mind is that lens effects do not change the appearance of the object to which they are applied. A circle with a magnify lens effect applied to it does not change its own appearance. The effect takes place when that circle is moved over another object.

12

Lenses can be assigned to any shape, or any closed object for that matter—not just to circles or ovals.

You can group objects that have lens effects applied. For example, to create the magnifying glass in Figure 12.1, I attached a line to the circle with a lens effect applied to it and grouped them. The lens effect will not apply to the line because there's no open area inside the line to act as a lens.

Types of Lenses

The Lens Docker window offers 12 different lenses. Those lens effects are No Lens, Brighten, Color Add, Color Limit, Custom Color Map, Fish Eye, Heat Map, Invert, Magnify, Tinted Grayscale, Transparency, and Wireframe.

A single closed object can have only one lens effect at a time. However, you can apply multiple lens effects by assigning different lenses to different objects, and stacking them up on each other.

I've illustrated all 12 of these effects (11, if you don't count No Lens) in Figure 12.4.

FIGURE **12.4**

Each of the lens effects has its own distortion effect.

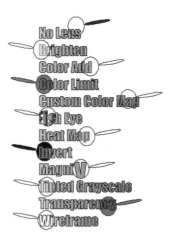

Lens Options

Many lenses come with these options: Frozen, Viewpoint, and/or Remove Face. A Frozen lens applies the effect of the lens permanently (more or less), because you can move or delete the lens and the distortion remains. Clicking on the Viewpoint check box produces an Edit button, which in turn enables you to move the center of the lens effect through x- and y-axis spin boxes.

The Remove Face check box is available for lenses that distort colors. This option enables you to turn off the section of a lens that doesn't cover any other objects.

How to Apply Lenses

Different lenses have different effects, but the process for applying them is basically the same. First, create an object over which you will place your lens. Then, create another object to be used as a lens. Often lenses are composed of circles, but you can use any closed curve (a rectangle, polygon, or closed curve you drew yourself).

Finally, select the object that is to act as the lens and choose Effects, Lens from the menu bar. Select a type of lens from the drop-down list, edit the lens options, and then click on the Apply button to apply your effect to your lens. Move the lens over your object to create the lens effect.

▼ To Do

12.1: Assign a Magnification Lens Effect to Artistic Text

In this exercise, you will create some Artistic text, and then apply a lens effect to a shape placed over the text.

1. Type some artistic text. If you're not poetically inspired this hour, just type Lens Effect.
2. Draw a circle.
3. Select Effects, Lens from the menu bar.
4. Click with the Pick tool to select your circle if it isn't selected.
5. Pull down the drop-down list in the Lens docker window and choose Magnify.
6. Change the degree of magnification by entering 1.5 in the Amount spin box, as I'm doing in Figure 12.5.

▼

12

FIGURE 12.5

You can adjust most lenses; for example, you can change the amount of magnification of the Magnify lens.

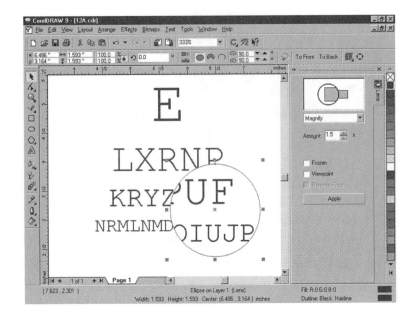

7. When you have defined your lens effect, click on the Apply button.

8. Drag your circle, with its attached lens property, over another part of the text object to experiment with the effect.

You can apply more than one lens at a time to an object, or you can use many lenses in an illustration. However, you'll quickly notice that the calculations CorelDRAW has to perform to achieve these awesome effects are an awesome drain on your computer memory. You might want to switch to Wireframe mode while you edit other parts of your illustration to speed CorelDRAW up a bit. However, you'll have to switch back to Normal view to see your lens effects on your screen.

Applying PowerClips

PowerClips take one selected object and places that inside another object. The object that is inserted into another object is placed in what CorelDRAW calls a *container*. The source for the container can be a closed path, a shape, or artistic text (but not paragraph text).

PowerClips do not change the size of either the container object or the target object. So, if you copy a large object into a small one, it will get cropped to fit the size of the target object. If you copy a small object into a large object, it will not fill the target object completely.

You apply a PowerClip by first creating the container object. Fill that object. Edit it. Touch it up, keeping in mind that you're about to use it to fill another object. Then, create the object into which you will inject the PowerClip.

With both the container and target objects created, select the container object with the Pick tool. Choose Effects, PowerClip, Place Inside Container. As soon as you do, a large black arrow appears on your screen. Point that arrow at the target for the PowerClip and click. The container object gets injected into the target object.

12.2: Insert a PowerClip into Artistic Text

▲ To Do

1. Draw a rectangle about the width of a page and fill it with a bitmap fill (you'll find bitmap fills in the Pattern Fill dialog box, accessible from the Fill tool flyout). Convert the filled rectangle into a bitmap (select Bitmap, Convert to Bitmap from the menu).

2. Type the word MINNESOTA in artistic text (all caps). Select Impact font and stretch the text so it is a bit narrower than the width of the page. Your page should look something like Figure 12.6.

FIGURE 12.6

By making my container object (the bitmap image) wider than the text, I'm ensuring that the entire text object will be filled when I use the pattern as a container.

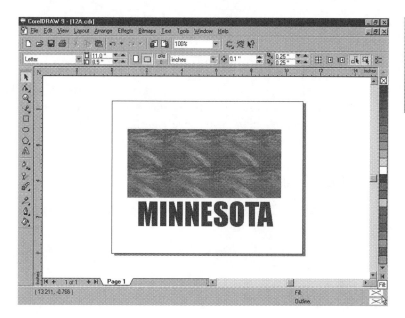

12

▼

▼   3. Use the Pick tool to select the bitmap image.

4. Select Effects, PowerClip, Place Inside Container from the menu bar.

5. Point the new, thick black arrow cursor at the text, as I am doing in Figure 12.7.

FIGURE 12.7

After you load an image into a PowerClip container, just point and click to insert that image into another object.

▲

Figure 12.8 shows the effect of a bitmap loaded into a PowerClip and injected into artistic text. You can edit the contents of a PowerClip by clicking on the (combined) object and selecting Effects, PowerClip, Edit Contents. After you edit the PowerClip container contents, choose Effects, PowerClip, Finish Editing This Level to place the container object back into the target object.

FIGURE 12.8

A bitmap image injected into artistic text.

Defining Interactive Transparency

The last effect you learn in this hour is interactive transparency. This effect works a bit like lens effects because it is applied to one object that is then placed over another object. What's unique about the Interactive Transparency tool is that you can define a graded degree of transparency within the "lens" object.

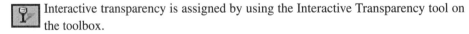 Interactive transparency is assigned by using the Interactive Transparency tool on the toolbox.

In Figure 12.3, I used interactive transparency to make an eyeball (really just a filled circle) partially transparent.

The Interactive Transparency tool enables you to apply varying degrees of transparency to a selected object.

12.3: Assign Interactive Transparency to an Object

▼To Do

In this exercise, you will assign interactive transparency to a shape.

1. Type a word in artistic text.

2. Create a closed object—a rectangle will do fine. Move the rectangle so it partially covers your text.

3. Select the rectangle and click on the Interactive Transparency tool. Click and draw across the rectangle, from right to left, starting at what will be the less-transparent end of the rectangle. In Figure 12.9, I'm defining less transparency in the upper-right of the rectangle and more in the lower-left.

FIGURE 12.9

The light square in the Interactive Transparency line indicates the less transparent end of the spectrum.

▲

4. Adjust the bar in the middle of the Interactive Transparency line to move the shift-point for transparency.

After you assign interactive transparency to an object, you can edit the shift-point by clicking on the Interactive Transparency tool in the toolbox and adjusting the shift-point. You can also move either end of the Interactive Transparency line to adjust the direction of the applied transparency. In Figure 12.10, I'm moving the endpoints to redefine the flow of the transparency gradient.

12

FIGURE 12.10

After you apply inter-active transparency, you can select the Interactive Transparency tool and move either endpoint to edit the direction of the transparency gradient.

When you select an object with the Interactive Transparency tool, the Interactive Transparency Property bar allows you to assign different shapes for transparency: Linear, Radial, Conical, and Square. Feel free to experiment with each of these methods for defining interactive transparency.

Summary

CorelDRAW 9 comes loaded with special effects that you can apply to objects. In this hour, you examined three effects that are applied by combining two different objects. Both Lenses and Interactive Transparency involve one object acting as a lens, being placed over another object.

PowerClips use more than one object to achieve their effect as well. A first object is loaded into a container and then "injected" into a second object.

Workshop

For this workshop, Paul created an illustration that is fun but challenging, as shown in Figure 12.11, so feel free to modify the following steps.

FIGURE **12.11**

Paul's illustration combines interactive transparency and lens effects.

1. Type some large artistic text, like what you see in Paul's model.
2. Assign interactive transparency to the text, as shown in Figure 12.12.

FIGURE 12.12

*Assigning interactive
transparency to artistic
text.*

3. Create an eyeball using two filled circles, as shown in Figure 12.13 (you can skip the eye outline if you wish!). Add interactive transparency to the outer and inner eyeball, as shown in Figures 12.13 and 12.14.

FIGURE 12.13

*Assigning interactive
transparency to the
outer eyeball.*

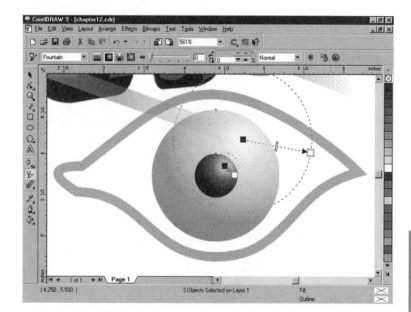

12

FIGURE 12.14

*The interactive trans-
parency inner eyeball
at an insane magnifi-
cation of 2464%.*

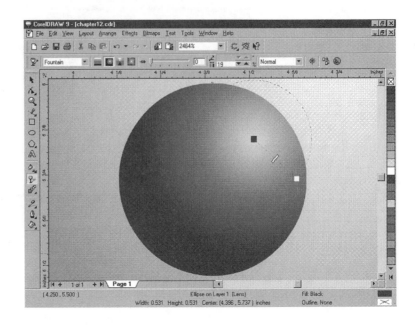

4. Add a shape that can serve as a lens. If you're ambitious, you can put together eye-
glasses as Paul did, or just create a circle or two to which you can apply lens
effects. Assign an Invert lens to your shape(s), as shown in Figure 12.15.

FIGURE 12.15

*The Invert lens effect
is applied to both eye-
glass lenses.*

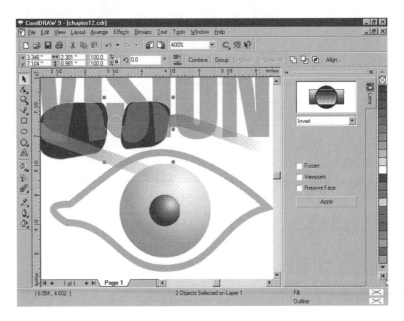

Quiz

Answers to the quiz questions can be found in Appendix A, "Quiz Answers."

1. How are lens effects different from fills?

2. Do PowerClips enlarge (or shrink) to fit the object into which they are injected?

3. What is so special about the Interactive Transparency tool?

4. Can you apply more than one lens at a time to an object?

5. How do you edit the contents of a PowerClip?

12

HOUR 13

Blends and Contours

In the previous hour, you started to experiment with the PowerClip, Lens, and Interactive Transparency effects that distort objects to which they are applied.

In this hour, you explore a couple effects that change objects based on duplicating them and distorting the clones.

The blend effect enables you to fill the space between two different objects with a set of new objects that change, step-by-step, from the first object to the second. Not only do the size and shape of blended images evolve from one object to another, but the color evolves as well. You can define a line along which the blend will take place. Figure 13.1 shows artistic text blending along a Bézier curve.

FIGURE 13.1

*Blends can convert
one object into another
along a defined line.*

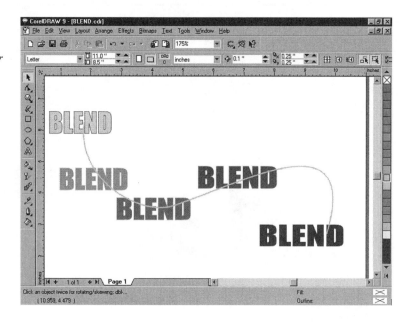

The contour effect enables you to create concentric lines inside or outside a selected object. This is a quick, easy way to draw concentric circles. Figure 13.2 shows the three ways you can apply contours: a defined number of lines inside the original object, a defined number of lines outside the original object, or as many lines as it takes to get to the center of the entire selected object.

The contour effect also has a feature that enables you to transform colors from an inside to an outside color, as you create contours. The concentric circles in Figure 13.2 transform from a dark color to a light color.

FIGURE 13.2

*Use contours to draw
concentric circles.*

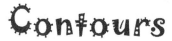

Working with Blends

Blends are an amazingly intelligent effect, and as such it's often hard to predict the exact effect you will create using them. If you are blending one object into another with a similar size and shape, the results are fairly straightforward. In Figure 13.3, I'm blending one oval into another, with slight color differences between the two objects. The results are a smooth, almost gradient, evolution from one color to the other.

FIGURE 13.3

Blends between similar objects are smooth and gradient.

However, blends between objects that are very different in size, shape, and color produce some wild transitional shapes, as you can see in Figure 13.4.

FIGURE 13.4

Blending a dark square and a bright star produces some unusual transitional shapes.

13

Defining Blends

Aside from the shapes that you blend into each other, you can control the effect of a blend by defining the number of steps (transformations) to take place and assigning rotation to the intermediate objects created by the blend effect.

13.1: Blend a Circle into a Square in Three Steps

1. Draw a circle and draw a square. Assign different color fills to each.

2. Click on the Interactive Blend tool in the toolbar. Click and drag to connect the circle and the square, as shown in Figure 13.5.

FIGURE 13.5

Defining a blend.

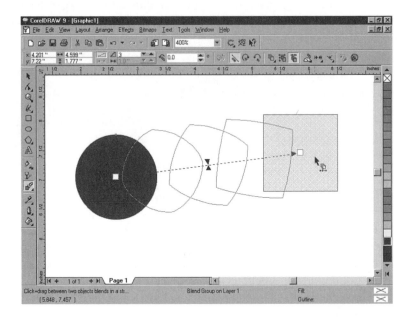

When you select the Interactive Blend tool, the Blend Property Bar becomes active. The Property Bar has a Number of Steps or Offset Between Blend Shapes spin box from which you can control the speed at which your objects transform into each other.

The more steps in a blend, the more transitional effects you create. A three-step blend has relatively dramatic changes between each intermediate object in the blend, whereas a 30-step blend has relatively imperceptible changes between intermediate objects.

3. Set the Number of Steps or Offset Between Blend Shapes to 3.

After you create a blend, you can edit the effect by changing the settings in the Blend Property Bar, or by editing either the starting or ending object. For example, when you edit the fill color of the square you used in the previous To Do exercise, the whole blend will change. Or you can edit (or remove) outlines from either the start or finish objects, or both. Resizing either the starting or ending object changes all the intermediate objects generated by the blend.

Blending Along a Path

The blend effect can generate intermediate objects along a defined path. To do this, you first draw a line and then blend two objects from the start to the finish of that line.

If you have two objects you want to blend into each other and a drawn path, you're ready to blend along that path.

In this exercise, you will create a blend that follows a Bézier curve.

▼ To Do

13.2: Blend Circles Along a Path

1. Draw one circle. Duplicate it and separate the circles.

2. Draw a Bézier curve. Any curve will do nicely.

3. Select the Interactive Blend tool in the toolbar. Click and drag from one circle to another to create a blend between the two circles.

4. Select 20 in the Number of Steps spin box in the Property Bar to create a smoother blend.

5. Click on the Path Properties button, and then the curved line button on the right side of the Blend Property Bar. Choose New Path from the menu that appears.

6. Point the curved line cursor that appears at the Bézier curve you defined in step 2. I'm doing that in Figure 13.6.

FIGURE 13.6

Blends can travel along custom-defined paths.

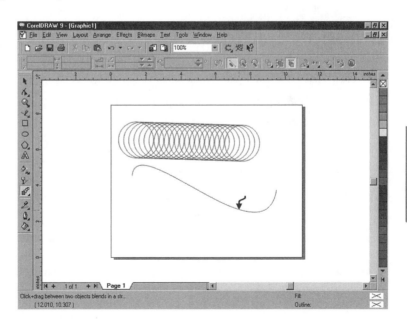

▼

13

▼   7. Select one of the circles (this can be a little tricky—click directly on the edge of the circle with the Pick tool to select it). Drag the circle along the path of the curve on which the blend is being effected, and note how the blend is affected. Drag the circle to the ends of the curve, as shown in Figure 13.7.

FIGURE 13.7

Moving blended objects along a path.

You can hide the line that forms the blend path by simply assigning no outline to it.

The Blend Property Bar has more features than will fit in this hour. One effect that you can experiment with easily is to use the two sliders found in the Object and Color Acceleration flyout button. Object and color acceleration change the impact of a blend from a smooth, gradual, equal transition to a distorted transition, so that most of the changes happen either toward the beginning or the end of the blend.

Blends are so flexible and have so many options that this book could be filled with nothing but blending! A good way to experiment is to just take the blend you created in the
▲   two To Do exercises so far and try applying the different effects in the Property Bar.

Defining Contours

At the beginning of this hour, you saw how you can use contours to create concentric circles. That's one quick, handy use of the Contour tool.

Illustrators also use contours to create blended effects. For example, you can transform a contoured rectangle into a picture frame. By combining contours with changed colors, you can often simulate the illusion of a 3D frame.

Defining Contour Lines

The most basic application of contours is to create lines around or inside a selected object. You can define how many lines and what distance they should be from each other.

The thickness and color of the generated contour lines is determined by the thickness and color of the original lines. You can define line properties the same way you define any outline color and thickness: Right-click on the color palette to assign outline color, and select outline width from the Outline flyout.

You can define a set number of contour lines inside or outside your selected object. Or you can define contours that completely fill your object (if your object is a closed curve).

Coloring Contour Lines

After you create contours, you can define color gradation between your original outline (or fill) color, and a contour outline (or fill) color. In this way, contours act a bit like blends—the color blends from the original to the contour color.

Contour color changes are defined in the Outline Color or Fill Color drop-down palettes in the Contours Property Bar.

13.3: Create Shape and Color Contours

To Do

1. Draw a circle, about an inch in diameter, and duplicate it twice. Move the circles so they are spaced a couple of inches apart.

2. Choose the Interactive Contour tool from the Interactive Blend flyout. Select the first circle in the Drawing window and click on the Interactive Contour tool.

 3. Click on the Inside tool in the Contour Property Bar.

4. Set the Steps spin box at 2 and select a color from the Outline Color drop-down palette in the Contour Property Bar, as shown in Figure 13.8.

FIGURE 13.8

Selecting a second contour color from the Property Bar.

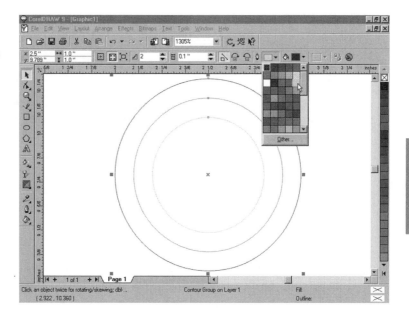

13

▼

 5. Select the second circle with the Contour tool cursor. Click on the Outside Property Bar button.

Leave the Steps and Outline Color settings the same.

 6. Select the third circle with the Contour tool cursor and click on the To Center Property Bar button.

The Steps spin box appears grayed out because CorelDRAW is going to compute how many steps are necessary to fill the circle. Set the Contour Offset to 0.25") and note the generated concentric circles. Experiment with other Contour Offset settings.

Your contours should look similar to the ones in Figure 13.2, near the beginning of this hour.

> After you generate objects using a blend or a contour, you can break the generated objects apart by selecting the contour or blend, and choosing Arrange, Separate from the menubar.

▲

Summary

Both the blend and contour effects apply gradual changes to selected objects. The blend effect requires two different objects, which are blended into each other by generating a series of intermediate objects.

The contour effect is useful for concentric circles or other concentric shapes. It is applied by defining a number of steps and the distance between steps.

Workshop

In this workshop, you combine blends and contours to create an illustration like the one Paul came up with in Figure 13.9. Some of the effects in this workshop are a bit of a challenge, so feel free to modify them to fit your current skill level. As long as you use the effects listed in each step, you'll reinforce your effects skills.

1. Start by creating the rectangular frame around the illustration. The frame is created by starting with a gray rectangle with no outline.

2. Select the Contour tool. Then choose white from the Fill Color drop-down palette in the Contour Property Bar.

FIGURE 13.9

Paul's illustration combines blends and contours.

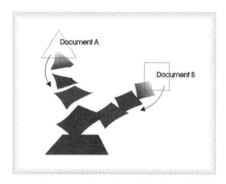

3. Select the Interactive Contour tool (from the Blend flyout). Click on the Center button in the Contour Property Bar and set the offset to 0.05", as shown in Figure 13.10.

FIGURE 13.10

The contour applied to the background rectangle creates a beveled-looking frame for the illustration.

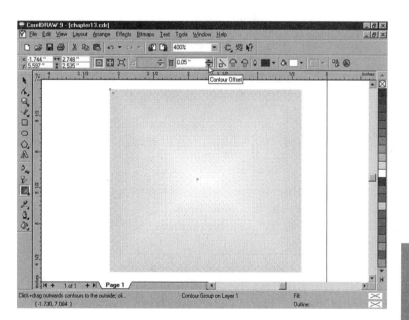

13

4. Start to create the blend diagram by drawing a triangle, a square, and a closed shape (use the Bézier tool to draw the shape, and use the Auto-Close button in the Bézier Property Bar to close the shape). Arrange the three shapes somewhat like those in the drawing in Figure 13.11.

FIGURE 13.11

A square, a triangle, and a third shape, prepared for blending.

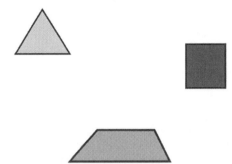

5. Create an interactive blend between the triangle and the center shape, and another interactive blend between the square and the center shape. Use three steps for each blend.

6. Finish your illustration by moving the contoured frame behind the drawing and adding text. You can embellish the diagram by selecting Arrange, Separate from the menu to break up the shapes created by the blend and adjust their location and fill colors.

Quiz

Answers to the quiz questions can be found in Appendix A, "Quiz Answers."

1. What does the Blend tool do?
2. What are the main ways to define the appearance of a blend after the objects have been selected?
3. How do you define the line thickness of the lines generated by the contour effect?
4. What happens when you edit one of the two objects used to generate a blend?

Hour 14

Working with Perspective

Adding perspective enables you to transform objects to create a three-dimensional look. The artistic text in Figure 14.1 appears to be coming off the page and toward the viewer.

You can apply perspective many ways, including extrusion, envelopes, and the Perspective effect itself. In this hour, you learn to work with vanishing points, which make any object appear to display three dimensions; such objects have *perspective*.

In this hour, you also explore applying interactive shading to objects to add dimensionality, and you'll have a little fun with Corel's Extrusion effects.

Applying Perspective

You apply perspective by moving specially empowered handles that appear when you
apply the Perspective effect. These perspective handles enable you to stretch your
selected object as if it were enclosed in a rubber band.

As you drag the perspective handles, the new version of your object is displayed in wireframe, as shown in Figure 14.2.

The small dots and dotted lines that appear when you apply perspective (visible in
Figures 14.2 and 14.3) form a perspective grid. By moving the handles that appear in the
perspective grid, you can create the illusion that the object is receding into the background, behind the page. Moving one node can create the illusion of the object receding
in one direction, and moving two nodes can create the illusion that the object has *vanishing points* (points at which it will disappear into the distance) in three dimensions.

Vanishing points are created when you apply perspective. This vanishing point is displayed in the Drawing Window as an "X." The X is visible when the object to which perspective has been applied is selected. You can adjust the vanishing point by clicking and dragging on it.

In this exercise, you'll create the illusion of artistic text vanishing in the upper left corner of the viewer's screen.

▼ To Do

14.1: Apply Perspective to an Artistic Object

1. Create a text object using artistic text (your name, my name, you'll figure something out). Size the object so it is about 4 inches wide and 2 inches high.

2. With the text object selected, choose Effects, Add Perspective from the menu bar.

3. Hold down Ctrl and drag the bottom perspective handle down, as I'm doing in Figure 14.3.

FIGURE 14.3

The perspective handles move the vanishing point.

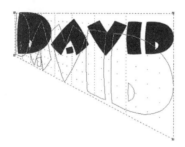

By holding Ctrl down as you drag on a perspective handle, you are constricted to pulling straight down, or at angles of 45-degree increments.

▲   4. Release the cursor and examine the effect of adding perspective.

Enclosing Objects in Envelopes

The Envelope effect gives you even more control over vanishing points and perspective. Envelopes provide a frame for whatever object is inside them.

14

You can apply four types of envelopes to an object: Straight Line, Single Arc, Double Arc, and Unconstrained. The Straight Line, Single Arc, and Double Arc envelopes enable you to change the shape of a selected object by applying a straight line segment, a single curve, or two curves respectively to a selected object. Unconstrained envelopes can be of any shape. Examples of all four are on display in Figure 14.4.

FIGURE 14.4

The Envelope effect comes with four ways to apply perspective.

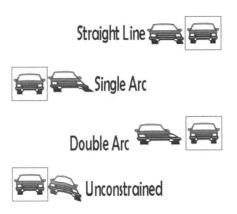

Envelope effects are available from the Envelope Property Bar. You can activate the Envelope Property Bar by selecting the Interactive Envelope Tool from the Blend flyout in the toolbox.

The main way to constrain—or control—the type of Envelope effect you apply is to select one of the four constraint tools in the Property Bar. Those are Straight Line, Single Arc, Double Arc, and Unconstrained, which means you can warp your selected object any way. You saw how the effects look in Figure 14.4, and Figure 14.5 shows the tools in the Property Bar.

FIGURE 14.5

You can assign Envelope effects from the Property Bar.

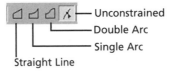

The Envelope Property Bar includes a Mapping Mode drop-down list. The four different mapping modes subtly affect the way envelopes are applied, and the best way to understand the differences is to experiment with them. The four options—Horizontal, Original, Putty, and Vertical—apply each of the four different envelope constraints somewhat differently. In Figure 14.6, I've applied a single arc envelope using each of the four Mapping Modes.

Most illustrators stick to Putty mode and rely on selecting an envelope constraint to control how an envelope is applied.

FIGURE 14.6

Mapping modes affect how envelopes are applied.

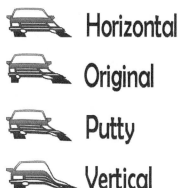

Horizontal

Original

Putty

Vertical

Creating Straight Line Envelopes

When you apply a straight line envelope, you are restricted to straight lines between each perspective handle. When you apply a single arc envelope, you can have a curved line serve as an envelope. Double arc envelopes enable complex curves between handles. Unconstrained envelopes are just what they sound like; they can be reshaped in any form.

14:2 Apply a Straight Line Envelope to Artistic Text

▼ To Do

1. Type your name in artistic text, and enlarge the object to four inches wide and about two inches high.

2. Select the Envelope tool from the Blend flyout in the toolbox.

3. With the Envelope Straight Line button selected in the Property Bar, hold down Shift, and drag in on the top-right handle.

▲

4. Use the Clear Envelope button in the Envelope Property Bar to remove the Envelope effect.

14

By holding Shift down as you drag on a perspective handle, you force your envelope to be symmetrical.

Creating Arc Envelopes

The single and double arc modes enable you to assign curved lines to the envelope shape. They work in a similar way, except that the double arc mode enables you to create more complex shapes.

14.3: Apply a Single Arc Envelope to Artistic Text

▼ To Do

In this exercise, you will distort artistic text using a single arc envelope.

1. Your name or some other artistic text should still be in your CorelDRAW drawing. If not, type your name in artistic text.

2. Select the Interactive Envelope Tool from the toolbox.

3. With the Single Arc mode selected in the Property Bar, hold down Shift and drag up on the bottom (center) handle, as shown in Figure 14.7.

FIGURE **14.7**

Using the Shift key applies a single arc envelope symmetrically to the selected object.

4. Use the Clear Envelope button in the Envelope Property Bar to remove the Envelope effect.

▲

Molding Objects with Envelopes

You can use the Envelope effect to mold an object to a preset shape. This can be a shape from a nice list of geometric shapes and popular symbols that are available from the Envelope rollup. Or you can define your own shape and use that to enclose your object. These techniques are often used to shape artistic text.

14.4: Place Artistic Text in a Shaped Envelope

1. Select artistic text.

2. Select Unconstrained mode in the Envelope Property Bar.

3. Pull down the Present palette in the Envelope Property Bar and click on the waving banner shape in the list of available shapes. Figure 14.8 shows this selection.

FIGURE 14.8

The Envelope rollup comes stocked with popular shapes that you can use to envelop text.

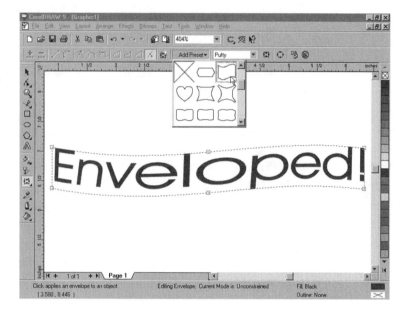

4. After you place your text in a shape, you can edit the shape handles to reform your text.

Wild Effects with Extrusion

Extrusion is another way of adding perspective to a selected object. Extrusion effects give text, curves, or shapes a 3D look.

Extrusion combines 3D effects with shading to create a whole range of wild effects. These are ideal for flashy, colorful, attention-getting text. Extrusion is a form of adding perspective. Extruded effects have vanishing points that you can edit, just like objects to which you apply perspective.

14

Although extrusion can be applied to any vector object in CorelDRAW, it's often used on text to add flair to a message, such as the text in Figure 14.9.

The Extrusion effect is potentially one of the most complex things you can work with in CorelDRAW. However, you can have a lot of fun with this effect without applying every element available in the rollup.

When you select text and then apply the Extrusion effect, you can define a vanishing point for the effect, rotate the extruded object, apply lighting from various angles, edit colors, and add beveling. This is done through four tabs in the Extrude rollup.

14.5: Extrude Text

▼ To Do

1. Type some text. Your name (first name) will work well for this. Assign a light-colored fill and a dark-colored outline to the artistic text. Then select the Interactive Extrude tool from the Blend flyout in the toolbox.

2. Select the Vector Extrusion Mode button in the Property Bar.

3. Click and drag from the center of your selected text up and to the left, as shown in Figure 14.10, to create an Extrusion effect.

4. Click on the Color button in the Property Bar and select the Use Color Shading button, the third option in the drop-down, as shown in Figure 14.11.

5. Select a light color for the From color and a dark color for the To color in the Color Shading drop-down palette.

6. Experiment with clicking on the vanishing point in the extrusion (marked by an X on your screen) and dragging it around the Drawing window, as shown in Figure 14.12.

▲ As you can see, you have almost unlimited effects that you can apply with Extrusion.

FIGURE **14.10**

Extruding text.

FIGURE **14.10**

Extruding text.

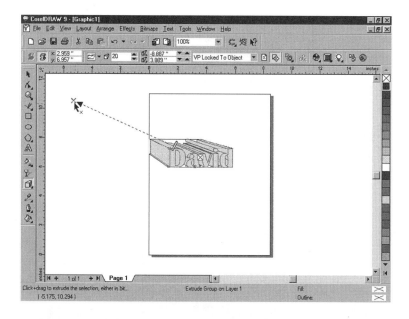

FIGURE **14.11**

Assigning shifting colors to an extrusion.

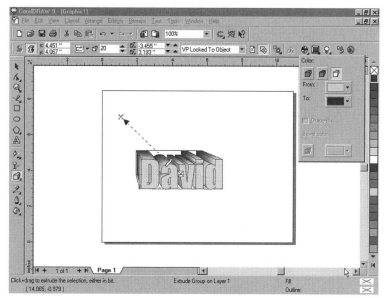

14

FIGURE **14.12**

*Changing the effect of
an extrusion by moving
the vanishing point.*

Adding Interactive Shadowing

Shadowing is yet another way to add perspective and the illusion of depth to an illustration. The Interactive Shadow tool enables you to draw shadows directly on a selected object.

To apply an interactive shadow, select an object and then select the Interactive Shadow tool from the Blend flyout in the toolbox.

With the Interactive Shadow tool selected, click and drag on your object to draw a shadow. When you first draw the shadow, it appears as a wireframe duplicate of your selected object, as shown in Figure 14.13.

FIGURE **14.13**

Drawing a shadow.

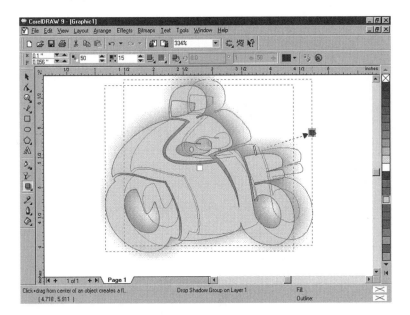

Like all interactive effects, the interactive shadow can be adjusted right in the Drawing window by moving either the start or finish squares in the interactive slider, or by moving the slider in either direction.

Summary

Perspective, envelopes, and extrusion are three ways to apply 3D effects to objects in CorelDRAW 9. Perspective is relatively restrained and subtle. Shadows can contribute to a 3D image. Envelopes provide more dramatic effects, and extrusion is just plain over the top.

Extrusion is defined by the location of a vanishing point, an imaginary spot where your object would disappear if it extended all the way to that point. You can change the impact of these effects by moving the vanishing point.

You can also create an illusion of depth by applying interactive shadows to an object.

Workshop

The familiar Webdings symbol character in Figure 14.14 includes an Envelope effect and an interactive shadow. Give it a try.

FIGURE 14.14

This symbol has been warped into an envelope, zapped with extrusion, and shadowed.

14

1. Drag Webdings symbol #144 onto the Drawing area (a shortcut for viewing the Symbols Docker window is Ctrl+F11). Assign a dark outline color and a light fill color, and enlarge the symbol to something like 3 inches square.

2. Select the single arc envelope tool and stretch the bottom-right and upper-left corners outward, as shown in Figure 14.15.

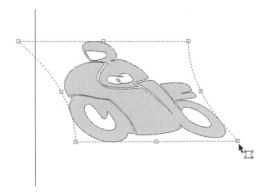

3. Apply an interactive shadow to the symbol.

4. Drag the interactive shadow slider toward the outer (dark) square to intensify the shadow effect, as shown in Figure 14.16.

5. Experiment with a bit of extrusion and modify the envelope (using the shape tool).

Quiz

Answers to the quiz questions are in Appendix A, "Quiz Answers."

1. How do you move the vanishing point in an extrusion?

2. What does a straight line envelope enable you to do?

3. How do you remove Perspective effects from an object?

4. How do you mold artistic text to a shape?

14

PART V
Handling Complex Drawings

Hour

HOUR 15

Designing with Paragraph Text

CorelDRAW's paragraph text features provide all the power of a modern word processor. The spell checker flags misspelled words as you type. A built-in automatic spell checker flags words not found in the dictionary with a wavy red underline and can even change DAve to Dave for you automatically.

You might be saying to yourself, "Yes, but I have all that with my word processing program." Okay, but can your word processing program take that text, shape it into a warped envelope, and apply an interactive fill as I'm doing in Figure 15.1?

FIGURE **15.1**

*Can your word
processor do this?*

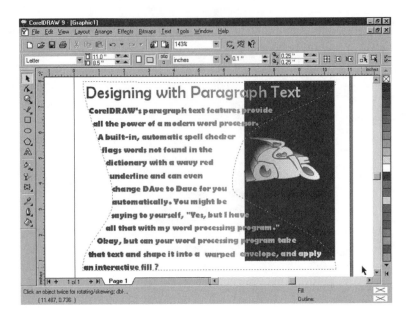

Figure 15.2 shows a display ad designed by Paul. It combines paragraph text with
envelopes, continued frames, shapes, and fountain fills.

FIGURE **15.2**

*CorelDRAW 9 enables
you to combine para-
graph text with graphic
objects.*

You use the same tool to create paragraph text that you used to create artistic text, the
Text tool in the toolbox. The difference is that when you create paragraph text, you start
by clicking and drawing a rectangle in the Drawing window (as opposed to just clicking
with the Text tool, which creates artistic text).

In this hour, you create paragraph text frames, and learn to check spelling and adjust
word and line spacing for frames of paragraph text. You also learn to shape paragraph
text with envelopes and flow text from one frame into another.

Create Paragraph Text and Check Spelling

CorelDRAW 9 has a spelling checker that flags words not found in the dictionary as you type. It even automatically corrects common spelling or capitalization mistakes.

15.1: Create a Paragraph Text Frame and Correct Spelling Automatically

1. Click on the Text tool.

2. In the Drawing window, drag to create a rectangle.

3. Type DAvid is teh man, with those spelling and capitalization mistakes. Note that the spelling and capitalization are corrected automatically.

4. Type nott and note the red, wavy line under the misspelled text. Right-click on the text and click on the correct spelling for not in the shortcut menu.

5. Right-click on the word man, that you just typed and choose Thesaurus from the shortcut menu. Use the Thesaurus to select a synonym for man.

6. Click on the Pick tool and use the Pick tool to select the text frame you just created. Press Delete on your keyboard to delete the text frame.

▲ That was easy, huh? Just like your word processor. Now let's see what CorelDRAW 9 can do with text that your word processor cannot do.

Assigning Effects to Paragraph Text

Most effects that you can assign to other objects can be assigned to paragraph text. For example, you can assign fill colors, outline colors, or fountain fills to paragraph text.

You can also assign special effects to paragraph text that are not available for other objects in CorelDRAW 9. The most useful of these special features is drop caps. Drop caps are extra large letters that you can place at the beginning of any paragraph.

Assign Drop Caps

You can assign a drop cap to the first word in a selected paragraph. Drop caps are available from the Effects tab of the Format Text dialog box.

In this exercise, you will create a frame of paragraph text, and define a drop cap.

15.2: Assign a Drop Cap to a Paragraph

1. Draw a paragraph text frame at least 4 inches wide and 4 inches high.

2. Type CorelDRAW's paragraph text features provide all the power of a modern word processor. Even a thesaurus is on call for content advice.

3. Select Text, Format Text from the menu bar and click on the Effects tab in the dialog box.

4. Select Drop Cap from the Effect drop-down list.

5. Click on OK in the dialog box. Your drop cap will look something like the one in Figure 15.3.

6. Save this document so that you can use it in the next To Do exercise.

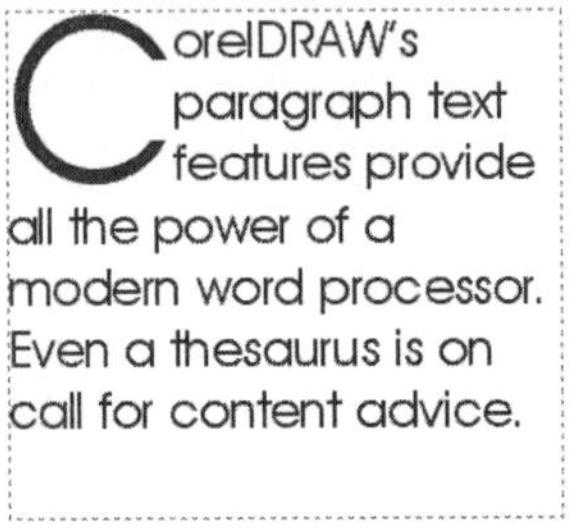

FIGURE 15.3

Easily assign a drop cap to any paragraph.

CorelDRAW's paragraph text features provide all the power of a modern word processor. Even a thesaurus is on call for content advice.

▲

Assigning Effects to Text

You can assign different effects that you've learned in earlier hours to paragraph text. Because you already learned these techniques and applied them to other objects, you can try them out on paragraph text.

Try these effects on paragraph text:

- Assign a fountain fill to the paragraph text (use the same fill techniques you learned in Hour 7, "Mixing Up Fills").

- Create a colored shape and move it behind the text.

- Drag with the Text tool to select some of your text (not all) and assign a color to that text from the color palette.

Adjust Line and Word Spacing

When you select a frame of paragraph text using the shape-sizing handles, you can adjust letter, line, word, or paragraph spacing interactively.

Dragging up on the bottom shape handle makes line spacing tighter (less). Dragging down increases line spacing.

When you drag to the right, with the right shape-sizing handle, you stretch spacing between letters. When you drag to the left, you compress letter spacing.

Holding down Ctrl while you drag on the shape-sizing handles changes the effect. If you hold down Ctrl while you drag on the right shape-sizing handle, you increase *word* spacing. If you hold down Ctrl while you drag on the down shape-sizing handle, you increase spacing between *paragraphs* instead of between lines.

15.3: Increase Line and Letter Spacing

1. Use the Pick tool in the toolbox to select the paragraph text frame you typed in the previous To Do exercise.

2. Click on the Shape tool in the toolbox and note the two shape-sizing handles, one in the lower-right corner and one in the lower left corner of the text frame. You can see them in Figure 15.4.

FIGURE 15.4

You can adjust character and line spacing interactively.

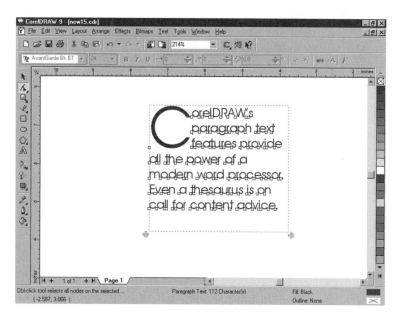

3. Drag down on the bottom shape-sizing handle. Note that line spacing increases.

4. Drag to the right on the right shape-sizing handle, as shown in Figure 15.5. This will increase letter spacing.

FIGURE 15.5

Stretching out letter spacing interactively.

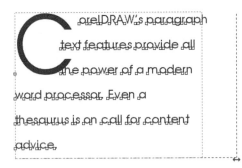

5. Hold down Ctrl and drag to the right on the right shape-sizing handle to increase word spacing.

Shape Text with Envelopes

In Hour 10, "Working with Shapes and Curves," you learned to edit shapes and curves around objects. When you edit the shape of artistic text, the shape of the letters themselves changes, and you create cool but strange effects with distorted text. However, when you place paragraph text in an envelope shape, the text flows in the shape without changing the look of the letters. Figure 15.6 shows paragraph text in a shape. Notice that while the text conforms to the shape of the envelope, the letters are not misformed.

FIGURE 15.6

You can shape paragraph text with envelopes.

When you edit the shape of artistic text, the shape of the letters themselves changes, and you create cool but strange effects with distorted text.

However, when you place paragraph text in an envelope shape, the text flows in the shape without changing the look of the letters.

To shape text to an envelope, use the Pick tool to select the paragraph text frame and then shape the envelope with the Interactive Envelope tool.

15

▼ To Do 15.4: Shape Text with the Interactive Envelope Tool

1. Click with the Pick tool to select the paragraph text frame you've been working with.

2. Select the Interactive Envelope tool from the Interactive Blend tool rollup, as I'm doing in Figure 15.7.

FIGURE 15.7

The Interactive Envelope tool enables you to shape text frames.

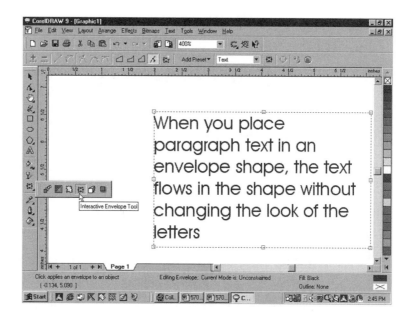

3. Click on the Envelope Straight Line button in the Property Bar.

4. Drag in on the lower-right corner shape handle, as I'm doing in Figure 15.8.

FIGURE 15.8

Shape text with line nodes.

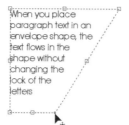

5. Click on the Envelope Single Arc Mode button in the Property Bar and reshape the text envelope using another node, as shown in Figure 15.9. All the techniques you learned for shaping envelope nodes in Hour 14 can be applied to paragraph text frames.

FIGURE 15.9

Shape text with complex curves.

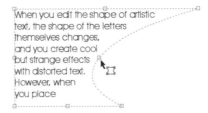

Flow Text Between Frames

If all your text does not fit in a single frame, you can flow it from one frame to another. This technique is essential for laying out presentations and documents that arrange text in multiple frames.

 You can resize text to fit a frame by selecting the text frame and then selecting Text, Fit Text to Frame from the menu bar.

15.5: Flow Text from One Frame into Another

1. Select a text frame by using the Pick tool.

2. Drag up on the bottom handle (not the shape-sizing handle, but the regular bottom sizing handle). Keep making your text frame smaller until not all the text you typed fits into the frame. When text does not fit in the frame, the bottom sizing handle changes from an open square to one with a triangle in it.

3. Use the Text tool in the toolbox to draw a new text frame. Select the original text frame with the pick tool, (the frame with overflow text) and click on the triangle at the bottom of the frame to "load" the cursor with the text that didn't fit in the frame.

4. Point to the new text frame into which you will continue the text. A large black arrow appears, as shown in Figure 15.10.

FIGURE 15.10

Flowing text into a new frame.

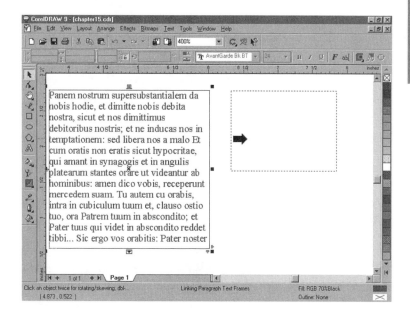

5. Click to pour the overflow text into the new frame. After you continue text, the bottom handle of the first text frame displays a box with lines, meaning this text is continued. A line appears connecting the original frame to the "continued to" frame, as you can see in Figure 15.11.

FIGURE 15.11

Flowed text is marked with lines.

> Panem nostrum supersubstantialem da nobis hodie, et dimitte nobis debita nostra, sicut et nos dimittimus debitoribus nostris; et ne inducas nos in temptationem: sed libera nos a malo Et cum oratis non eratis sicut hypocritae, qui amant in synagogis et in angulis platearum stantes orare ut videantur ab hominibus: amen dico vobis, receperunt mercedem suam. Tu autem cu orabis, intra in cubiculum tuum et, clauso ostio tuo, ora Patrem tuum in abscondito; et Pater tuus qui videt in abscondito reddet tibbi... Sic ergo vos orabitis: Pater noster

> qui es in caelis, sanctificetur nomen tuum; adveniat regnum tuum; fiat voluntas tua sicut in caelo et in terra. Panem nostrum supersubstantialem da nobis hodie, et dimitte

6. Enlarge your second text frame until all the continued text fits, as I'm doing in Figure 15.12. When there is no more text to display, the bottom handle of the final frame displays as an open square.

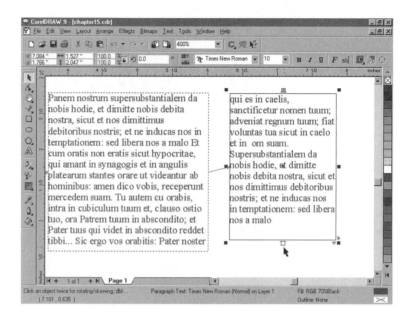

FIGURE 15.12

An open box indicates that all the continued text fits in the "continued to" frame.

Summary

Paragraph text combines the features of a word processor with CorelDRAW's graphic features. You can create, edit, and spell check text in the Text Edit window. After you create paragraph text in CorelDRAW, you can apply effects to the text frame, including color fills and shaping.

If your text does not fit in your text frame, you can continue that text into other text frames. This is especially helpful if you lay out a brochure that mixes graphics with text.

Workshop

In this workshop, you sharpen your paragraph text skills by creating a display ad like the one Paul designed in Figure 15.13.

1. Create a new drawing with a landscape-oriented, letter-size page. Enter the large-font text you see in Figure 15.13 (or some other text of your own choice).

FIGURE 15.13

This layout includes paragraph text shaped by an envelope and continued text between frames.

2. Create a text box and enter some text. You can select the text and use the Copy and Paste tools to create a bunch of text to experiment with.

3. Use the Envelope tool to reshape the paragraph text, as shown in Figure 15.13.

4. If all the text fits in the text frame, make the frame smaller until the triangle icon indicates that not all text fits in the frame.

5. Draw a new text frame on the page and continue the text that didn't fit in the first frame into the second frame.

6. Add illustrations, if you want, to create a page layout similar to the one in Figure 15.13.

Quiz

1. How do you enter paragraph text, as opposed to artistic text?

2. How do you assign font type and size to paragraph text?

3. How do you shape paragraph text?

4. If you want to resize your text to fit in a text frame, what's the quick, easy way to do that automatically?

HOUR 16

Managing Layers and Pages

You can add, delete, and navigate between pages in CorelDRAW 9. This is useful for creating multipage brochures or newsletters, or working with longer documents that you want to publish with CorelDRAW.

The Object Manager Docker window works like an organizing tool to help you arrange and edit objects in complex illustrations. Even at this point, in working with one page, you might have noticed that keeping track of the wide variety of objects you create in an illustration can get crazy. Some of the illustrations our resident artist Paul designs involve hundreds of objects. You can often find objects more easily using Wireframe view than you can in Normal view, but when you have stacked a dozen objects on top of each other, even Wireframe view isn't much help in sorting through or finding objects.

If you're used to the old Layers rollup in earlier versions of CorelDRAW, it's gone. But that's okay, because all its features have been incorporated into the new and improved Object Manager. The Object Manager makes it easy to find objects. You can even assign unique names to each object you create, such as "Dave's big ol' red rectangle." Or something more creative.

Finally, in this hour, you'll explore the process of creating a Master Page using the Object Manager. Objects on a Master Page appear on every page in your drawing. This is handy, for example, if you want to place a logo or text such as "Zoo News" on every page in your drawing.

Working with Multiple Pages

You can add pages to your publication, delete them, and even name them. After you create several pages, you can navigate between them using the navigation bar and tabs at the bottom of the Drawing window (just above the status bar).

To add pages, select Layout, Insert Page from the menu bar. You'll see the Insert Page dialog box, shown in Figure 16.1. This dialog box enables you to define how many pages you want to insert and whether you want those pages before or after the current page. In addition, you can define the page size and orientation for your new page(s).

FIGURE 16.1

You can insert and define new pages before or after the current (selected) page.

16.1: Add Three Pages to a Drawing, Name Your Pages, and Delete Pages

▼ To Do

1. Open a new CorelDRAW file.

2. Select Layout, Insert Page from the menu bar and enter 3 in the Insert Pages spin box.

3. Leave the After radio button selected.

▼ 4. Click on OK.

▼   5. Note that you now have four page tabs on the bottom of your Drawing window.

> You can view all four Drawing window tabs at once by dragging on the divider between the page tabs and the scrollbar. In Figure 16.2, I'm enlarging the page tabs area so I can see all four tabs.

16

FIGURE 16.2

You can resize the area dedicated to page tabs.

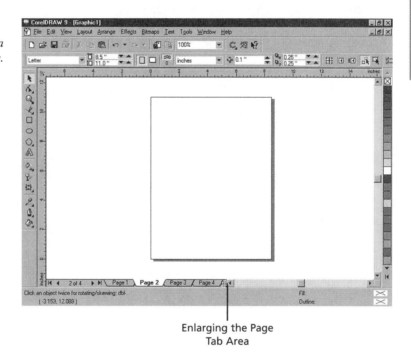

Enlarging the Page
Tab Area

6. Right-click on the Page 1 tab and select Rename Page from the shortcut menu.

7. Enter a new name, Cover, in the Rename Page dialog box, as I'm doing in Figure 16.3.

FIGURE 16.3

You can name pages.

▼

▼   8. Name the last page (Page 4) Back on your own.

        9. Right-click on Page 3 and select Delete Page from the shortcut menu. Delete
▲   Page 2 as well, so only the Front and Back pages remain.

After you create a couple different pages, you can navigate between them by clicking on
a page tab, or by using the arrow navigation buttons to the left of the page tabs. These
arrows differ, depending on how many pages are in your publication and which page you
have selected. But the ones on the left move you to the front of the publication, and the
ones on the right move you toward the end. If two arrows point one direction, the one on
the outside takes you to the beginning or end of the publication.

Navigating with the Object Manager

The Object Manager enables you to navigate from one page to another and also from one
object to another. You view the Object Manager Docker window by selecting Window,
Dockers, Object Manager from the menu bar.

The Object Manager has four icons on top, as shown in Figure 16.4.

FIGURE 16.4

*The icons on top of the
Object Manager
enable you to add lay-
ers, control how much
you see about each
page, and control your
editing.*

New Layer

Show Object Properties

Edit Across Layers

Layer Manager View

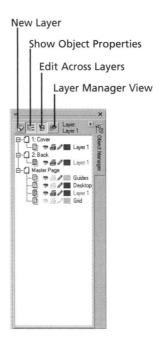

For now, just be aware of these four icons, and refer to Figure 16.4 if I ask you to click on one of them.

The Object Manager displays all the pages you have created and an extra page called the Master Page. Objects on the Master Page apply to *all* pages in your publication.

Navigating Layers

You can have more than one layer on a page. Why would you want to do that? There are a number of uses for multilayered pages:

- You can view one layer at a time, so you can see only part of your illustration. Sometimes that makes it easier to work with a complex drawing.

- You can print only one (or selected) layers on a page. That way you can use one layer for nonprinting objects, such as shapes you use to help design your page.

- You can make one (or more) layers "uneditable." So, for example, if you have a number of objects on a page that you don't want disturbed, you can place them on a noneditable layer. You won't accidentally delete or change these objects while you work with objects you do want to edit.

These examples illustrate the three properties on every layer that you can control: View/Not View, Print/Not Print, and Edit/Not Editable. These properties are set by selecting or unselecting the Eyeball (View/Not View), Printer (Print/Not Print), and Pencil (Edit/Not Editable) icons next to each layer.

> The page property icons are only visible for individual layers. That's why they don't appear next to the page title in Figure 16.5.

16.2: Create a Nonprinting Layer to Mark a Photo

In this exercise, you will add a layer to a publication that marks the location of a pasted-up photo, but does not print.

1. If not already open, open the two-page CorelDRAW file that you created in the previous To Do exercise. Open the Object Manager Docker window if it is not visible (select Window, Dockers, Object Manager).

2. Click on the small minus sign (–) next to each page to display only the page itself. In Figure 16.5, I've compressed the Cover and Back pages, and I'm compressing the Master Page.

Unlike other pages, the Master Page doesn't show up as a tab at the bottom of the window.

FIGURE 16.5

Page display can be shrunk so only the Page title appears in the Object Manager.

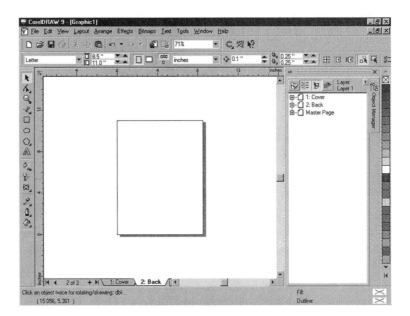

3. Switch to the Back (or 2) page by clicking on the Back (2) page in the Object Manager. Note in the page tab of the Drawing window that you are now looking at Page 2.

4. Switch back to Page 1 and click on the plus symbol (+) to see all layers and objects on that page. Click on the New Layer icon at the top of the Docker window. Name the new layer Non-printing, as shown in Figure 16.6.

Selected layers display with a red page icon.

5. Click on the small printer icon next to the new nonprinting layer. The little printer should turn gray, indicating that this layer will not print.

6. Draw a 3-inch-by-3-inch square in the upper-right corner of the Drawing page.

FIGURE 16.6

Creating a new non-printing layer.

16

7. Click on the + next to the nonprinting layer in the Object Manager Docker window. You see your new rectangle listed as the (so far, only) object on this layer.

8. Click twice (slowly, don't double-click) on the new rectangle name in the Object Manager. Enter a new name for this object, Paste-up photo goes here, as I am doing in Figure 16.7.

FIGURE 16.7

Naming an object in the Object Manager.

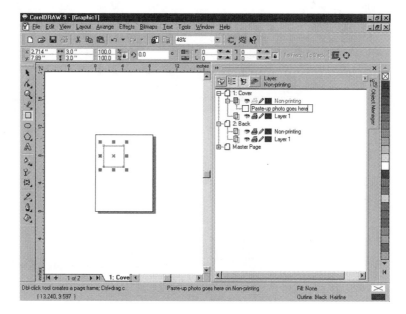

9. Look at the properties of your selected object by clicking on the Show Properties icon at the top of the Object Manager Docker window. After you see your object properties, click on the Show Properties icon again to unclutter the window.

> The information displayed by the Properties button depends on the type of object selected. For example, if you select a paragraph text frame, you'll see the font and color of the text, among other attributes. If you select a shape, you'll see the type of shape, the outline and the fill attributes.
>
> The information displayed by the Properties button takes quite a bit of space to display. To read all the properties for a selected object, you can enlarge the Object Docker window by clicking and dragging (to the left) on the border between the Docker window and the Drawing window.

10. Switch back to Layer 1 on the Cover page in the Object Manager by clicking on the small page icon next to Layer 1. Create a couple text frames and fill them with a word or two of copied text. Make sure the text frames do not overlap with the rectangle you created to mark the spot where a photo will be pasted up (see Figure 16.8).

FIGURE 16.8

Combining a printing layer with a nonprinting layer on the same page.

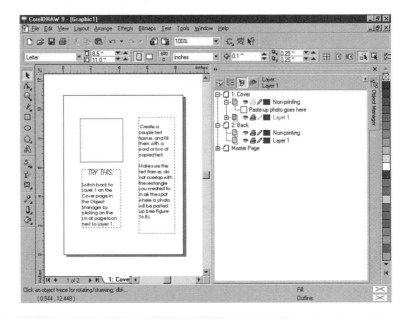

▼ 11. Select the Pick tool. Then, click on the Eyeball icon next to the nonprinting layer to hide the nonprinting rectangle.

12. Click on the Pencil icon next to the nonprinting layer so that this layer cannot be edited. The nonprinting layer will not be visible, as in Figure 16.9, nor can it be edited. The object on the nonprinting layer looks grayed out in the Object Manager because it cannot be edited.

FIGURE 16.9

Any layer can be hidden onscreen or declared off-limits to editing.

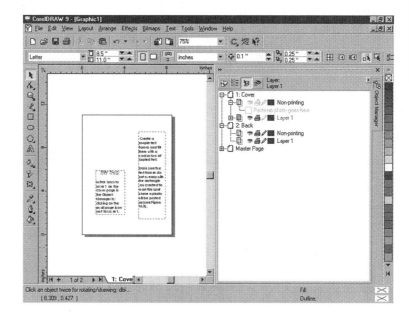

16

13. If you have access to a printer, print the page and note that objects on the nonprinting layer will not print. (For more information about how to print your
▲   CorelDRAW files, see Hour 18, "Printing.")

Another handy thing you can do with the Object Manager is select objects in cluttered, hard-to-edit illustrations. In Figure 16.10, I located an ellipse in the page by clicking on it in the Object Manager.

FIGURE 16.10

Finding objects is often easier in the Object Manager than in the Drawing window.

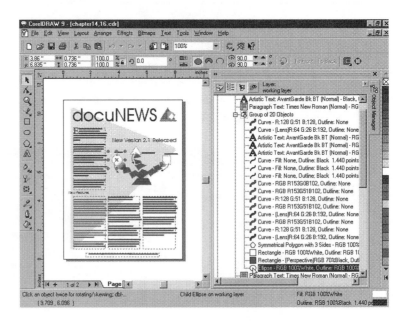

Creating a Master Layer

Objects on Master Layers appear on every page. The default Master Layer generated with each new drawing includes nonprinting Master Guides, Master Grid, and Desktop Layers. These layers simply support the CorelDRAW Drawing window. The Desktop Layer is the area outside the Drawing page in the Drawing window, and normally it does not print.

You can also include printing objects on Master Layers. The best way to do this is to create a new layer on one of your pages and define it as a Master Layer. Then, place objects on that layer that you want to print on each page. Master Layers are defined by right-clicking on any existing layer and choosing Master Layer from the shortcut menu.

Because DRAW's terminology is a little confusing, let's review: As soon as you define a layer as a Master Layer, that layer becomes part of the Master Page.

16.3: Create a Master Page with an Icon

1. Click on any page in the Object Manager and click on the New Layer icon.

2. Name the new layer Every Page, as I am doing in Figure 16.11.

FIGURE 16.11

Creating a new layer that will be a Master Layer.

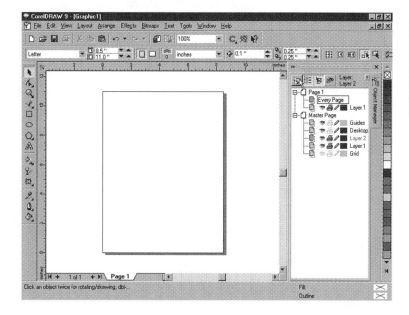

16

Because CorelDRAW already includes a Master Page, I'm avoiding calling my new layer Master Page to avoid confusion.

3. Right-click on the new Every Page layer and choose Master from the context menu. As soon as you do, this layer will jump down to the Master Page in the Object Manager.

4. Make every level on every page invisible, except for the new Master Every Page layer. Click on that layer in the Object Manager to select it, and enter some text on the page, as I'm doing in Figure 16.12.

FIGURE 16.12

Master Layer objects will appear on every page.

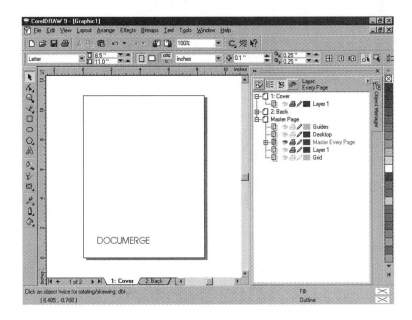

5. Make every layer on both pages in your drawing visible and examine both Pages 1 and 2.

Because the Master Layer text is visible (and will print) on both pages, you should see it in the same place on both the Cover and the Back Page of your drawing.

You can edit the Master Layer text from any layer on any page. So, if the Master Layer text is not located right, you can simply move it while you edit your regular pages. If you want to restrict yourself from editing the Master Layer while you're working on other layers, click on the Edit Across Layers icon on top of the Object Manager (the icon on the right). With Edit Across Layers deselected, you can edit only the layer that you have currently selected in the Object Manager.

Summary

By adding more than one page to your drawing, you can use CorelDRAW as a desktop publishing tool to design publications. You can easily navigate from one page to another or rename pages.

The Object Manager Docker window is a powerful way to locate and work with objects in your drawing. It's useful to find objects in crowded illustrations. The Object Manager can also be used to create layers and assign layer properties. Those properties can include nonprinting layers, layers that cannot be edited, or layers that are not visible on the screen.

Workshop

In this workshop, you practice working with two pages and layers. You will create a two-page brochure, with a nonprinting layer and a Master Layer, like the one in Figure 16.13.

16

FIGURE 16.13

The triangle and logo on the page are Master Layer objects.

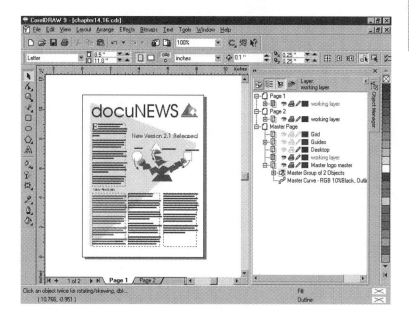

1. Open a new drawing. Add a second page. Name the two pages.
2. Use the Object Manager to create a second nonprinting layer on Page 2. Name this layer `logo master`, and make it a Master Layer.
3. Working on the Master Layer, draw a triangle on the left side of the page and design a small logo from shapes in the upper-right corner, as shown in Figure 16.14. Hide all layers except the Master Layer.
4. Name these shapes in the Object Manager.
5. Examine your document, and note the Master Layer objects on both pages.
6. View all layers of your drawing.
7. Get creative. Add some text and images to create a two-page brochure.

Figure 16.14

The triangle and logo will appear on every page.

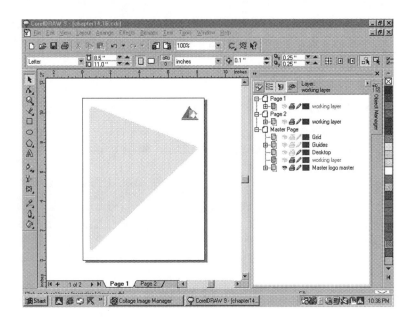

Quiz

1. How do you make the Object Manager Docker window appear?

2. How do you add pages to a drawing?

3. How do you make a layer nonprinting?

4. Can you rename pages?

HOUR 17

Importing and Exporting Objects

DRAW's feature-packed, vector-based essence has always been a wonderful environment in which to create illustrations. The knock on DRAW has often been that it was difficult to publish the finished product.

Two things are working to make it much easier to integrate DRAW into the wider world of publishing:

- DRAW has increased support for exporting images to other formats.
- The growing demand for Web output mitigates the difficulties in sending DRAW output to service bureaus for commercial printing projects.

Corel has made it even easier to export and publish DRAW 9 illustrations. In Hour 18, "Printing," we'll look at how you can take your DRAW files to a commercial printer. In Hour 19, "From CorelDRAW to the World Wide Web," I'll show you how to export DRAW objects to the two universally recognized Web graphic formats. In this hour, you'll see how you can import files from a variety of bitmap file formats and export DRAW objects and files to other file formats.

In addition to Corel stretching out a hand to other applications, other software standards are beginning to acknowledge CorelDRAW files as well. For example, Microsoft Office 2000 documents will list CorelDRAW as a support format for imported files, as you can see in Figure 17.1. The importing process in Word will prompt you to select a support file format in which to import the file (among the options is the *.wmf Windows Metafile format, which works well with DRAW files).

FIGURE 17.1

Microsoft Word acknowledges CorelDRAW files.

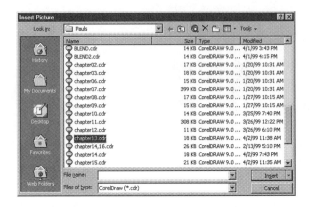

Even when you cannot import a CorelDRAW file directly into another application, in most cases, transferring graphic images between CorelDRAW 9 and other programs is a smooth process. Usually, you can handle the process by copying objects from CorelDRAW into other applications and choosing from various Paste options in the target application.

When you copy and paste CorelDRAW objects into other applications, you rely on the Clipboard to translate those objects into a format readable by the target application. If you select the Paste Special command in the Edit menu, many Windows offers two basic options: picture or bitmap. Picture pasting is vector-based, like DRAW, and preserves more detail and color, and is more memory efficient than bitmap pasting.

Moving objects from other programs into CorelDRAW is a bit different. Copied bitmap images enter CorelDRAW as bitmap images, not as vector-based objects. But when you get those bitmap images into CorelDRAW, you can edit them just as you would any other bitmap object in CorelDRAW. You explored that process in Hour 11, "Working with Bitmap Images in CorelDRAW 9."

Many Ways to Transfer Objects

Before you walk through some specific examples of importing and exporting different types of other files, it will be helpful to understand the different ways you can move objects in and out of CorelDRAW. Importing, opening files, exporting, copying, pasting—you can use all these techniques to transfer objects in and out of CorelDRAW.

Importing Versus Opening

You can bring files from other programs into a CorelDRAW file either by importing them or by opening them. The main difference is that opening foreign files creates a new drawing, whereas importing brings the file contents into your drawing. What happens if you import a file from Adobe Illustrator, for example, into a blank new document? You get the same result as if you opened that Illustrator file using the CorelDRAW Open menu.

You can open the Import and Open dialog boxes from buttons in the toolbar, as shown in Figure 17.2. Figure 17.2 also shows the Export button.

17

FIGURE 17.2

You can bring files from other formats into CorelDRAW through either the Import or the Open dialog boxes.

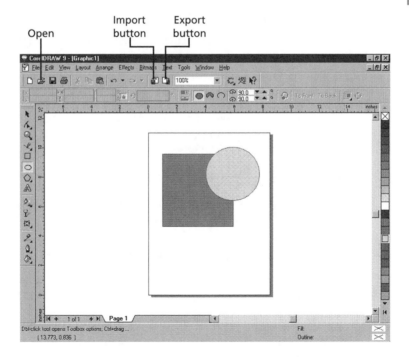

DRAW imports dozens of file formats, ranging from Excel worksheets to Auto-CAD files.

Exporting Versus Saving As

Although there is a subtle difference between opening foreign format files and importing them, there is no substantial difference between exporting files or using the Save As dialog box to save them to other formats. Okay, one exception to that rule exists.

When you learn to export files to Encapsulated PostScript format at the end of this hour, you will use the Export dialog box. Whether you export your CorelDRAW drawing or save it as another format, you have the option of saving the entire drawing or just selected objects as another file format.

In short, there's not much difference between Exporting objects from CorelDRAW into other file formats and using the Save As dialog box to save them in other file formats.

Copying and Pasting

Most of your transfer problems between CorelDRAW and other programs can be handled by copying and pasting objects. When you select an object, or objects, you can copy them into the Windows Clipboard and then paste them into other applications. In this hour, you explore those options and when to use which one.

In other words, the Windows operating system manages many, if not most, of your importing and exporting problems.

Exporting Paragraph Text

Text frames can be exported to word processing files. The text that you create in CorelDRAW can be saved as a WordPerfect, Word, or generic RTF file format.

17.1: Export Text to a Word Processor

▲ To Do ▼

1. Create a paragraph text frame by dragging with the Text tool from the toolbox.
2. Type some text in your frame.
3. With the text frame selected, click on the Export button in the Standard toolbar.
4. Click on the Selected Only check box in the Export dialog box.

▼   5. Pull down the Save File as Type drop-down menu in the Export dialog box and
             choose RTF (Rich Text Format—a universally recognized format that preserves
             most formatting) or a word processor. Enter a filename in the File name field of the
             dialog box.

          6. Click on the Export button to save the selected text in your word processor format.

          7. If you have a word processor installed, you can open the file to see that this
▲   worked. If you do this, make some editing changes and save your file again.

Importing Paragraph Text

You are more likely to import word processing documents into CorelDRAW than you are
to export them. When you import text into CorelDRAW from a supported word processing format, that text automatically gets poured into a new paragraph text frame. You cannot open word processing documents as new CorelDRAW files, but you can always open
a new blank CorelDRAW file and import the text into it. Your options are to let
CorelDRAW figure out the size of that frame, or to define your own frame as you
import.

17

17.2: Import a Text File into CorelDRAW

▼ To Do

          1. To start, you will need a text file. If you have Windows Notepad on your system,
             you can create a short text file and save as a TXT file. Or you can create a docu-
             ment with a word processing program and save it to RTF format.

          2. Click on the Import button in the toolbar. Select All Files in the Files of Type drop-
             down menu and navigate to your text file.

          3. Click on the text file, and then click on the Import button in the Import dialog box.

          4. Your cursor will become a paragraph text cursor, with the name of the imported
             text file, as you see in Figure 17.3.

          5. Drag with your imported text cursor to define a frame for the imported text. If your
             text does not fit in the paragraph text frame, you can enlarge the frame or use the
             flowing text techniques you learned in Hour 15, "Designing with Paragraph Text,"
▼   to continue the text into other frames.

FIGURE 17.3

The imported text cursor enables you to define a paragraph text frame to pour your text into.

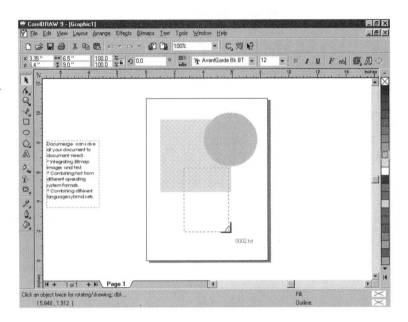

Your other option is to simply click with the import text cursor. If you do that, CorelDRAW will create a text frame large enough to hold the entire text file.

Importing Graphic Objects into CorelDRAW

As you learned earlier in this hour, importing and opening files from other formats is very similar. The difference is that importing brings the file into an open CorelDRAW drawing, whereas opening the file creates a brand new CorelDRAW file.

To import a file from another format, open an existing drawing or create a new one in CorelDRAW. Then, click on the Import button in the toolbar, and select All Files in the Files of Type drop-down menu in the dialog box. This way, CorelDRAW figures out the type of file.

When you click on the Preview check box in the Import dialog box, you see a thumbnail of supported images in the Preview area of the dialog box.

If your imported image is in a bitmap format, the drop-down menu with Full Image showing becomes active. You can select Crop from this drop-down list to crop the file before you import it. If you select the Crop option and click on the Import button, you can crop your image in the Crop Image dialog box before you bring it in. In Figure 17.4, I'm selecting Crop from the drop-down menu.

FIGURE 17.4

You can crop bitmap images as you import them.

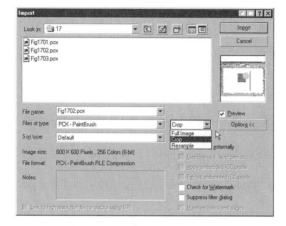

After you select Crop as the import method and click on the Import button in the Import dialog box, a Crop Image window appears. In the Crop Image window, you can click and drag on handles in the viewing area, or define cropping digitally in the Select Area to Crop spin boxes in the lower part of the window. In Figure 17.5, I'm cropping an image interactively using the crop handles.

FIGURE 17.5

Cropping an image before importing it.

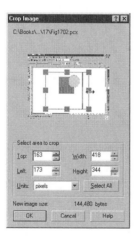

Imported vector-based images from Adobe Illustrator cannot be resampled or cropped as they are imported. However, they can be edited using all the vector-based editing options in CorelDRAW.

Copying Objects from CorelDRAW

You can copy files from CorelDRAW into any Windows application. Some applications provide several options for pasting the CorelDRAW file. For Microsoft Word 2000, for example, paste options include Bitmap File, CorelDRAW Object, and Picture (vector-based) Image.

These are the three main options for pasting CorelDRAW objects into other applications:

- If you paste your objects from CorelDRAW as bitmap objects, your objects will be converted into bitmap format and pasted into the target application.
- If you select CorelDRAW objects, your objects will be pasted into the target application as vector-based images, and you can then edit them in CorelDRAW from within the target application.
- If you choose Picture format, your graphic will be placed in the target application as a vector-based image format, usually Windows Metafile (*.wmf), but it will not be linked to CorelDRAW.

17.3: Copy a Graphic from CorelDRAW into Another Application

1. Create a graphic image (or several) in CorelDRAW. Select the image(s) you want to copy to another application.

2. Open another application into which you want to paste your selected object(s).

3. Select Edit, Paste Special (or Edit, Paste, if Paste Special is not an option) from the target application menu bar.

> *Don't* right-click and choose Paste from a shortcut menu. In most cases, this doesn't provide you with as many Paste options. The Paste option on the Edit menu provides you with more control over the format in which you import your object, as you will see in the next step.

4. Choose one of the radio button file format options. These differ from application to application but, in general, will fit into three categories: copy as bitmap, copy as CorelDRAW object, or copy as a vector format.

In Figure 17.6, I've opened Word 2000 and am attempting to paste a CorelDRAW object. I'm presented with five options. The first option imports the copied graphic as an object that can be edited in CorelDRAW. The second option is available only because I have text included in the objects I am copying and will import only the text. The Picture option imports the graphic as a vector-based graphic, maintaining the high resolution and small file size qualities of the CorelDRAW original. The bitmap option imports the image as a memory-heavy bitmap. The Windows Enhanced Metafile format is similar to the generic Picture format, but sometimes does a better job of handling text and images. You can experiment when you have more than one vector or bitmap option to see which one looks better when you copy your graphic.

17

FIGURE 17.6

Paste format options break down to three types: CorelDRAW object, (other) vector-based, or bitmap.

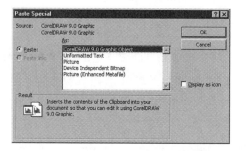

When you select a format, click on OK in the target application Paste Special dialog box.

Some older applications that still run under Windows 95 do not support Paste Special options. In those cases, you are restricted to pasting in a format defined by the target application.

Most applications to which you copy objects have some way to edit those pasted graphics. If you choose to paste as CorelDRAW objects, you can edit those objects in CorelDRAW when you double-click on them.

Exporting Objects from CorelDRAW

You might have situations where copying and pasting, even using Paste Special options, is not enough. One of those options is when you have to convert a CorelDRAW file to a file format that a printing service bureau can handle.

Sending files to a professional printer is discussed in more detail in Hour 18. However, here we'll look at two quick, easy, and reliable ways to make a CorelDRAW illustration available to almost anyone: Exporting to a PostScript file, and publishing your illustration as a PDF file that can be opened (and printed) by anyone with Adobe Acrobat Reader, a program that can be downloaded for free from the Internet.

Exporting to PostScript Files

Try calling your favorite printing service bureau or find one in the yellow pages. Ask what kinds of output it can create and the employees will impress you with a list of brochures, billboards, posters, and so on. But ask if they have a lot of experience printing CorelDRAW 9 files and they'll probably put you on hold, ask around, and tell you no, not really. However, almost every printing service bureau can work with EPS files, and CorelDRAW files can be saved to PostScript format.

You export drawings to PostScript files in the Export dialog box.

17.4: Export a Drawing to a PostScript File

1. Create a drawing in CorelDRAW or open an existing one.

2. Click on the Export button in the Standard toolbar and choose EPS Encapsulated PostScript from the Save As Type drop-down list, as shown in Figure 17.7.

FIGURE 17.7

Exporting a CorelDRAW illustration to a PostScript file.

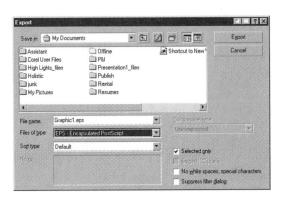

3. Navigate to a folder if necessary in the Save In drop-down list.

4. Enter a filename in the File name box.

5. Click on the Export button.

6. In the EPS dialog box, you can choose to export text as curves or text. Consult with your printing service bureau to find out how they want you to set this and other options in the dialog box. Or leave the options in the default setting.

▲   7. Click on OK in the dialog box.

CorelDRAW can open EPS files, but you will find the objects in them do not edit well; many effects cannot be applied to objects in these imported files. EPS is not a good format to use for files that you intend to edit. If you save a file as an EPS file for a printer, save the drawing as a CorelDRAW file as well.

Exporting to Adobe Acrobat Reader

Adobe Acrobat has gained acceptance as a universal file format for both printed and Web publications. The Adobe Acrobat Reader, which enables you to open and print files in Acrobat's PDF format can be downloaded free at Adobe's Web site. Last time I checked, the exact URL was

`http://www.adobe.com/prodindex/acrobat/readstep.html#reader`

If it's moved, you can find a link to it at the `www.adobe.com` site.

CorelDRAW 9 can publish files directly to PDF format. You have several predefined PDF style options: You can save PDF files formatted for document distribution, for editing, for Web sites, or for professional printing prepress.

Each PDF style has a set of dialog box settings that correspond to the type of publication you are creating. For example, if you select the PDF For Web style, the default graphic image compression type becomes Web-compatible JPEG images. On the other hand, if you choose the PDF For Prepress style, images are saved using LZW compression, preferred by print service bureaus.

17.5: To Publish a File to PDF

▼ To Do

1. Create the publication in CorelDRAW 9 and select File, Publish to PDF. The Publish to PDF dialog box appears.

2. In the General tab of the Publish to PDF dialog box, you can use the File name box to name and locate the file. Use the Export range options to save part or all of your publication.

3. Select the Generate Job Ticket check box to create either an internal (embedded) set of printing instructions or an external file in jtf format (which can be opened either with Adobe Acrobat or a text editor). These instructions (shown in Figure 17.8) can tell a printer how to handle your publication.

▼

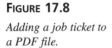

FIGURE 17.8

Adding a job ticket to a PDF file.

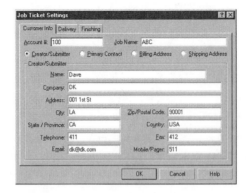

4. The Objects tab in the dialog box enables you to change default settings for how Corel will translate your images and text into a PDF file. For example, you can either convert text to curves (ensuring the maximum integrity between your Corel drawing and the PDF file), or not (allowing text to be edited later).

5. The Advanced tab has even more detailed options for handling color and image conversion to the PDF file. The settings in this tab provide options that may be required by a commercial printer for whom you are preparing the file.

6. The Document tab enables you to include bookmarks and thumbnails as part of the PDF file. Bookmarks and thumbnails help readers navigate your document in a PDF reader. Figure 17.9 shows a two-page publication, which has been published from CorelDRAW 9 to a PDF file, being viewed in the PDF Reader, with thumbnails on the left side of the page.

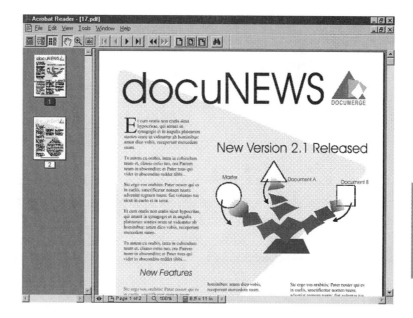

FIGURE 17.9

Viewing a two-page DRAW publication in Adobe Acrobat.

Summary

Much of the work of moving objects, either text or graphics, in and out of CorelDRAW can be handled by copying objects. When you copy objects, you can usually paste them into other Windows applications as CorelDRAW objects, other vector-based (Picture) formats, or bitmap images.

When you copy graphic images in or out of CorelDRAW 9, the Paste Special option on the Edit menu gives you control over the format of the graphic image.

The Import button in the CorelDRAW toolbar enables you to bring objects, or even entire files, into CorelDRAW. When you use the Import dialog box, you can bring objects into CorelDRAW even if you don't have the software in which those imported objects were created.

You can also export images from CorelDRAW to other file formats. You can export either selected objects or entire files. One useful export application is to export CorelDRAW files in Encapsulated PostScript format, which is recognized by almost every printing service bureau.

Workshop

In this workshop, you experiment with exporting and importing graphic objects and text.

1. Create a paragraph text frame. Enter a paragraph of text. Apply text formatting including font size, font type, italics, boldface, and text colors.

2. Select the paragraph text frame and click on the Export button. Export the selected text frame as a document file using the RTF option in the Export dialog box.

3. Open the exported file in your word processor. How did CorelDRAW do in exporting your formatting? Don't close your word processing file.

4. Create a drawing in CorelDRAW. Keep it simple, like a shape or a symbol. Copy the drawing to the Clipboard and switch to your word processing program.

5. Select Edit, Paste Special in your word processor menu, and if available, choose the Picture or Enhanced Metafile option in the Paste Special dialog box.

6. Click on OK in the Paste Special dialog box and note the look of your object in your word processor.

Quiz

The answers for this quiz can be found in Appendix A, "Quiz Answers."

1. What's the difference between importing objects from other file formats and opening files of other formats?

2. Can you change imported images as you import them?

3. What do you do when your printing service bureau cannot handle CorelDRAW files?

4. What's the quick, easy way to transfer CorelDRAW objects into other Windows applications?

Hour 18

Printing

In the hours that you put into learning CorelDRAW, you learned to create some complex illustrations. How do you share those graphic images with the world? You can print them or you can display them onscreen, for example, in a Web site. In this hour, you learn to print your CorelDRAW illustrations. You learn to move your CorelDRAW 9 objects into a Web page in the next hour in this book.

Printing can be easy or complex. If you print your CorelDRAW illustrations with your own laser printer, the process is basically governed by the Windows operating system. This is true for both color and black-and-white printing. If you've looked at the displays at your local copy shop, you've seen some spectacular color printer output, including full-color posters with near-photographic quality.

CorelDRAW also comes with a full set of printer options that make it easy to print business cards, labels, and other odd-sized output. You learn to print cards and labels in this hour.

Things get tricky when you want to translate your CorelDRAW illustration into a mass-produced printed publication. That requires bringing something—a file or printed layout—to your printer. You learn to manage that process in this hour as well.

Printing with Your Printer

If you are preparing a limited number of copies of your illustrations, you can get excellent quality from a color printer. Home-quality color printers are extremely low-cost, and office-quality color printers are more accessible as well.

For the next step in quality, your local Kinko's, Copymat, or the equivalent has color printers with output quality that will create impressive posters and displays. If you need 100,000 copies of your illustration, this isn't a viable option. But if you need one or two copies, or even a hundred prints, the new technology in color printers is your best option.

In the previous hour, you learned how to deal with exporting your CorelDRAW illustration on machines that don't support CorelDRAW. You can export your illustration to a program that is supported by the computer connected to a quality color printer. Or if CorelDRAW is on your laptop, take your laptop to your local printer and have them print from your computer.

A Look at Printing Options

If you print the final output for your illustration on your own printer, your print options are basically those available to all Windows applications. You can print selected objects, select pages when you have a multipage document, and print multiple copies. If you have multiple copies of a multipage document, you can click on the Collate check box.

The Collate check box organizes your copies so that your documents print in sets. For example, if you have a four-page document and you want to print two copies, collating prints pages 1, 2, 3, and 4, and then prints pages 1, 2, 3, and 4 in that order again. If you do not select the Collate check box, your two copies print in the order of two copies of page 1, followed by two copies of page 2, two copies of page 3, and then two copies of page 4. Collating makes it easier to organize your work, but it slows down the printing process by up to 40%.

To access printer options, don't click on the Print button in the Standard toolbar; instead select File, Print from the menu bar. You see the General tab in the Print dialog box, shown in Figure 18.1.

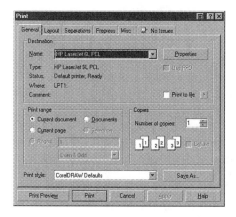

FIGURE 18.1

*The General tab of the
Print dialog box has
the basic controls
for printing your illus-
tration.*

In the General tab of the Print dialog box, you can select an installed printer from the
Name drop-down menu, and choose which pages to print in the Print range area. If you
print more than one copy of your file, you can click on the Collate check box in the
Copies area to place your copies in order. If, for example, you print 20 uncollated copies
of a four-page publication, you'll get 20 page ones, 20 page twos, and so on. If you collate your copies, you'll get 20 sets of the complete document.

One interesting option is the Even and/or Odd selections available from the drop-down list
in the Print Range area. Of course, this option is active only if your publication is longer
than one page; if it's a one-page document, the Even and/or Odd options is grayed out.

You can use the Even/Odd drop-down menu to print two-sided copies with a single-side
printer. Do this by first printing odd pages, then even pages. Double-sided printing is
handy for creating small numbers of pamphlets or two-sided handouts. You can also use
double-sided printing to create models of a publication that a printer will publish.

There's an easier way to print duplex (double-sided) pages using printers that print on
only one side of the page. The Layout tab of the Print dialog box has an option that walks
you through the process of printing double-sided pages and helps you avoid printing twice
on one side of the page, and not at all on the other. To access that option, select the
Layout tab and pull down the Signature Layout drop-down list. Choose Double Sided Full
Page. You can then click on the Print Preview button to see how your publication will look
when it's printed back-to-back on pages. Figure 18.2 shows the Double Sided option.

18

FIGURE 18.2

*Even if your printer
doesn't print duplex,
you can print double-
sided pages with
CorelDRAW.*

After you preview your double-sided document, you can click on the Close button in the
Preview window toolbar to return to the Print dialog box. Then, after you click on the
Print button in the Print dialog box, CorelDRAW patiently walks you through the process
of double-sided printing. Be prepared to waste a few sheets of paper while CorelDRAW
tests your printer and asks you some questions. You supply the answers to a wizard,
which determines how your printer works. After that, you get explicit directions on how
and when to load sheets of paper to achieve double-sided printing.

Printing Business Cards or Labels

Business cards and labels are created a bit differently than they are in some other desktop
publishing programs or word processors. Rather than duplicating a full sheet of cards or
labels, you simply choose an appropriate page layout, and then create a single card or label.

CorelDRAW's Page Layout options dialog box supports hundreds of label and card layouts from several major publishers. Your local office supplies store has standardized-size
labels for everything from video cassettes to CDs. They also sell full-sheet business card
paper that separates into individual business cards.

18.1: Design and Print a Business Card

To Do

It's not necessary to purchase laser business card sheets to try this; you can experiment
with a regular sheet of paper.

1. Open a new drawing in CorelDRAW.

2. Select Layout, Page Setup from the menu bar.

3. Double-click on Label in the Options window.

▼   4. In the Label area of the window, click on the label size that matches the business
        card size on the sheets of business cards you bought. If you're experimenting with
        a plain sheet of paper, you can choose Avery 5371, as I have in Figure 18.3.

FIGURE 18.3

*CorelDRAW comes
with hundreds of preset
card and label sizes.*

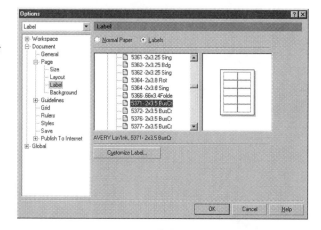

     5. Click on OK in the Options window and design a business card. In Figure 18.4,
         I've made myself a bigshot at Data Munchers.

18

FIGURE 18.4

*Designing business
cards or labels is as
easy as creating any
other CorelDRAW
illustration.*

     6. Select File, Print, and click on the Preview button in the Print dialog box. You see a
         page full of business cards. The preview screen is shown in Figure 18.5.

You can also see the Preview screen by selecting File, Print Preview from the
menu.

▼

FIGURE 18.5

Previewing a sheet of business cards.

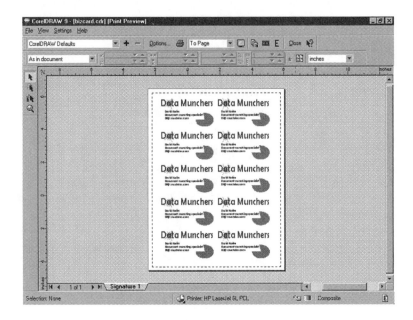

Bringing Your Publication to a Commercial Printer

If all you need is professional black-and-white printing, you can take your CorelDRAW file to a commercial printer and let them print it. Or export your CorelDRAW file to a file format your printer can work with. In Hour 17, "Importing and Exporting Objects," you learned to export your CorelDRAW objects to other file formats, including the universally recognized EPS file format and the widely accepted PDF format.

If you need to prepare your CorelDRAW pages for commercial color printing, you have many different qualities of output available to you. Commercial, large-quantity printing requires separate plates for different colors. Two ways that colors can be separated for color printing are spot color or process color. Spot color is typically used for two-color printing. For example, if you have a brochure you want to print in red and black, you can arrange with your printer to provide him with a black master and a red master page. Both the black and red masters will be converted to printing plates and printed over each other to produce two-color output.

Spot color printing is a relatively low-tech printing option that can be managed by inexpensive print shops. All your printer needs to do is cut two print plates and apply Pantone spot colors. This solution enables you to produce color brochures, catalogs, calendars, business cards, and so on with a small budget.

Process color is exponentially more complex and expensive. It is used for high-quality color printing, such as magazines and high-quality catalogs. Process color involves combining four (or sometimes even six) color plates. When colors are composed by combining four inked plates, those colors are usually cyan, magenta, yellow, and black (abbreviated as CMYK). With process color, you provide your printer with four (or six) different masters for each page, and these are then used to create different color plates.

Reproducing complex or spectacular color-mix fountain fills is beyond the capability of spot color separations. You can use one-color fountain fills, such as from black to white, with spot coloring. But, even with process color printing, fountain fills sometimes appear as bars of color. Fine-tuning very complex color mixes for process color printing is a complex art that requires a lot of experimenting and experience.

Although transferring coloring from monitor to paper is very complex, your color images translate into Web graphics much more easily, as you'll see in the next hour on Web graphics.

Preparing Spot Color Separations

Scenario: The next issue of your newsletter or brochure is going to be printed in color. Your printer will accept your 600dpi output to create printing plates with and can duplicate Pantone colors.

To see exactly what colors you'll get from your printed output, do not rely on what you see on your monitor. Instead, ask your printer for a sample book showing the way Pantone colors will look when printed.

The first step in preparing your publication for two-color spot color printing is to make sure that all the fills and outlines in your publication are confined to two colors. If you've created a publication already, you can use the Object Manager (see Hour 16, "Managing Layers and Pages") to determine the fill and outline properties of all your objects. Pick the two Pantone spot colors that you will assign to objects, and change the assigned colors of every object to those colors.

Most printers define two-color spot printing as black plus a second color. Some enable you to use any two colors, but most pass on some additional charge for washing out black plates. Check with your printer about the policy on charging for two-color printing.

One way to check your publication and see what colors are assigned to every object is to view the Object Manager Docker window. You explored the Object Manager in Hour 16. You can display the Object Manager Docker window by selecting Layout, Object Manager from the menu bar. Among the displayed object properties are the exact color of each object on your page.

After you assign two (and only two) colors to all the objects in your publication, select File, Print from the menu bar. Normally, if you prepare master pages for a printer, you want to select all pages and one copy in the General tab of the Print dialog box.

Click on the Separations tab in the Print dialog box. In the Separations tab, click on the Print Separations check box. If you have restricted your publication to two colors, you see those two colors in the list at the bottom of the dialog box, as in Figure 18.6.

FIGURE 18.6

The Print Separations tab lists all the colors assigned to your publi- cation.

Most of the other check boxes in the tab are not relevant for spot color separations. But the Print Empty Plates check box is useful. It prints two master sheets for each page, even if only one color is used on that page. This makes it easier to keep your pages organized.

You can print an additional set of your separation masters, which have information on them identifying which color goes with that plate. This is helpful in avoiding mixed-up colors when plates are printed. You can add this information in the Prepress tab of the

Print dialog box. Click on the Position Within Page check box to print color information on each page.

Before you print your two different spot color separations for each page, you can click on the Preview button in the Print dialog box to see how the separations will come out. Figure 18.7 shows a single-color separation without the reference color information. This is the sheet that your printer will use to create a printing plate.

FIGURE 18.7

Spot color separations can be previewed.

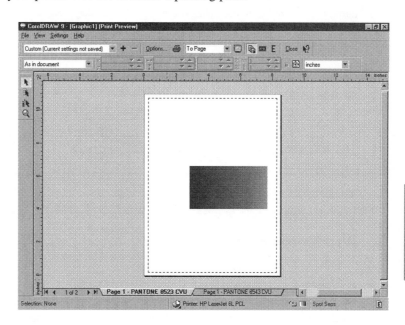

Preparing Four-Color Masters

Printing process color separations is similar to creating spot color separation. The results are much less predictable because all colors and fountain fills are broken down into four colors. CorelDRAW does this automatically for you.

The main rule in creating process color separations is to first consult with a service bureau that will prepare your file to be taken to a print shop. Process coloring is a complex process, and each service bureau has its own way of handling your files. Note the specifications given you by the service bureau, and apply them to the general outline below for process printing.

To convert spot colors to process colors, click on the Convert Spot Colors to CMYK check box in the Separations tab of the Print dialog box. The spot colors you assigned break down to mixtures of the four CMYK colors.

To create four-color CMYK process color separations, select File, Print from the menu bar and click on the Separations tab in the Print dialog box.

If you applied only process colors to objects in your publication, you see four colors listed in the color list: Cyan, Magenta, Yellow, and Black. If you mixed process colors and spot colors, no problem. Click on the Convert Spot Colors to CMYK check box, and the spot colors you assigned will be broken down to mixtures of the four CMYK colors.

When you separate your colors into the CMYK colors, you can follow the same steps you learned for printing spot color separations. The difference is, you get four sheets per page if you click on the Print Empty Plates check box.

For high-quality CMYK color separation, you need to rely on a very high-quality service bureau printer to create your copy-ready masters. You can, of course, print lower-quality copies on your own laser printer to get a basic idea of what your color plates will look like.

PostScripting Your Files

To bring your file to a service bureau, find out from them what printer output they use and how you can send your printer output in a compatible file. Many times, the printer can provide you with printer drivers for a compatible printer. You don't need the printer itself, only the software that creates files for that printer. If you already have a PostScript printer installed, you can often select that printer.

To create a file for a service bureau, select a compatible printer in the General tab of the Print dialog box. In Figure 18.8, I've selected an Imagesetter printer. I don't have an Imagesetter. I can't afford one! But my service bureau has one. By selecting the Print to file and For Mac check boxes (because my service bureau uses a Macintosh), I can create a file that I can take to my service bureau.

When you click on the Print button in the Print dialog box after selecting the Print to File check box, you'll be prompted to choose a folder and filename for your print file. Take that file to your service bureau. It can use the file to create high-quality output that your printer can use to shoot printing plates for the production process.

Figure 18.8

*Print output can be
sent to a file and taken
to a service bureau
for high-quality
copy-ready output.*

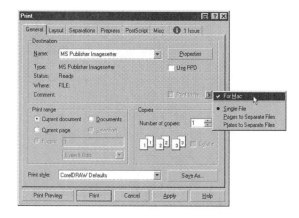

Summary

Printing with CorelDRAW can be as simple or complex as your needs. If all you need is
output on your laser printer, CorelDRAW provides you with complete control over pages
and can create back-to-back duplex output.

If you need to take your CorelDRAW file to a commercial printer for color printing, your
two options are spot colors or process colors. Spot colors are typically used for two-color
printing. Process colors mix four colors to create a full array of colors. You can create
color separations in CorelDRAW and print them, or create a file with print output to take
to a commercial service bureau for high-quality copy-ready output.

Workshop

In this workshop, you first print mail labels. Then, you create a two-color publication and
print color separations.

1. Open a new CorelDRAW file and define a label output by selecting Layout, Page
   Setup and double-clicking on Label in the Options dialog box. Click on the Labels
   radio button. If you have labels, use the appropriate size; if not, choose AVERY
   Lsr/Ink, 5160, as in Figure 18.9. Click on OK.

2. Design a cool-looking return-address label with text and a symbol.

3. Select File, Print Preview to see how the labels will look when printed.

4. Click on the Close button in the Preview window to return to the dialog box. Then
   either close the dialog box or click on the Print button to send your labels to the
   printer.

18

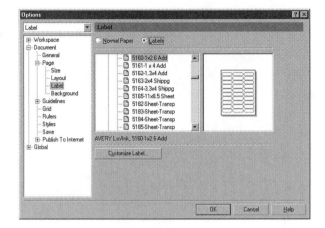

FIGURE **18.9**

Label and card layouts in the Options dialog box.

5. Create a four-page newsletter or brochure. You can open and edit the brochure you have worked on in previous hours.

6. Assign only Pantone Process Black CV or Pantone Process Red 032 CV to each object. You can assign less than 100% of either of these colors to any object.

7. Create color separations by selecting File, Print and clicking on the Print Separations check box in the Separations tab.

8. Click on the Print Preview button to see the two plates for each page that you will print.

9. Close the Preview screen. Either close the Print dialog box or print separations for your publication.

Quiz

Answers to the quiz questions can be found in Appendix A, "Quiz Answers."

1. Where do you define layout for different size paper such as business cards or labels?

2. If you bring a two-color brochure to a commercial print shop, which color separation process works best?

3. When you print color separations, how do you know what color is associated with each plate?

4. Can you print CMYK color separations if you used process color in designing your publication?

HOUR 19

From CorelDRAW to the World Wide Web

There's no need for me to tell you how strategic Web sites have become. Both sites on the World Wide Web and sites on internal intranets are becoming an important way to share information, and that includes graphics.

In Hour 18, "Printing," you saw that when you transfer your CorelDRAW illustrations to printed output, it is often difficult to re-create the coloring of your onscreen illustration on the printed page. It's fun to transfer your CorelDRAW images to Web sites because viewers see your fountain fills and colors in full living color.

You can place your CorelDRAW illustrations on Web sites in two ways: Save individual objects as Web-compatible graphic images and then import them into a Web page you are designing with another Web publishing program, or create the HTML (HyperText Markup Language) code yourself. That works fine if you already know how to create Web pages.

If you don't know HTML from WWW, you can still create full-fledged Web pages with text, graphic images, backgrounds, and links to other sites in CorelDRAW. I've written many books about Web-design packages, and I still find the process of generating Web pages in CorelDRAW 9 pretty smooth and easy to use. Figure 19.1 shows a Web page I threw together in a half hour, although I admit I got some help from Paul, who provided the images.

FIGURE 19.1

You can easily publish a CorelDRAW 9 page as a Web page.

Using Web-Compatible Colors

Web colors are easier to deal with than printed colors because there are not as many options. Printing presents innumerable options, ranging from black and white, or one spot color, to hexachrome (six-color) plates.

Web graphics are restricted to 216 colors by the limitations of Web browsers (the programs that interpret Web pages for visitors). Technically, you can use 256 colors, but 40 of those are reserved for use by the operating system.

CorelDRAW provides two Web-compatible color palettes, one for Internet Explorer and the other for rival Netscape Navigator. The palettes are similar, but unfortunately you have to select one. I won't get involved in the "browser war," so you have to decide which browser you think is going to be used by the majority of visitors to your site.

To use either of the Web-compatible color palettes, select Window, Color Palettes, and then choose either Microsoft Internet Explorer or Netscape Navigator. While you're at it, you might want to use this same routine to unselect any other palettes you have displayed.

> What happens if you create Web graphics (or assign colors to Web text) that are not on one of the Web palettes? Frequently, you get a color that is not very close to the one you intended to assign. Web browsers will try to recreate color not in their palettes by dithering (mixing) pixels from the set of 216 colors that they do have. Sometimes this creates a reasonable illusion of the missing color, and sometimes the results are a gross mismatch. That's why the safest way to design Web graphics is to stick to the colors available in one of the two Web color palettes (Netscape Navigator or Microsoft Internet Explorer).

Saving Objects as Web-Compatible Graphics

This short hour can only scratch the surface of Web-compatible graphics, but that's okay. You don't need to know a lot of graphic file format theory to transform your CorelDRAW images into graphics for the World Wide Web. Here's the 30-second crash course.

Most Web browsers—the programs that folks use to visit Web sites—can interpret only images saved in the GIF or JPEG file formats: GIF and JPEG are bitmap-based images—as opposed to DRAW's vector-based files.

19

- GIF files have the advantage of having a transparent color assigned to them so the backgrounds appear invisible on a Web site.

- GIF files can be *interlaced* to appear to fade in while a viewer waits for a site to completely download. Most people think this reduces boredom while visitors wait to see your images.

> JPEG images can also simulate being "interlaced" by using Progressive JPEGs.

- The file format of JPEG images mixes colors in such a way that it often reproduces color photographs better than GIF files. So if you have a photo, save it as a JPEG file. Save other graphics as interlaced GIF images.

Now that you've been introduced to the two universally recognized Web-graphic formats, you can convert your CorelDRAW objects to either one of them.

Saving Objects as GIF Images

Any object (or group of objects) in CorelDRAW can be saved to the GIF file format. Those GIF images can be placed in a Web page.

19.1: Save a Graphic as a GIF File

In this exercise, you transform artistic text into a Web-compatible graphic.

1. Type the name of your company or organization, or your own name in artistic text. Feel free to add your slogan or address as well, but remember to use artistic text, not paragraph text.

Don't worry about whether the font you select can be interpreted by Web browsers or your visitors' systems. Because we are converting the text into a Web-compatible graphic, the font and effects will be maintained regardless of what fonts a visitor has on his or her system.

2. Add a fountain fill.
3. Click on the artistic text and click on the Export button in the toolbar.
4. Choose the Selected Only check box in the Export dialog box.

Choosing the Selected Only check box exports only the selected objects in your illustration. If you don't choose the Selected Only check box, all objects in the Drawing window are exported.

5. Choose CompuServe Bitmap GIF (that's the full, formal name for GIF files) from the Save as Type drop-down menu. Enter a filename. Figure 19.2 shows the Export dialog box configured to transform the selected text into a Web-compatible GIF file.

FIGURE 19.2

Exporting selected text to a GIF file prepares it to be placed in a Web site, retaining as much as possible of the effects and fonts applied to the text.

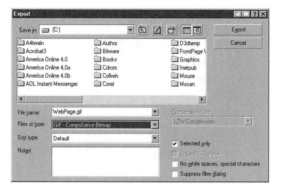

6. Click on the Export button. The Bitmap Export dialog box appears.

7. In the Bitmap Export dialog box, choose Paletted (8-bit) from the Color drop-down menu. The Anti-alisasing Normal radio button smoothes out rough edges in your object when it converts to a 72dpi bitmap image.

> Graphic images destined for the Web should be saved at 72dpi. Saving at a resolution other than 72dpi can distort the size of your image when you place it in a Web site.

8. Click on the Dithered check box to reduce the effect of any color loss when you convert your image to a limited color palette graphic.

9. Click on OK. The next dialog box is the Gif Export dialog box. Click on the Interlace Image check box to create the fade-in effect while visitors wait for your graphic to download. Click on the Image Color radio button to choose a background color to make transparent. Then use the Eyedropper to click on the white background in the Original Window, as you see in Figure 19.3.

19

FIGURE 19.3

CorelDRAW 9's Gif Export dialog box enables you to add interlacing and transparency to your Web graphic.

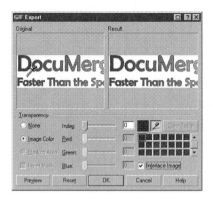

9. Finally, click on OK. Your image is ready to be placed in a Web site.

Saving Objects as JPEG Graphics

Saving an image to JPEG file format is less common than saving images to GIF format. But if you have a scanned photo, JPEG images will probably reproduce the colors better on a Web site.

To export an image to JPEG format, start by selecting the object(s) and clicking on the Export button in the toolbar. Click on the Selected Only check box in the dialog box.

Choose JPEG Bitmaps (JPG) from the drop-down menu and enter a name for the file in the File name box. Click on the Export button.

You will probably want to select the Anti-aliasing and Dithered check boxes. Anti-aliasing will reduce "jaggies," and dithering will help compensate for the limited color palettes available in browsers. You will also want to assign 72dpi resolution to your image in the Bitmap export dialog box. After you click on OK in the Bitmap Export dialog box, you can preview your image in the JPEG Export dialog box.

If you want to experiment with the two sliders in the JPEG Export dialog box, you can. Increasing the value setting for the Compression slider makes the file smaller but of poorer quality. It will load faster but look worse. Increasing the Smoothing slider value rounds off rough edges produced when you convert a vector-based image to a bitmap. The downside is that more smoothness also means blurrier images. To see the effect of your slider settings before you assign them, click on OK. The Progressive check box causes your JPEG file to fade in as GIF images do, but this feature is not

> recognized by all browsers. The Standard (4:2:2) setting in the drop-down list in the Encoding Method area is more memory-efficient than the other (Optional 4:4:4) setting, and the quality difference is usually unnoticeable.

This quick hour gives you enough skills to transfer your graphics to Web sites. For expert-level Web graphic design, check out the many Web graphics books entirely devoted to creating graphics for Web sites.

Publishing Your Illustration as a Web Page

CorelDRAW 9 comes with all the tools you need to create a Web page that can be posted at a Web site. You can design a page layout with a tiled background image. You can automatically transform all the objects on your page to Web-compatible text and images. And you can even define links from your Web page to other Web sites.

In this section of the hour, I'll share a few tips to get you through this process without crashing into some of the pitfalls that can make this a bit frustrating. In no time, you'll have a Web page designed. Do you have a Web browser installed on your computer? If so, get ready to see your own Web page in 40 minutes.

Designing a Web Page

I find that the best page layout to use for designing Web pages in CorelDRAW 9 is a regular 8 1/2-by-11-inch page, laid out in Landscape orientation. You can select Layout, Page Setup from the menu bar, choose Letter for paper size, and click on the Landscape radio button. Click on OK, and your page is ready to become a Web page.

I won't attempt a crash course in the aesthetics of Web page design except to give you one piece of advice: Keep it simple. That doesn't mean you can't have a sophisticated CorelDRAW illustration on the page. It just means keep your Web page to as few objects as possible. The page I shared in Figure 19.1 won't win design awards for flashiness, but it will open quickly and the information is easy to find. Most Web pages have a title, a basic explanation of the page, and buttons composed of text and shapes that enable visitors to navigate to other Web pages. Don't worry for now about defining those links, but you will probably want to put some on your page.

19

19.2: Create a Basic Home Page

In this exercise, you create a Web page with text and graphics.

1. Open a new CorelDRAW page, letter size, Landscape orientation.

2. Type a title for the page; your own name is okay.

3. Assign a fountain fill to your page name.

4. Type a short explanation of your Web page in paragraph text.

5. Add two or three buttons, composed with a light color-filled shape and dark text. These can let visitors navigate to other sites or to other pages you will create. You can always copy my site in Figure 19.1 if you want a simple model.

6. Save your page.

Creating a Page Background

Web page backgrounds are created by taking a small graphic image and *tiling* it—that is, placing it side-to-side and top-to-bottom to fill the whole page. Why take a small image and tile it, instead of creating a background image large enough to fill the whole page? Mainly to keep the file size down and help the page load faster.

CorelDRAW handles this for you. You can save any object as a GIF (or JPEG) image and then use it as a tiled-page background.

19.3: Create a GIF Image to Use as a Background Tile

In this exercise, you create a small image that will serve as a tiled background for your Web site.

1. Create a rectangle about 1-inch square.

2. Fill the rectangle with a subtle fill from the Bitmap Pattern Fill list (you can flip back to Hour 7, "Mixing Up Fills," to refresh your fill skills). In Figure 19.4, I'm selecting a light-colored fill pattern. Assign no outline to the filled square. (Right-click on the X at the top of the color palette.)

3. Click on the new filled square and click on the Export button. Click on the Selected only check box in the Export dialog box, choose GIF as the file type, and name the file BG1. Click on the Export button.

4. In the Bitmap Export box, set the Resolution to 72dpi, select the Anti-aliasing and Use Color Profile check boxes, and click on OK. Then, click OK in the GIF Export dialog box, accepting the default settings.

5. Select Layout, Page Setup from the menu bar.

FIGURE 19.4

You can define your own custom Web page background tiles in CorelDRAW.

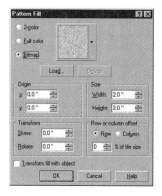

6. Double-click on Background in the left side of the Options window.

7. Click on the Bitmap radio button and then click on the Browse button to open the Import dialog box. Navigate to the BG1.GIF file you just created and double-click on it, as I'm doing in Figure 19.5.

FIGURE 19.5

After you export an object as a GIF bitmap file, you can use it as a page background for your Web page.

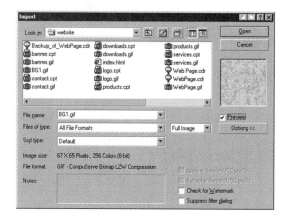

19

8. Click on OK. Your image will be tiled as a background for your page. When you save your page as a Web page, this background will be attached. My background is illustrated in Figure 19.6.

FIGURE **19.6**

Any tiny filled rectangle can be a Web page background.

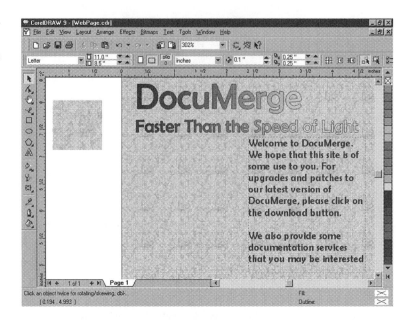

Creating Web-Compatible Text

You can make text Web-compatible two ways. Earlier in this hour, you learned to save selected artistic text as a Web-compatible GIF image. That ensures that all the effects and fonts you assign to the text will display in a uniform way, regardless of the font capabilities of visitor's browsers or systems. The limitations of converting text to graphics include

- The text is slower to download.
- The text cannot be edited as easily by Web page editing programs.
- The text cannot be copied as text from the Web site by visitors.

If you do send regular text to a Web page, CorelDRAW will help by checking the text and identifying compatibility issues you might run into with Web browsers.

19.4: Make Paragraph Text Web-Compatible

To Do

In this exercise, you let CorelDRAW check your paragraph text for Web compatibility.

1. Select your paragraph text frame with the Pick tool.
2. Choose Text, Make Text HTML compatible from the menu bar.

▼   3. The text Property Bar changes. The formatting features available from the new Property Bar assign formatting that can be interpreted by Web browsers. A third drop-down menu exists, to the right of the Font List and Font Size List. This is the HTML Font Size List, shown in Figure 19.7. When you choose a font size from this list, you are pretty much guaranteed that all Web browsers can interpret it.

FIGURE 19.7

The HTML Text Property Bar comes with preset font sizes that are interpreted by most Web browsers.

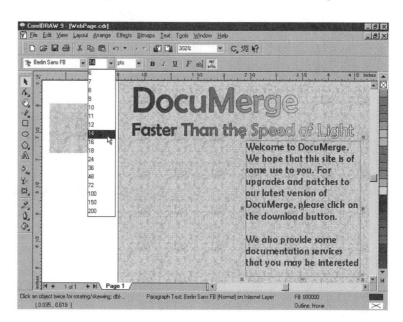

▲

You can edit HTML-(Web site)compatible text the same way you edited regular paragraph text. But when you assign format features, choose attributes from the HTML Text Property Bar.

Defining Links to Other Web Sites

Links to other Web sites are most easily defined using the Internet Objects toolbar. To view this toolbar, choose Window, Toolbars from the menu bar, and then click on the check box next to Internet Objects in the Options window. Click on OK to see this toolbar in your Drawing window.

19

19.5: Assign a Link to an Object on Your Page

In this exercise, you define an Internet link for text.

1. Click on an object on your page to which you want to assign link properties. You can use the Text tool to click and drag on text to select it as the link object. Visitors to your Web page who click on this object will jump to the assigned Web page.

2. Click in the Internet Address drop-down list in the Internet Objects toolbar, and type the URL to which you want to assign a link. If you don't have any good links in mind, share mine: http://www.ppinet.com. In Figure 19.8, I'm assigning a link to that site from the text on my Web page.

FIGURE 19.8

Links to other Web sites can be assigned to any object, including selected text.

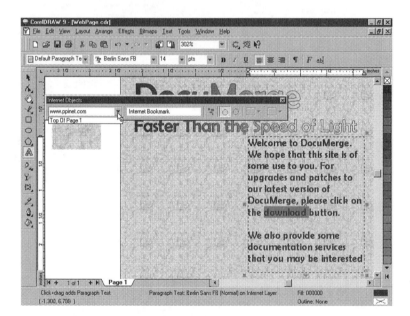

3. Assign links to additional objects on your page.

Publishing Your Page as an HTML File

The Web page you have defined needs to be converted to an HTML file before it can be published on a Web site. To do that, select File, Publish to Internet from the menu bar.

The first Publish to Internet Wizard dialog box gives you four choices for HTML style types. The first radio button, HTML, is the most reliable. Click on it in the Save HTML Layout Method to Use drop-down menu. Then, use the Please Select a Folder box to name your file, and select a folder in which to store the files needed for your Web site. Click on the Next button.

The second wizard box asks what kind of graphic image files you want to use. Click on the GIF radio button and the Interlaced check box to convert your images to GIF files that will fade in when visitors go to your Web page. If, as in the exercises you did earlier in this hour, you already made your text Web-compatible, you don't have to check the Render All Text as Images check box. Click on the Next button one last time.

In the final wizard box, enter a Page title filename for your Web page. Click in the File Name column and type a filename with an extension of .htm. Enter a title for your page as well, in the Title column. Browsers use page titles to identify the page to visitors.

Many Web servers, the computers that store your Web page, require the .htm filename extension. Some require an .html filename extension. Other Web servers accept either one, so it's best to check with the folks who administer the Web server to which you are sending your Web page, and find out what filename extensions they require.

Here, I need to explain that simply saving your file as an HTML file will not place your page on the World Wide Web or on an intranet site. Transferring HTML files to Web servers, computers that are accessible to Web browsers, is beyond the scope of this book. Many Internet service providers, such as AOL, give you access to free Web page space, and you can find out from them how to transfer your HTML-compatible files to their server. You can assign any name to your Web page; but you should check the rules of the server to which you will publish your Web site to find out what filenames are acceptable.

19

If you plan to create and manage a Web site that includes Web pages, input forms, and sophisticated page design, you might want to check out the wide assortment of good books on Web page publishing. I happen to have one out with David Elderbrock called *FrontPage 2000 Bible*. That book covers the entire process of bringing together pages, input forms, and other Web page components (such as sound and video) and working with Web servers to make your program available on the World Wide Web or your intranet.

Whatever route you take to publish your Web pages, you'll find that the graphics and pages you create in CorelDRAW 9 will mesh smoothly as you put together a site for the Web.

After you name your Web page, click on the Finish button in the final wizard page. After you do, CorelDRAW 9 checks your page for any problems that will prevent it from publishing. You can elect to see those errors in the HTML Conflict Analyzer Docker window, as shown in Figure 19.9.

FIGURE **19.9**

Corel will check your Web page for potential HTML conflicts.

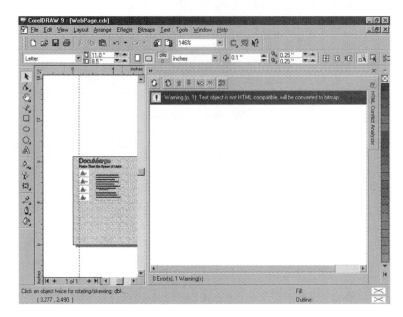

The most common conflicts are

- You didn't make your paragraph text HTML-compatible. Check each frame of paragraph text and make sure you used the Text, Make Text HTML Compatible menu option.
- You didn't convert your artistic text to curves. Make sure you choose each artistic text object and select Arrange, Convert to Curves from the menu bar.
- You have objects in the Drawing area that are not in the Page area, and those objects won't make it onto your Web page. You can delete objects off your Drawing area or move them onto the Page area so they become part of the Web page.

After you fix your HTML errors, if any, run the wizard again to save your illustration as an HTML page.

Even if you haven't made arrangements to publish your HTML page to a server, you can still use the File, Open option in any Web browsing software to open your file. You might get a warning message from CorelDRAW stating that it is unable to find your URL (uniform resource locator, or Web site address). Just click on OK and don't worry about that warning if you haven't transferred your page to the World Wide Web. This just means that your site isn't on the Web yet.

In Figure 19.10, I'm viewing the Web page I created in CorelDRAW 9 using Internet Explorer (IE). IE recognizes the link to another Web site and displays the target of the link in the IE status bar.

FIGURE 19.10

Web browsers will interpret the links you assign to objects in CorelDRAW 9.

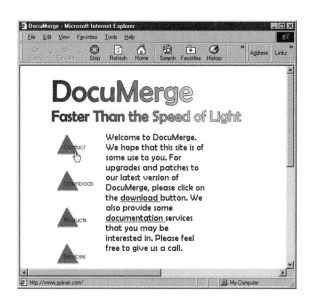

Final Advice on CorelDRAW 9

This is the last hour in this book concerned with CorelDRAW. The next five hours introduce you to PHOTO-PAINT. At this point, you've been introduced to enough of CorelDRAW 9 to have a lot of fun and create some impressive illustrations. You've also seen that CorelDRAW 9 is an extremely powerful software package, and a full investigation of its features is beyond what can be covered in 24 quick hours.

You have several resources to help you move up to the expert class of CorelDRAW illustrators. Corel's support site for DRAW 9 is at

```
http://www.designer.com/
```

Finally, let me invite you to keep in touch via a site associated with this book at

`http://www.ppinet.com`

where you'll find color illustrations from the book, as well as links to additional CorelDRAW resources   .

Summary

You can add CorelDRAW illustrations to Web sites in two ways: You can export individual objects as GIF or JPEG files, or you can use CorelDRAW 9's Internet Publishing Wizard to convert an entire drawing to a Web page.

When you convert an illustration to a Web page, text, graphics, and page background are converted to Web-compatible file formats.

Workshop

In this workshop, you publish a Web page as an HTML file that can be placed on a Web server and visited by Web browsers.

1. Start by designing a simple page that can be a home page for your Web site. Use a letter-sized page, oriented in Landscape. Include artistic text and paragraph text.

2. Create a 1-inch square and fill it with a bitmap fill. You can find these fills in the Pattern Fill dialog box that is opened from the Fill flyout.

> The image you use to create a background fill will be saved and then deleted from your Web page. Use the saved file version of the image as a page background.

3. Delete the outline for this square by right-clicking on the X at the top of the color palette. Export this object as a GIF file by clicking on the Export button and choosing GIF from the Files of Type drop-down menu. Click on the Selected Object check box in the Export dialog box. Name the file `BGX.GIF` and accept all defaults to save the file. After you save this object as a GIF file, delete it. The image is saved on your disk and can be used as a page background tile fill.

4. Select all the paragraph text in your drawing, and choose Text, Make Text HTML Compatible from the menu bar.

5. Select each artistic text object and select Arrange, Convert to Curves from the menu bar.

6. Select Layout, Page Setup and double-click on background.

7. Click on the Bitmap radio button, and use the Browse button to navigate to the BGX.GIF file you created in step 3. Double-click on that file in the Import dialog box; then click on OK in the Options window.

8. Select File, Publish to Internet from the menu bar. In the first Publish to Internet Wizard dialog box, click on the HTML radio button and click on the Next button. In the next window, leave the HTML tables radio button checked and click on the Next button again. In the third wizard box, click on the GIF radio button and the Interlaced check box to convert your images to interlaced GIF files. Click on the Next button for the last time. Enter a filename for your Web page and click on Finish.

If you have a Web browser installed on your computer, open the HTM file you just created and test it in the browser.

Quiz

Answers to the quiz questions can be found in Appendix A, "Quiz Answers."

1. How do you prepare a single object you created in CorelDRAW to be embedded in a Web page you are defining in HTML code, or with a Web page layout program?

2. What does transparency do to GIF images?

3. How do you assign links to CorelDRAW objects?

4. What should you watch out for when you convert text objects to HTML?

19

PART VI
PHOTO-PAINT

Hour

Hour 20

Diving into PHOTO-PAINT

CorelDRAW is an excellent tool for creating fine looking illustrations and graphics. So why does Corel offer another program to deal with graphic images? PHOTO-PAINT works in a different realm. Corel PHOTO-PAINT is a tool that works exclusively and expertly with bitmap images. The world of bitmap images is the world of photographic quality images. The best way to modify these images is to use PHOTO-PAINT 9.

PHOTO-PAINT 9 includes some new effects, tools, and techniques that make image manipulation easier and even more effective. Anytime a tool becomes easier to use it frees the user to be more productive and creative, and to have more fun.

A Brief Introduction to Bitmap Images

PHOTO-PAINT 9 manipulates bitmaps. A *bitmap* is an image that has been broken up into little squares called *pixels*. Figure 20.1 shows an example of a bitmap image loaded into PHOTO-PAINT 9.

FIGURE 20.1

A bitmap image.

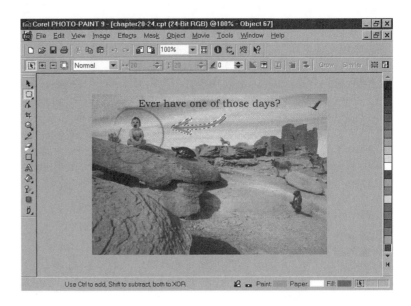

When an image is stored in a computer as a bitmap, it is stored as a grid of pixels. Photographs can be converted into bitmap images by using a digital camera or a scanner. In both cases, the image is converted into a grid of pixels that represent the image. Figure 20.2 shows a close-up of the same bitmap image shown in Figure 20.1, but in Figure 20.2 I have zoomed in to a level at which the individual pixels that make up the image are visible.

FIGURE 20.2

Pixels in a bitmap image. Notice how the image is made up of small squares.

Size and Color

The two main properties of a bitmap are its size and its coloring. The size of a bitmap image is usually expressed as the number of pixels in the image's height and width. (Bitmap images can also be measured by inches, centimeters, and other units). When an image is digitized, the color of each pixel is the average color of the area encompassed by the pixel.

When you use more colors and create larger images, a larger file is required to save your image. This becomes a factor, particularly when you want to use your image in a Web site, where larger file sizes mean slower download time for your Web page.

Resolution

Resolution is the density of the pixel grid. Resolution is measured in pixels per inch, and commonly expressed as dots per inch (dpi). Resolution is important because it affects the viewing quality of an image. A low resolution results in a *blocky*—or *pixilated*—image. Resolution of an image is also affected by the device on which the image is displayed. We'll explore resolution and color changes shortly.

Setting Up the Environment

PHOTO-PAINT's environment (see Figure 20.3) is similar to the CorelDRAW environment. There are some differences, but they mainly involve functionality and the type of tools specific to PHOTO-PAINT.

By default there is a toolbox on the left, a color palette on the right, a status bar on the bottom, a Standard toolbar on top and, as with Draw, a floating Property Bar. Like CorelDRAW, the interface of PHOTO-PAINT can be customized to suit your needs and desires. Each toolbar can be detached to become a floating toolbar; conversely the toolbar can be docked just about anywhere.

When you begin to work in PHOTO-PAINT, you will see that desktop space becomes limited when the rollups, toolbars, and Docker window start to appear. If you want as much room on the screen as you can get, maximize PHOTO-PAINT by clicking the square at the top right of the PHOTO-PAINT window or double-clicking in the PHOTO-PAINT title bar located at the top of the window. Figure 20.4 shows the Options dialog box.

20

FIGURE 20.3

The PHOTO-PAINT environment.

Title bar   Menu bar   Standard toolbar

Property Bar

Toolbox

PHOTO-PAINT
Image window

Status bar

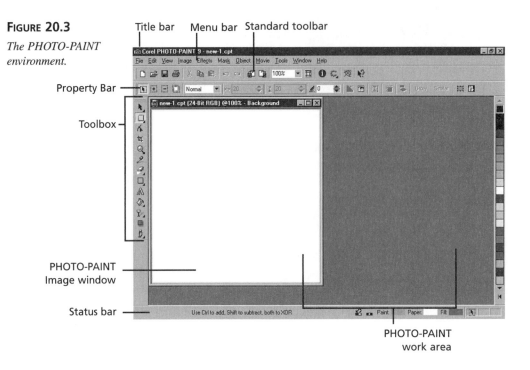

PHOTO-PAINT
work area

Most customizations to the PHOTO-PAINT interface are made from one place. To customize the interface, select Tool, Options. Spend some time browsing the Tools, Options hierarchy and experimenting with the many customizable features.

FIGURE 20.4

The Options dialog box.

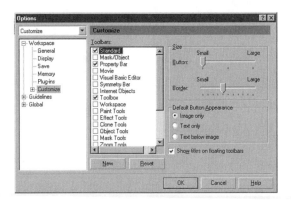

Creating a New Bitmap Image

To create a bitmap image in PHOTO-PAINT, simply click the New icon from the Standard toolbar at the top of the screen (located just below the menu items) or choose File, New. PHOTO-PAINT opens a dialog box asking for the type of bitmap image to create (see Figure 20.5).

FIGURE 20.5

The Create a New Image dialog box.

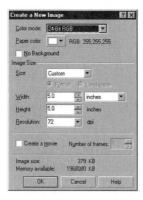

The first thing that PHOTO-PAINT needs to know is the color mode for your new bitmap. To create an image that displays on the monitor, select the 24-bit RGB Color Mode.

Next select the paper color. This determines the color of the background of the image. Notice that the white paper color has an RGB value of 255,255,255. This means that all colors are turned on at full intensity to create white. You can also select the No Background check box to tell PHOTO-PAINT that you want a transparent background.

RGB refers to a measurement of a color's quality based on the proportions of red, green, and blue in the color. In the RGB color mode, values ranging from 0 to 255 represent the amount of red, green, and blue in the color. For example, a value expressed in the RGB mode as 0, 150, 175 should have a red;green;blue ratio of 0:150:175, and be the color of the blue green sea.

20

If you select No Background, the background displays a checkerboard pattern. The checkerboard pattern serves only as a visual cue when working with transparent objects, and it does not print. We will cover objects and their transparency later.

The next section in the Create a New Image dialog box asks questions about image size and resolution. The Image Size list box offers some predefined sizes. You may also select Custom and set a specific height and width for your new image.

In order to ensure that the image size reflects a real size that is not affected by the selected resolution, you need to select a measurement unit other than pixels. In this case, I chose inches in the Measurement Units list box and set the height and width boxes to 5 inches. This guarantees an image that is 5 inches square when it prints, no matter what the resolution setting. Remember that though this image will be 5 inches square when printed, the image will not necessarily be 5 inches square on your monitor. The size on the monitor will depend on the zoom level. To let the resolution determine the size of the image, select a measurement unit of pixels for the height and width settings.

Defining Image Resolution

Image resolution means the density of pixels per inch. High resolution is required for printed output. If an image is destined for a monitor, the most frequently used setting is 72dpi. Determine the optimal resolution for a new image by following these guidelines:

- If the image is to be viewed on a monitor, choose the final size of the image in inches (or centimeters) and set the resolution between 72 and 96dpi.
- If the image is a photographic quality image destined for high quality inkjet printers and laser printers, choose a resolution between 150 and 200dpi.
- If, however, the image is a black-and-white line art image, set the resolution to the maximum resolution of the printer. You can set printer resolution up to the maximum in the Properties dialog box for your printer, which is opened by clicking on the Properties button in the Print dialog box.
- For printing to offset presses, it is best to talk to a service bureau about its recommended resolution settings and file types for bitmaps images. Usually, images destined for magazines need to be at a resolution of 266dpi or higher.

> The Create a New Image dialog box contains another important and exciting setting: Create a movie. Selecting the Create a Movie option enables you to create an animation or movie using PHOTO-PAINT 9—but first, get familiar with the basics.

Choose OK and a new image window appears in the PHOTO-PAINT work area. The window contains a white area that represents the bitmap image surface. The name of the file and the current color mode of the image are located in the window title bar. PHOTO-PAINT creates a file name starting with new and ending in the file name extension cpt for new images. The gray area around your white image (assuming you selected white for paper color) is not part of the final image. Figure 20.6 shows a new 24-Bit file, ready for an illustration.

FIGURE 20.6

A new image file created.

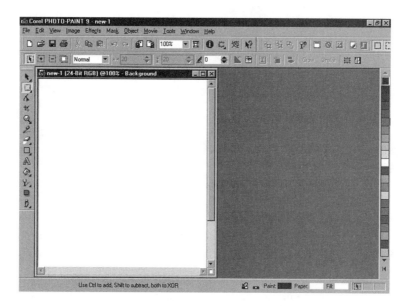

Notice the name of the file. The letters cpt in the title bar of the new image window indicate that this is a Corel PHOTO-PAINT document. The number indicates how many images have been created since opening PHOTO-PAINT. To change the name of the file, select File, Save As. Enter a new name in the File Name text box and click Save. The blank bitmap will be saved under the new name, and the title bar will reflect the change.

20

Setting the Zoom Level

Click the small square located in the top-right corner of the new image window to maximize the new image window so that it fits into the entire PHOTO-PAINT work area.

Create a new image where the values are identical to the previous example, but set the resolution to 150dpi. Click OK. The first thing to notice is that the image area (the white area) is much larger than 5 inches square. Figure 20.7 shows this larger image area. This is due to the resolution difference between the image and the resolution of the monitor. Remember that the image's resolution is 150dpi, and the monitor's resolution is approximately 72dpi.

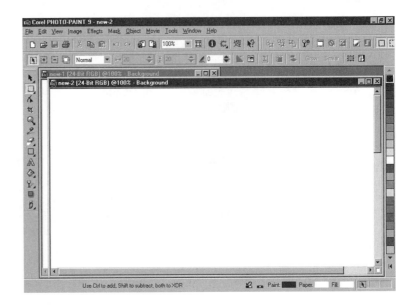

In the Standard toolbar, locate the Zoom Level drop-down list box. Here, by default, the
image is zoomed in at 100% (refer to Figure 20.7). Zooming does not affect the image; it
is akin to moving closer and farther away from the surface of the image. When an image
is viewed at 100% it will match, in size, a pixel from the image to a pixel on the monitor.
Because our image has twice the density of pixels than the monitor, it apparently grows
to about twice its actual size.

To view the image at actual size, select 1 to 1 in the Zoom Level list box, or choose the
Zoom tool from the tool box and select 1 to 1 from the Property Bar. The background
white area should now appear at actual size, 5 inches square. To display the document
information dialog box, choose File, Document Info.

Notice that this file has a resolution of 150dpi and is 5 inches square. To set the ruler to
inches, choose Tools, Options, then select Document, Ruler, and change the units for the
ruler to inches. Select the image window and press Ctrl+R, the keyboard shortcut to display the ruler.

More than one image can be open at the same time (see Figure 20.8). For
example, open as many images as you want to view at one time and then
choose Window, Tile Vertically. All the images appear tiled vertically in the
work area. To make an image the current image, click on its title bar. To
close an image, click the X on the top-right corner of its window's title bar.
To maximize an image to fill the work area, double-click on its title bar.

FIGURE 20.8

Viewing two images at one time.

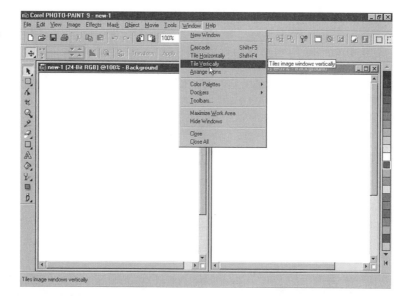

Setting Colors and Fills

There are three color swatches on the status bar: Paint, Paper, and Fill (see Figure 20.9).

FIGURE 20.9

Paint, Paper, and Fill color swatches on status bar.

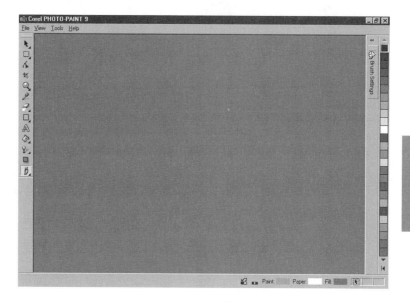

20

Each of these swatches represents the currently selected Paint color, Paper color, or Fill color. The Paint color affects tools such as the Paintbrush and Text tools. The fill color affects the fill of objects created using the rectangle, ellipse, line, and polygon tools or using the Fill tool itself. Setting the Paper color affects only the color of the paper when creating new images.

> In PHOTO-PAINT, you need to choose the Paint and/or Fill colors before painting on the image. You cannot change the color of the paint after you apply it to the image. You can change it later by selecting the area to change and then painting over it or by replacing the pixel colors, but you cannot change its color as you can in CorelDRAW, where you select the object and simply change the fill color. The same is true of painting shapes; the fill color must be selected prior to drawing the shape.

To change the currently selected paint color, left-click a color in the palette; to modify the currently selected fill color, right-click a color in the palette. To load a new type of palette, choose View, Color Palette and select the type of palette to use.

> For a full discussion of selecting color palettes for various types of output, see Hour 7.

Summary

In this hour you have received your first introduction to the PHOTO-PAINT 9 environment. PHOTO-PAINT works solely in the realm of bitmap images—images composed of a grid of colored squares called pixels. The two essential measurements of a bitmap image are its size and its resolution.

PHOTO-PAINT's environment is similar to CorelDRAW's. But PHOTO-PAINT allows you to manipulate and modify digital images—scanned photographs and photographs made with a digital camera.

Workshop

1 Start PHOTO-PAINT 9 and select File, New to create a new image.

2 Select Tools, Options and make sure a check is in boxes adjacent to Standard, Property Bar, and Toolbox.

3 Set the size and resolution of your image. Set the size at 7 inches wide by 2 inches high, and set the resolution to 72 dpi.

4 Select File, Save As, and name your first PHOTO-PAINT 9 image. You will return to it in the next Hour.

Quiz

Answers to the quiz questions can be found in Appendix A, "Quiz Answers."

1. What is a bitmap?

2. What does dpi mean?

3. How do you know what resolution size to set?

4. How do you create a new PHOTO-PAINT image?

20

HOUR 21

Painting Text

The Text tool of Corel PHOTO-PAINT 9 has many important new features. The Corel Text Engine is now the basis for PHOTO-PAINT's Text tool. This means that text made with the PHOTO-PAINT Text tool can be created in artistic flavor, as well as text flavor.

To create text, choose the Text tool. The mouse cursor changes from the object picker arrow to an I-beam cursor. Position the I-beam cursor on the image surface and left-click. A vertical line appears on your image surface. This is the text cursor that represents the size and starting position of the text that you are about to type. Type some text. To use a font, style, format, and size other than what appears in your image, modify the options on the Property Bar (font, size, character/line spacing, character style, and alignment) just as you would in CorelDRAW.

To access options for the Text tool, use the Property Bar or double-click the Text tool in the toolbox to display the Tool Settings rollup. This rollup is sensitive to the currently selected tool and will display options appropriate to the tool. Go to the Format Text options by clicking on the Text tool Property Bar, and experiment with the array of available options. A new feature of PHOTO-PAINT 9 enables you to edit the outline color of selected text by right-clicking on a color swatch in the color palette.

If you want to create an image containing only text, it is usually best to use CorelDRAW. CorelDRAW has some built-in editing features that PHOTO-PAINT does not have.

Choosing Different Types of Fills

PHOTO-PAINT, like CorelDRAW, has the capability of creating complex fills, such as the fountain fill, pattern fill, bitmap fill, and texture fill. Because the concept of PHOTO-PAINT fills is very similar to CorelDRAW fills, please refer to Hour 7, "Mixing Up Fills," for general information regarding the types of fills and their general options. Because PHOTO-PAINT is a bitmap tool, there are some PHOTO-PAINT   specific options that have been added to the fills that need explanation. These options—Tolerance and Anti-aliasing—are accessed on the Property Bar, or by double-clicking on a particular tool to display the Tool settings rollup.

Anti-aliased Text

Anti-aliasing gets rid of those dreaded *jaggies,* the jagged edges along bitmap objects. Jaggies, or aliasing, occur because sometimes there is more than one color in a particular pixel grid. This will result in a staircase-type effect along the edges of an image. PHOTO-PAINT's Anti-aliasing tool severely reduces the jagged look of an image's borders.

To see the difference between an anti-aliased text image and regular text, try the following: On the Standard toolbox, choose 100% for a zoom level. Then select the Text tool, deselect the Anti-aliasing check box, set your font to Arial size 48, and type some text. You can zoom into the text using the Zoom tool (the magnifying glass on the toolbox) by clicking on the text until you can see the jaggies clearly. Notice the jagged edges around the letters (see Figure 21.1). Letters that contain diagonal lines will be more susceptible to the jaggies, so make sure you type something with angled lines, a w or z, for example.

Now choose the Text tool and click on your text. Turn anti-aliasing on by choosing Anti-aliasing in the Tool Settings rollup, or click the Anti-aliasing button on the Property Bar. Nothing happens, right? No problem, PHOTO-PAINT does not anti-alias until you choose a different tool or click your text cursor to another position away from your currently typed text. This is a time-saving feature so that PHOTO-PAINT does not anti-alias your image until you are satisfied with its size, position, format, and so on.

FIGURE 21.1

Text with jaggies, zoomed at 100%.

Choose the Pick tool (the arrow) and PHOTO-PAINT will anti-alias the edges of your text, as shown in Figure 21.2. See the difference? Most of the time you will want anti-aliasing enabled. You may find it useful to turn anti-aliasing off for text when your text size is very small (under 8 points). At such a small size, the text characters are so small that it takes only a few pixels to draw them, and the anti-aliasing just smudges so that they become illegible (although at 6 points or less they cease to be legible anyway).

FIGURE 21.2

Anti-aliased text with the jaggies mini-mized.

21

If the Text tool is still selected, you can type more text in a different position in the image by left-clicking in the image at the new position. At this point, the original text that you typed becomes a PHOTO-PAINT object. The same occurs when you finish typing your original object and choose another tool—for example, the Pick tool.

> After your text becomes a PHOTO-PAINT object, it works the same way and has the same properties as other objects. You can select it, drag it, and so on, just as you can with any other object. The only time that these objects are affected is when the objects are combined with the background or when you save a file as a file format other than native PHOTO-PAINT format.

Editing a Text Object

When text becomes an object—that is, when you no longer have the I-beam text cursor in the text and the object handles have appeared—you cannot modify the font, color, style, or format of the text as you can in CorelDRAW. You cannot select the object and pick a new fill color. If you try, nothing appears to happen.

To modify a text's properties, use the Text tool to select the text object again. Any object transformations that have been applied to the text object (rotation, for example) will be discarded, and the text cursor (the I-beam) will appear in the text. Moreover, if you have changed the paint color since the creation of the text, PHOTO-PAINT will apply the new paint color to the text.

The best way to resize text is to use the Text tool to select the text object and choose a new font size in the Property Bar. This method ensures that the text is the highest quality that it can be. It is possible to change the size of the text by dragging the object handles (drag the corners to keep the aspect ratio and use the other handles to stretch or shrink the text horizontally or vertically), but this is not as effective in keeping the quality of the text.

> When manipulating objects in PHOTO-PAINT so that they change shape or size, PHOTO-PAINT does not commit the change until you tell it to commit the change by double-clicking on the object or right-clicking anywhere and choosing Apply. To abandon the change, right-click the object and choose Reset. This enables you to undo your change before it changes the bitmap that represents the floating object.

To delete a text object, select the object and press the Delete key or choose Object, Delete. You can also duplicate a text object (and, as it turns out, any PHOTO-PAINT object) by pressing Ctrl+D or choosing Object, Duplicate.

Select a PHOTO-PAINT object consecutively and you will notice that the object handles change from scaling handles to rotation/skew handles, distort handles, and perspective handles (see Figure 21.3). This is similar to CorelDRAW objects. Selecting an object consecutively means to click on it repeatedly, but not with quick clicks (not double-clicking).

FIGURE 21.3

Selecting an object more than once displays different object handles for different transformations.

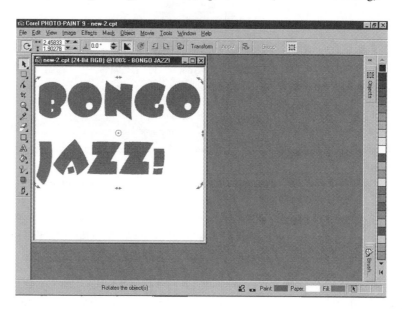

Using the Objects Docker

The Objects Docker window is very helpful. It can be opened by choosing Window, Dockers, Objects. Click the double arrow in the upper-left corner of the window to expand the window; when the window is expanded, click the double arrow in the upper-right corner to collapse the window but keep it active. This enables you readily to access the window without leaving the primary window (see Figure 21.4).

The Objects Docker window contains a list of all the objects that can be found in the current image. Type objects are listed using the first letters of the text that the user creates with the Type tool.

To rename an object, right-click on the object and select Properties from the context menu. The Object Properties dialog box appears, and you can change the name by typing a new name in the Name box. The Object Docker window will be covered more in the next hour.

21

FIGURE 21.4

The Objects Docker window.

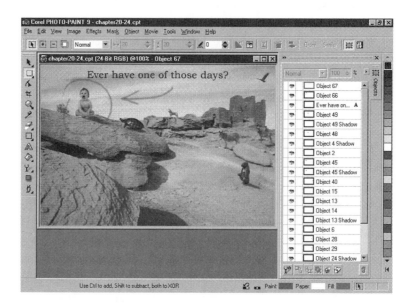

The eye next to the thumbnail in the Objects Docker indicates whether the object is currently visible. Any text that you have typed appears as individual objects. Selecting an eye toggles the visibility of the object on the same line. Text, Shadow, and Lens objects can be identified by the icons to the right of each object's name.

Summary

In this hour, you've covered a lot of ground. You learned how to begin using PHOTO-PAINT 9 and how to work with zoom levels, colors, fills, and text objects.

Because you have covered so much in so few pages, you may still have questions about such aspects of PHOTO-PAINT 9 as aliasing, resolution, and color modes. If so, be sure to check out the companion Web site at www.ppinet.com. And remember—experiment and explore!

Workshop

Let's put some of what you have learned to practice by creating an image that has a resolution of 72dpi and that contains a couple copies of a text object layered on top of each other to create a simple, but pleasant, effect. You can aim for a text object like the one in Figure 21.5.

FIGURE 21.5

Duplicated text.

1. Create a new image that is 7 inches wide by 2 inches high with a 72dpi resolution.

2. Select the black color for the text object by left-clicking a color on the palette. Then select the Text tool.

3. Change the font size and style of the text to something you like and to something that will fit nicely into the space in your image (a good choice is Times New Roman at 96 points). Then click on the image near its left and type some text. Position the text object with the Pick tool to center it in the image.

4. Duplicate the text by selecting the text object and typing Ctrl+D.

5. Change the paint color to another color, and with the Text tool, select the topmost text object. The top text object color will change to the new color. Nudge this object up and to the left using the Pick tool. The result should look something like Figure 21.5.

If you like the effect, save your image. Images saved as PHOTO-PAINT files enable them to be further edited.

Quiz

The answers to the quiz questions can be found in Appendix A, "Quiz Answers."

1. When should the paint and fill colors be selected?

21

2. Can you easily change the color of a text object?

3. What is the Objects Docker?

4. How do you turn on anti-aliasing?

HOUR **22**

Painting Bitmap Objects

In this hour, you begin to learn about masks—a powerful image manipulation feature of PHOTO-PAINT 9. Since masks are the most exciting feature of PHOTO-PAINT, I want to give you a taste of what you can do with them now. In Hour 24, we'll explore masks in more detail.

In this hour you will also begin to learn about creating and painting bitmap shapes and putting borders around them. PHOTO-PAINT 9 offers numerous tools that enable you to make varied and creative artistic expressions. So let's get going!

A Quick Introduction to Masks

A mask can have many different uses, but the fundamental idea behind the mask is to enable you to select a portion of a bitmap image. One way to accomplish this is using a Mask tool, which isolates an area of the bitmap. When you use a Mask tool to select an area, the selected area is modifiable or selected, while a mask covers the rest of the area. This enables you to protect areas of your image from changes when applying effects and when painting. You can also use this selected area (and it need not be contiguous —an area that is connected) to create a floating object, which is what we want to do here. Open a photographic-quality image in PHOTO-PAINT. You can scan one of your own photographs into PHOTO-PAINT, for example. Choose File, Open and locate any photographic image. Figure 22.1 shows an image you saw in Hour 21, "Painting Text"—the baby in the desert. Several photographs were scanned and manipulated by our resident artist, Paul Mikuleckey to create this striking image. Now, using the Mask tool and other tools, the image can be manipulated further.

FIGURE 22.1

Baby in the desert.

When you select the rectangle mask flyout from the toolbox (on the left side of the PHOTO-PAINT window), the masking tools shown in Figure 22.2 appear.

FIGURE 22.2

The mask flyout tools.

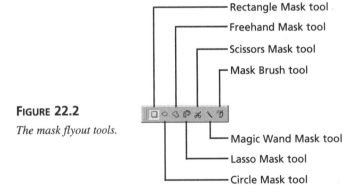

In the next few steps, the Rectangle Mask tool manipulates the image of the baby and animals in the desert.

22.1: Create Objects with the Rectangle Mask Tool

▲ To Do

1. Choose the Rectangle Mask tool and select a starting point in your image; then, while holding the left mouse button down, drag to encompass a portion of your image with the tool. In this example the Rectangle Mask tool surrounds the monkey. The result is a *marquee*—a rectangle of "marching ants" that surrounds the selected area (see Figure 22.3). If the animated rectangle does not appear, choose Show Mask Marquee on the Standard toolbar.

   This marquee does not affect the image. The rectangle within the marching ants signifies the modifiable section of the image, and a mask now protects the rest of the image.

FIGURE 22.3

Marquee of marching ants surrounding the monkey.

When you find yourself trying to modify an image that you cannot seem to modify, it may be that you have a mask selected. To remove any and all masks from your image, choose Mask, Remove.

2. To create a new object from the area you've just selected, choose Object, Create, Object Copy Selection. This will create a PHOTO-PAINT object that floats over the original bitmap background without destroying the selected area.

▼

3. Choosing Object Cut Selection removes the object from the selected area. You can see this object in the Object Docker and the object's object handles should now appear on the image.

4. You can also see all objects in your image by choosing Show Objects Marquee from the Standard toolbar. This will outline all your objects with a blue marquee.

5. You can now manipulate this object. Experiment with it by repositioning, scaling, and rotating the object (see Figure 22.4).

FIGURE 22.4

The selected area is now a transformed object sitting next to the baby.

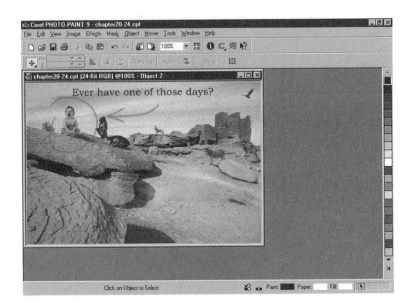

When you mark an area of your image, PHOTO-PAINT analyzes the area and generates objects within the mask. Note that PHOTO-PAINT created both a monkey object and a separate shadow object—both of which have to be moved separately. In Figure 22.4, the monkey's shadow is still back at the original location.

Painting Shapes

Painting PHOTO-PAINT shapes is somewhat similar to drawing CorelDRAW shapes. As in DRAW, you select a shape from the Rectangle Tool flyout, and then draw that shape.

The main difference is object attributes are defined *before* you draw the shape. In a
minute (or two) I'll walk you through the process of defining borders and fills for shapes
in PHOTO-PAINT. But first, it might be helpful to list some of the differences between
shapes in DRAW and PHOTO-PAINT:

- You need to set the shape's options prior to painting the shape (this includes setting
  fill and outline colors).

- If you do not select the Render to Object button, the painting of objects will modify the selected object or background. That is, the shape paints over the pixels
  underneath it, effectively replacing the object's (or background's) pixels with the
  selected fill color of the currently selected shape.

- When a Paint Shape tool (Rectangle, Ellipse, Polygon, or Line) is selected,
  PHOTO-PAINT reflects the selected tool by changing the mouse cursor to a
  crosshairs, with the currently selected tool's icon in the crosshairs's upper-right
  quadrant.

- To choose a different Paint Shape tool, click the small black triangle on the cur-
  rently selected Shape tool (by default, the first Shape tool to appear is the
  Rectangle tool). This triggers the flyout toolbar, which contains the Ellipse,
  Polygon, and Line tools.

> If you accidentally paint over a white background, you can choose Edit,
> Clear and the background will be wiped. If your background is an image, it
> too will be erased, so be careful. Also, make sure that your background is
> selected when you Clear the image (use the Objects Docker to select the
> background). If an object is selected and Edit, Clear is activated, the object is
> erased.

In PHOTO-PAINT, shapes can also include an outline (see Figure 22.5). To add a different colored outline to a shape, choose the paint color (the border color), click the Shape
tool of choice, and enter a thickness in the Width box on the Property Bar. Experiment
with different thicknesses to get the desired effect. In PHOTO-PAINT, the object is a
bitmap and the outline is painted onto the object. That is, the pixels on the border of the
object will be modified so that their color reflects the paint color.

FIGURE 22.5

Rectangle with an outline.

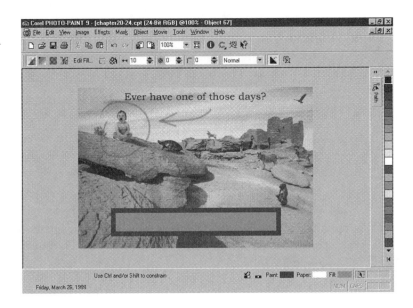

Painting Rectangles

22.2: Paint a Rectangle

In this exercise, you will paint rectangle shapes. Choose the Rectangle tool. The Rectangle tool is the default tool in the Rectangle tool flyout in the toolbox (on the right side of the PHOTO-PAINT window).

1. Assign a border color for your rectangle by clicking on a color in the color palette (left mouse button).

2. Modify the width option for the rectangle using the Width spinner in the Property Bar.

3. Modify the roundness of the rectangle corners by entering a value in the Roundness spinner box on the Property Bar.

4. Choose a fill color for the rectangle by right-clicking on a color swatch from the palette.

5. Using the Rectangle tool, paint the rectangle by selecting the start point of the corner of the rectangle on the image and then drag the mouse and release the mouse at the end corner of the rectangle.

> To constrain a square from a rectangle, hold down the Ctrl key as you draw the rectangle shape.

Painting Ellipses

Painting an ellipse is similar to painting a rectangle. First, select the Ellipse tool from the Rectangle tool flyout in the toolbox. Then, select a border color by (left) clicking on a color in the color palette. Then, select a width in the Property bar. Right-click on a color in the color palette to define a fill color for the ellipse.

After you define paint and fill properties, drag the ellipse (or circle if you hold the Ctrl key while painting the ellipse) to a desired shape and size. Figure 22.6 shows rectangles and ellipses painted with borders.

FIGURE 22.6

Rectangles and ellipses with borders.

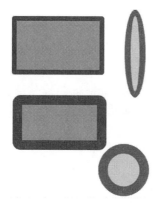

Painting Polygons

Polygons are shapes with three or more sides. Choose the Polygon tool from the Shape tools flyout.

The following steps walk you through creating a polygon (be sure to select the Polygon tool before beginning with step 1).

22.3: Create a Polygon

In this exercise, you will create a polygon.

1. Select a paint color for the polygon by clicking on a color in the color palette.
2. Choose a fill color for the polygon by right-clicking on a color in the color palette.
3. Define a width for the outline using the Width spinner in the Property bar.
4. Left-click this cursor in the image area. This is the first point on the first edge of a polygon. Attached to this point is a rubber band line that follows the mouse cursor.

▼ 5. Choose the endpoint for the first edge of the polygon by left-clicking on the image surface. The outline of the first edge is painted, and the rubber band continues to follow the mouse cursor.

6. Continue to place polygon edges on the surface of the image in this manner.

7. When you are on the last point of the last edge of the polygon, double-click the left mouse button.

The polygon is then complete, and PHOTO-PAINT fills it with the selected fill and outlines it with the current paint color.

> To constrain the polygon edges to 45-degree increments, hold Ctrl down while moving and pressing the left mouse button.

Polygons can have edges that intersect, and can be any shape or size and have any number of edges. See Figure 22.7 for examples of polygons, with and without borders.

Figure 22.7

Painting polygons.

▲

Painting Lines

Painting lines is very similar to painting polygons. The main difference is that the Line tool will not connect the first and last point and use a fill. Moreover, the fill does not determine the color of the line; rather, the paint color determines the color of the line.

To draw a line, select the Line tool, the fourth and last tool in the Rectangle tool flyout. Click once to begin the line, and click to create additional line segments.

To stop painting line segments, double-click. The width setting (on the Property Bar) determines the width of the line.

Lines have an additional option called the Shape Joints option. When you select the Line tool from the Toolbox, you can choose from one of four types of shape joints. The options are Butt, Filled, Round, and Point. The four types of joints are illustrated in Figure 22.8.

FIGURE 22.8

The use of different line joint options: Butt, Filled, Round, Point.

Modifying Paint Modes

A painted shape or a PHOTO-PAINT object can interact with the bitmap underneath the shape in a variety of ways. This interaction between the color of the shape or object paint and the color of the paint of the pixels is called the Paint Mode when painting shapes, and is called the Merge Mode when working with objects.

To modify the Paint Mode, choose a new Paint Mode in the Property Bar prior to creating your object. To modify the Merge Mode for existing floating objects, use the Merge listbox in the Object Dockers window. Different types of Merge Modes exist. For example, if you select the Add mode, the colors between the object and the image beneath it are added to make a brighter and usually different color. Experiment with the effects of different modes on objects and painted shapes. For some examples, see Figure 21.9.

FIGURE 22.9

Merge Modes painted over the bongos. Left to right from top: Normal, Difference, Screen, LogicalAND, Multiply, Overlay, Subtract, Hard Light, and Exclusion.

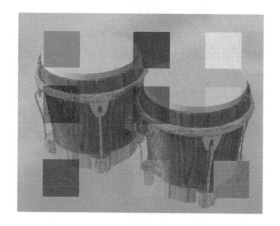

22.4: Apply Merge Modes

In this exercise, you will experiment with a few different merge modes.

1. Draw a circle with yellow fill and paint colors.

2. Draw a smaller square with a blue fill and paint color. Move the square so that it intersects with the circle.

3. Select Window, Docker, Objects (or press the Ctrl+F7 shortcut key) to display the Object Docker window. Note that the Merge Mode drop-down menu is set to the default of Normal (unless you have selected another Merge mode earlier).

4. From the Merge Mode drop-down menu, select Difference and note the effect where the two objects intersect.

5. Experiment with the Multiply, Texturize, and Subtract effects.

Changing Fill Colors

Changing fill color in PHOTO-PAINT works differently than changing fills in DRAW. In PHOTO-PAINT, fills are applied to contiguous groups of like-colored pixels. In other words, if you have an object that is part red and part blue, you can replace either the red or the blue pixels in that object.

22.5: Change a Fill Color

In this exercise, you will change the fill color for an object's inside color, and then change the object's outline color.

1. Select the Rectangle shape tool. Set the Width spinner in the Property bar to 10 to create a thick outline around the rectangle that you are about to draw.

2. Choose a red fill color (right-click on red in the Color palette), and a blue paint color (left-click on blue in the Color palette).

3. Draw a rectangle. The fill should be red, the outline blue.

4. Change the fill color to green by right-clicking on green in the Color palette.

5. Select the Fill tool from the Toolbox and click in the center of your rectangle. The fill color should turn to green. Press Ctrl+Z to undo the fill.

6. With the Fill tool still selected (and the bucket cursor visible), carefully click on the blue outline of the rectangle. The *outline* should change color, but the inside should remain the same.

Now that you've experimented with the basic routine for changing fill color, I'll briefly introduce you to some more advanced concepts that you can explore on your own.

PHOTO-PAINT decides which pixel colors to replace based on the *tolerance value*. The smaller the tolerance value setting, the more precise the fill. That is, the fill affects pixels of colors similar to the one you select. The higher the tolerance, the more pixels fit, and more of your image fills. So, for example, if you wanted to replace colors and precisely distinguish between shades of purple, you would set the tolerance level around 5. If you wanted to replace all colors ranging from blue to purple, you would set the level around 50.

You can change the tolerance settings for a fill by using the Color Similarity or Hue Levels spinner in the Fill Property bar.

Fills do not have to be applied to objects; you can also use the Fill tool to change page background color. To do that, click on the page background with the Fill tool. For example, in Figure 22.10, I used the Fill tool to create a green background for part of my illustration, by tweaking the settings in the Color Similarity or Hue Levels spinner.

FIGURE 22.10

Filling to replace selected colors.

Summary

In this hour, you learned the basic functions of Mask tools. Mask tools protect part of the image on which you are working, while enabling you to modify one or more areas in the rest of the image. You learned how to create objects using the Mask tools.

You also learned to create bitmap objects by using the Shape tools. You learned how to add outlines to shapes, and how to fill them with color. You learned how to create polygons, and you learned about the different types of lines you can create.

Workshop

1. Open a new PHOTO-PAINT 9 file by selecting File, New. Set the height and width to 400-by-400 pixels, and set the resolution to 96.

2. Select colors. In this example, purple paint and deep yellow fill were selected.

3. Select the Ellipse tool. Set the border width to 10 and the transparency to 0.

4. Create several overlapping circles (remember to hold down the Ctrl key when using the Ellipse tool, which will constrain the shape to be circular).

5. Select the Polygon tool and select round in the Shape Joints box. Draw a polygon on the bottom of your canvas, beneath the overlapping circles.

6. Select the Text tool. Type `Going in Circles?` inside the polygon. Make the text an object, and position it in the center of the polygon, as in Figure 22.11.

FIGURE 22.11

Circles and a polygon with text.

Quiz

Answers to the quiz questions can be found in Appendix A, "Quiz Answers."

1. What does a mask do?

2. How do I place or border or outline on an object?

3. Can I change the color of a rectangle object after I paint it?

4. What determines the color of a line?

HOUR 23

Working with Objects

In this hour, you look more at PHOTO-PAINT 9 objects and what they can do. Then, you take a peek at some of the paintbrush tools and their many variations. You will also begin to explore the Effect tools, such as the Clone tool and the Image Sprayer tool—tools even more intriguing than their names.

PHOTO-PAINT objects are a powerful feature in PHOTO-PAINT. In this section, you discover more things you can do with objects: order objects on top and behind one another, feather an object's edges, add drop shadows to objects, and make objects transparent.

Ordering Objects

To order an object behind another object, select the object and right-click the object to display a menu near the cursor. Then choose Arrange, Order and select a position option: To Back, To Front, Behind One, or Forward One.

You can also order objects (from front to back) in the Object Docker by selecting the object to order and dragging the object above or below a desired object. The order of objects in the Object Docker reflects the relative position of all the objects above the background.

Grouping Objects

After you select a number of objects, you can group them just as in CorelDRAW. These grouped objects then behave, in most circumstances, as one object. To group the selected objects, choose Object, Arrange, Group, or press Ctrl+G. To ungroup objects, choose Object, Arrange, Ungroup, or press Ctrl+U. You can also group and ungroup objects by right-clicking on the selected object(s) and choosing Arrange, Group (or Ungroup).

When objects are grouped they maintain their order relative to each other, but the group itself takes on the order position of the topmost object in the group. The objects are linked together in the Object Docker window by a solid black line.

Aligning Objects

Just as in CorelDRAW, you can align PHOTO-PAINT objects relative to each other vertically and horizontally. Moreover, you can make the spacing among objects consistent using the distribute option.

To align or distribute objects, select the objects to align. With the objects selected, choose Object, Arrange, Align and Distribute. The alignment options are similar to those you explored in CorelDRAW 9 in Hour 5, "Setting Up Page Layout."

Transforming Objects

As you have seen, there are a number of different transformations that we can apply to objects in PHOTO-PAINT. Clicking on an object toggles between four different transformation handles. They are described in Table 23.1.

TABLE 23.1 TRANSFORMATION OBJECTS

Icon	Name	Description
Position	Position	You can move an object by clicking and dragging on the center of it, or resize it by clicking and dragging on a handle.
Rotation	Rotation	Rotates (spins) a selected object.
Distortion	Distortion	You can stretch different sides of the selected object by clicking and dragging on a single handle.
Perspective	Perspective	Creates the illusion that the object has a vanishing point somewhere on (or beyond the edge of) the illustration.

You can add the same transformations to multiple objects by selecting them, grouping them, and then applying the transformations.

Defining Object Opacity

Opacity measures how well you can see through an object. The higher the opacity, the harder it is to see through. You can find the opacity setting for an object in the Object Docker window at the top of the window. To change the opacity, move the slider to the desired position For example, in Figure 23.1 the opacity for the selected object (Object 67) is 50%.

FIGURE 23.1

Changing opacity of an object. The rectangle has an opacity setting of 50%.

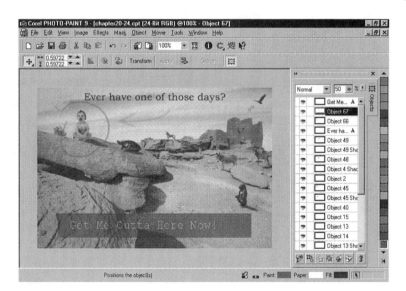

The opacity changes to objects that have been grouped will affect all the individual objects that make up the group.

The overall opacity of an object is modifiable as long as the object remains an object. After the object is combined with another object or the background (see the section "Combining Objects," later in this hour), the opacity of an object cannot be changed using this method.

23

Object Feathering

The edges of objects in PHOTO-PAINT can be faded to nothing, revealing the background (or other objects beneath) on the edges. This is called *feathering*.

Select an object and choose Object, Feather. In the Feather dialog box, select a width for the feather option in pixels. With the Preview button selected (in the Feather dialog box, the eye left of the OK button), an increase in the spinner for the feather width will display the new increased feathering immediately on your object (see Figure 23.2).

FIGURE 23.2

Object feathering.

Combining Objects

Objects can be combined together or combined with the background. Do not confuse this with grouping objects. Grouping maintains an object's identity. Combining combines objects to create new objects (or modified backgrounds). When objects are combined together or combined with the background, the pixels between the two bitmaps will be combined permanently. (Be careful: Only Undo can get you out of a jam here.)

To combine objects, first select them. Then, choose Object, Combine and then select the type of combination you want. You can combine multiple objects together to create a new object, combine the object with the background, or combine all objects in the image with the background.

Object Transparency Tool

The Object Transparency tool gives you the ability to add a number of different types of transparent gradients to an object. The Object Transparency is not editable. When you apply another transparency type to an object, it will add it to the already modified object. To apply the current interactive transparency, select another tool or object.

To add a transparent gradient to an object, choose the Object Transparency tool and select the type of transparency to apply to the object.

23

> For a better interface to the Object Transparency tool settings, double-click the Object Transparency tool to display the Tool Settings rollup.

To apply Linear transparency, choose the Object Transparency Tool, select Linear type, and left-click the part of the object that you want to be the least transparent. Drag the mouse to another portion of the object and release the mouse button to select the most transparent part of the object. You can modify the start and end transparency values by modifying the Node Transparency slider on the Property Bar. Select the node to adjust and slide the slider to the desired transparency value.

In Figure 23.3, I placed an ellipse on top of text, and I've added transparency that increases from left to right.

FIGURE 23.3

Adding transparency to an ellipse.

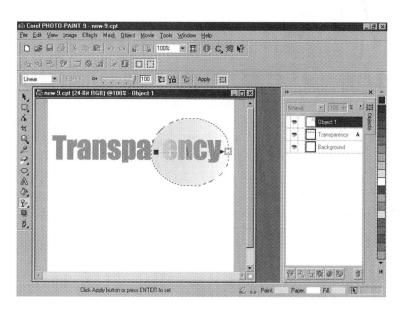

Working with Paintbrushes

PHOTO-PAINT has a set of tools that emulate paintbrushes. These tools modify pixels of a bitmap image using the selected paint color. This is similar to the way that real paint-brushes modify paint on a canvas. These tools include the Paint tools, Effect tool, Clone tool, and the Image Sprayer Tool. See Figure 23.4.

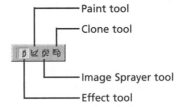

FIGURE 23.4

Paint tool flyout.

If you plan to use the Paint tools a lot in your work, I would suggest the purchase of a tablet. A *tablet* is a computer-input device that acts very much like a mouse or trackball, but you use a pen to move the cursor.

Corel PHOTO-PAINT 9 has special pen settings which facilitate greater artistic control, but you must first install a pressure sensitive pen and tablet, along with their Windows drivers.

Paint Tool

Paint tools enable you to add the paint color to your image in a way that depends on the type of paintbrush and paint color you choose. When you select the Paint tool, the Property Bar displays some of the modifiable options of the Paint tool. Double-click the Paint tool to display the Tool Settings Docker to access Paint tool options. When you select the Paint tool from the toolbox, a brush appears in the upper-left corner of the Property Bar. Click on the arrow next to this brush to see available brush options. Figure 23.5 shows the Paint Tool Docker and the brush options.

Each of the settings in the Docker window contains several options that affect the Paint tool, and which you can change. As with many aspects of PHOTO-PAINT, the choices are many and varied; experiment with different settings to learn more about them and to develop your own artistic style. Figure 23.6 shows a sample of some of the many possible effects.

Paint tool Docker

FIGURE 23.5

Paint tool settings and paintbrush options.

Brush options

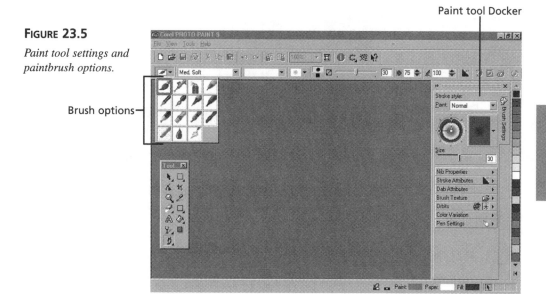

FIGURE 23.6

Using different brushes with the Paint tool.

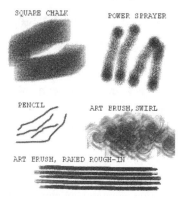

Effect Tool

The Effects tools are similar to the painting tools, but rather than adding color to the image surface, the Effect tools modify the pixels in different ways. There are a number of different effects that you can apply to your painting. Some of the more common effects are Smear, Smudge, and Brightness. The Smear tool, for example, acts like a cotton swab by smearing color underneath it, making it appear as if the paint colors are being moved to the front and sides of the tool (see Figure 23.7).

FIGURE 23.7

The Smear tool. The rectangle on the bottom-left has not been smeared; different smear effects are evident on the other three rectangles.

The Effects tool can be found in the Paint Tool flyout. Double-click the Effects tool to see the Effects Docker and the drop-down window of available options.

Spraying Images

The Image Sprayer is a tool that effectively sprays selected images onto the screen. You can "spraypaint" on an image using these steps:

23.1: Experiment with the Image Sprayer

▲ To Do

In this exercise, you can have some fun trying out Image Sprayer effects.

1. Choose the Image Sprayer tool from the Paint tool flyout.

2. Paint on your image. The result is a spray of the currently selected image.

3. To change the sprayed image, choose an image from the Brush Type drop-down menu in the Property bar. Or, to load your own image from a file, use the Load Image Sprayer List button in the Property bar.

4. Try modifying the size of the images, the rate at which they come out of the sprayer, and so on. See Figure 23.8 for an image created using the Effect tool and the Image Sprayer tool.

▲

In Figure 23.9, the entire illustration was made with the Image Sprayer tool.

FIGURE 23.8

"Hot Jazz"—an image created using the Effect tool and the Image Sprayer tool.

FIGURE 23.9

An illustration created from sprayed images.

Cloning

The Clone tool uses a part of an existing image as paint on the brush. By using the clone tool, you can transform any object in your illustration into a paintbrush. After you select the Clone tool, you can use the Round/Square Nib button to select either a round or square area to clone, and the Nib Size slider in the Property bar to adjust the size of the cloned area.

23.2: Create a clone

In this exercise, you will use the clone tool to transform your paintbrush into an object in an illustration.

1. With any image open, choose the Clone tool from the Paint Tool flyout.

2. Use the Round/Square Nib button in Property bar to select either a round or square nib to define the clone area.

3. Use the Nib Size slider in the Property bar to define the size of the cloned area.

4. Right-click the area of an image for the source of the cloning.

5. Left-click at the place where you want the source image to copy. Depending on your Clone tool settings, the source image will be painted where you apply the Clone tool. See Figure 23.10 for an example of the use of the Clone tool.

FIGURE 23.10

The Clone tool selected the bongos, which were then painted over the desert image.

When using the Clone tool, you can select an image source from a file other than the one you are currently working on.

23.3: Select a New Image Source to Clone

In the exercise below, you will select an image source from one image, and apply it to another image.

1. Open an image that you will use for the source of a clone.

2. Select the Clone tool and right-click the part of the image to copy.

3. Then create a new image and start painting with the Clone tool in the second image. The source image should now start to appear in the destination image.

If you select the source of the clone effect from an object, the Clone tool will honor the boundary of the object. That is, it will not select paint from past the boundary of the object. However, if you select the background source for the clone effect, objects that lie on top of the background will be ignored when selecting paint from the source image. For best effect, it is usually best to combine all the objects with the background in the source image.

Summary

In this hour, you learned that there are many ways to create, manipulate, and transform bitmap objects. You began to learn how to order, group, align, and transform objects. You learned how to adjust the opacity of an object, and how to feather and combine objects.

You also learned about the paintbrush options and the Paint tool, and began exploring the different settings you can select when painting. Finally, you learned about the Effect tool, Image Sprayer tool, and Clone tool.

23

Workshop

Try putting some of what you have learned into practice by creating an image using some of the tools and object techniques that you have learned in this hour. The following steps create the image in Figure 23.11. Feel free to modify the workshop to suit your own level of expertise.

FIGURE 23.11

Paul's illustration combines image sprayer effects, masking, and sprayed images.

1. Start PHOTO-PAINT and select File, New to create a new image.
2. Select a size for your image. In this example, 5-by-5-inches square, and set the resolution to 72dpi.
3. Select the Image Sprayer tool from the Paint Tool flyout.
4. Double-click on the Image Sprayer tool to display the Tool Settings Docker. Click on the small arrow to see available images. In this example, the first selection is raindrops. Spray raindrops in the center of your canvas.

5. Select the Magic Wand Mask tool and click on the white background. Select Mask, Invert to select the balls. Convert the clouds to an object so you can change their opacity. To do this, select Object, Create, Object Cut Selection. Then modify the opacity to 50% in the Object Docker.

6. Create another new image and repeat steps 2 thru 5, except this time use the butterfly image and spray around the left and bottom borders of the canvas. After you create the butterfly object, change its opacity to about 60%. Create another new image, using foliage, and spray around the top and right borders of the canvas. Once again, make this an object and change the opacity to about 60%.

7. Create another new image and repeat steps 2 thru 5 using the planets image. Spray a spiral through the center. Do not modify the opacity of this object.

8. Create another new image. One at a time, select each object that you created in the previous images and choose Edit, Copy. Then immediately select this new image and choose Edit, Paste. Do this for all three of the objects created previously.

9. Organize the objects in this new image so that the raindrops are at the back, the butterflies and foliage are in the front, and the planets are in the middle.

Remember to save your image by choosing File, Save As. Save the image as a PHOTO-PAINT file so that the object information is maintained. This image will not be used in further workshops, so it is not necessary to save the image. Play around with feathering the edges of some of these objects and changing each object's opacity to see what kinds of different images you can created. Most of all, have fun!

Quiz

Answers to the quiz questions can be found in Appendix A, "Quiz Answers."

1. What is the difference between grouping and combining objects?

2. What if I want to put an object behind an area that is not a floating object?

3. What is the difference between the Paint tool and the Effect tool?

4. How does the Clone tool work?

HOUR 24

Having Too Much Fun with Masks

So far, you have covered only a small fraction of the features available in PHOTO-PAINT. Even the features covered have many more aspects to explore. The same can be said for the new features I introduce to you in this hour. After reading a section, be sure to experiment with the new things that you learn. In this way you will be better able to remember the things learned and discover new techniques, effects, and shortcuts.

In this hour, you learn more about masks and also some clipping features. So have some fun!

Working with Masks

In previous hours, you began to see what the Mask tools can do. They define the area of an image that is editable and apply a mask to the rest of the image, thus effectively protecting the rest of the image. To create an object from an editable area, choose Object, Create and then choose the type of object creation.

To view a mask, select the Show Mask Marquee button on the Property Bar, or select Mask, Marquee Visible. The mask marquee appears. It looks like a parade of "marching ants," and by default the color of the "ants" is black. With the mask marquee visible, you can clearly see which part of your image you can further manipulate, and which part is protected.

Object marquees can also be made visible. To see the object marquee, select Show Object Marquee on the Property Bar, or select Object, Marquee visible. The object marquee looks like blue marching ants.

> A mask marquee outlines *all or part of particular objects*. A mark marquee defines an area of your total image that is editable while the rest of the image is protected. An object marquee, on the other hand, outlines *the border of selected objects*.

Removing and Inverting Masks

To remove an existing mask, choose Mask, Remove or press Shift+Ctrl+R. This makes the entire image editable and removes the mask from your image.

An area selected with a Mask tool is the currently editable area. To invert the mask so that the editable area becomes masked or protected and the masked area editable, choose Mask, Invert.

Masks and Objects

Masks over the top of selected objects mask only the currently selected object, not the entire image. In Figure 24.1, a rectangular mask is applied to the image, then Object 4—the coil of planets—is selected in the Object Docker. Select Edit, Cut or Edit, Copy to remove the editable area from the object. The result is the removal of a rectangular section of the planets. Note how the butterflies and raindrops balls are unaffected.

To cut through the entire image, combine all the objects with the background, and then cut the rectangular area. Exceptions to this rule are the Lasso, Scissors, and Magic Wand tools, about which you will soon learn more. You can select editable areas of an image using these tools as if the image's objects were all selected, if the Mask Visible button on the Property Bar is clicked before using the Mask tool.

FIGURE 24.1

Using the Mask tools on objects. The image created in Hour 23, "Working with Objects," with a portion masked and removed.

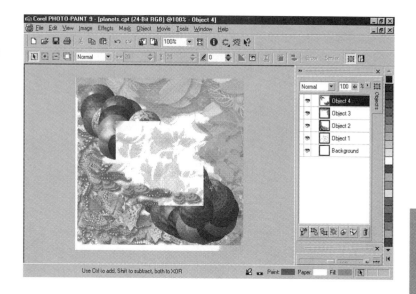

If you try to select a transparent area of an object using a Mask tool, you cannot create a new object from that area. However, you can select the object above or below that contains the colored area you had originally intended to use for your new object.

Moving the Contents of Selected Areas

You can move an area selected by the Mask tool by creating the mask and then right-clicking and dragging the selection. When you release the right mouse button, a small pop-up menu appears asking what you want to do with the selection; copy, move, or cancel the action.

The moved selection does not become an object unless you convert it into an object by choosing Object, Create, Object: Copy from selection (or Cut from selection). Figure 24.2 shows the masked rectangle moved to another portion of the image created in Hour 23.

Moving the Mask Marquee

The mask marquee can be manipulated like any object by using the Mask Transform tool.

FIGURE 24.2

*Moving a selected por-
tion of an image.*

Create a selected area using a Mask tool. Then display the Pick tool flyout and select the Mask Transform tool. The marquee of the selected area will turn into an object that can be transformed like any other object (see Figure 24.3). You may drag or scale the marquee.

Click on the marquee object again and PHOTO-PAINT will display rotation handles that you can use to rotate the marquee. All object-like transformations can be applied to the marquee object. When your marquee is positioned and transformed to your liking, select the Pick tool (or any other tool) to apply the changes to the mask marquee.

FIGURE 24.3

*Modifying the mask
marquee using the
Mask Transform tool.*

Mask Modes

You can work in one of four different modes when creating masks: Normal, Additive, Subtractive, or XOR. When Mask, Mode is selected, the currently active mode is checked.

In Normal mode, the Mask tool creates an editable area on the image. If a mask already exists, it goes away and the new mask is applied to the image.

The Additive mode adds to the editable area of the image by removing sections from the currently created mask. For example, in Figure 24.4, the Rectangle Mask tool in the Additive mode enables an additional three editable rectangular areas to be added to the already existing editable area.

FIGURE 24.4

The Rectangle Mask tool being used to add rectangular areas to an image that already has a mask.

24

The Subtractive mode expands the masked area by removing editable sections of the image. (If there is no mask, Subtractive mode masks the entire image and makes the selected area editable.) See Figure 24.5 for an illustration of the Subtractive mode used on the rectangular mask.

FIGURE 24.5

The Subtractive mode used to alter the masked area.

The XOR mode creates a mask in which overlapping regions are protected. This means that if you create two overlapping rectangles using the Rectangle Mask, the overlapped section will be masked and the other areas of the rectangle will be editable.

You can switch between modes by choosing Mask, Mode and the desired mode. You can also select the mode interactively by selecting a Mask tool and then pressing the Ctrl key while drawing the mask.

Render Text to Mask

When using the Text tool, the Render to Mask button creates a mask that outlines the currently selected font style and size. Select the Text tool, and on the Property Bar, click the button called Render Text To Mask (see Figure 24.6).

FIGURE 24.6

The Render Text To Mask button.

This option outlines the typed text with a mask. The text area is the modifiable area, and a mask protects the rest of the image.

After text has been rendered to a mask, you can create an object from the mask or apply an effect to the masked area. Figure 24.7 shows text rendered to a mask.

FIGURE 24.7

Text rendered to a mask.

When text is rendered to a mask and the editable area is then copied to the Clipboard and pasted back as an object, the resulting textlike object is not a real text object. Although you cannot modify the object like a regular text object, you can modify the object like any other regular object—that is, rotate, skew, change opacity, feather the edges, and so on.

More Mask Tools

You have already seen the Rectangle Mask tool in action, but other Mask tools can also isolate areas of an image. A combination of these Mask tools enables you to isolate complex parts of images, including parts of images that are a certain color and that fall within a color's tolerance value. In the following sections, you take a look at the other Mask tools.

Circle Mask Tool

The Circle Mask tool creates an elliptical or circular editable area. Select the Circle Mask tool from the Mask tool flyout. Press the Ctrl key while drawing the Circle Mask tool to constrain the mask to a circle. Figure 24.8 shows an example of a circular mask.

FIGURE 24.8

A circular mask.

24

Freehand Mask Tool

The Freehand Mask tool makes an irregularly shaped editable area. Select the Freehand Mask tool and click on the image surface. Then move the cursor to another location and click again (the marquee line will connect your first point with the next point). Continue clicking around your irregular object and double-click on the last point to close the mask.

You can also use the Freehand Mask tool to trace an editable area. With the cursor positioned on your image, press the left mouse button and, while holding the mouse button, trace the object that you want to make editable. Double-click when finished. Figure 24.9 shows an editable area selected using the Freehand Mask tool.

FIGURE 24.9

A Freehand mask.

Lasso Mask Tool

The Lasso Mask tool selects an editable area in a similar way to the Freehand Mask tool.
The crucial difference is that the Lasso Mask tool uses your original selection point on
the image as a seed color. (The *seed color* is the color used to determine the extent of the
mask.) The mask defining the selectable area then shrinks until it finds a pixel that does
not fall in the tolerance value of the seed color.

Use the Property Bar to define the tolerance value for the currently selected Mask tool.
Figure 24.10 shows a marquee selection using the Lasso Mask tool.

FIGURE 24.10

*A Marquee mask dis-
playing an editable
area after using the
Lasso Mask tool.*

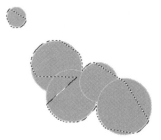

The initial point for the Lasso Mask tool in this image was in the white area just above
the small circle in the upper-left of the image. After dragging the Lasso Mask through
the image, the resulting editable area can be seen in Figure 24.10, earlier in this hour.
Any white area is masked until the tool meets a pixel (light blue in this case) that falls
past the tolerance value of the pixel we originally selected (white). At this point the mask
stops shrinking.

Scissors Mask Tool

The Scissors Mask tool selects an area by using the color of a currently selected pixel to move the mask's marquee to its nearest contrasting pixel. It effectively places the mask marquee at the edges of contrasting colors.

Select the Scissors Mask tool and click near the area you want to make editable. When you click on the image, two things happen. First, a square appears around a part of the image centered on the point you clicked. See Figure 24.11 for an example on our baby-in-the-desert photo. This square shows the maximum boundary that the mask marquee searches for contrasting edges.

The second thing that happens is a rubber band line becomes attached to the originally selected point, which follows your scissors cursor. This rubber band line is where PHOTO-PAINT thinks there is an edge and is where the mask marquee appears if you double-click or go on to select another point (see Figure 24.11). If you double-click, the mask is closed and the editable area is selected. Figure 24.12 shows the selected area.

24

FIGURE **24.11**

The Scissors Mask tool.

FIGURE **24.12**

The Scissors Mask tool selected area.

You can also use the Scissors Mask tool as a Freehand Mask tool by holding the left mouse button down and dragging the scissors around the object that you wish to select.

Magic Wand Mask Tool

The editable area selected by the Magic Wand tool includes the pixels that fall into the tolerance value of the original pixel you select. This editable area expands as long as there are connected pixels to your original pixel that fall into the tolerance value. When no more pixels connected to the original pixel are found, the masking is complete and the mask marquee is displayed to show the editable area.

Use this tool for selecting areas that consist of similar colors. To change the tolerance value, enter a value in the Color Simliarity box on the Property Bar.

Mask Brush Tool

The Mask Brush tool is another excellent way of creating a freehand editable area. The Mask Brush tool acts like a brush. The area where you apply the brush is the editable area. You can select different brush widths and nib styles in the Property Bar or in the Tool Settings rollup.

Figure 24.13 shows an image with two editable areas selected using the Mask Brush tool. To add additional brushstrokes to existing ones, be sure to choose the Additive mask mode from the Property Bar.

FIGURE 24.13

A mask created using the Mask Brush tool and the Additive mask mode.

Mask Effects

There are many more things you can do with masks after they are created. You can feather the edges of a mask, create a mask border, create lenses using masks, and clip masks. After learning the basics of a new effect, experiment to see what you can come up with.

Feathering Masks

Feathering increases the transparency along the edges of a selected area or object, thus blending the edges and making the demarcation between the two areas less evident. Just as you can feather the edges of an object, you can feather the edges of a mask by choosing Mask, Shape, Feather.

In the Feather dialog box, enter the width of the feather and its direction (average, middle, inside, outside). If you do not select average you must also choose whether you want the edges of the feather to be curved or linear. I generally prefer the softer transition of curved edges, but it is best to experiment with the different effects so you can achieve the results you desire on a particular image.

24

Mask Borders

The mask marquee can itself be converted into an editable area by choosing Mask, Shape, Border. Enter the border width of the area and the edge type in the dialog box. A soft edge has a more gradual blend than the hard-edge type. The border width is the total width of the selectable area on both sides of the mask marquee.

The result is an editable border area that surrounds what used to be the old mask marquee. Figure 24.14 shows the Mask Border dialog box on the planets image with an elliptical mask in its center.

FIGURE 24.14

The Mask Border dialog box.

Smooth and Remove Holes

A color isolation tool such as the Magic Wand can create an editable area that is imperfect (see Figure 24.15). PHOTO-PAINT has effects that enable you to create a cleaner looking mask marquee and editable area, by smoothing the edges of the mask or removing holes in the mask. To clean up the editable area, choose Mask, Shape, Smooth or Remove Holes.

FIGURE 24.15

An editable area selected using the Magic Wand tool, which contains holes or islands of masked areas.

To see the effect of smoothing or removing holes most effectively, choose Mask, Mask Overlay. A reddish-colored blanket is overlaid on the image surface (see Figure 24.16). This reddish blanket does not affect the image. The darkest red represents the most protected area of the image. Colors that can be seen through this red blanket are the most editable areas of the image. Shades of red determine the strength of the mask at those pixels. The darker the shade, the more the pixel is protected from modification.

FIGURE 24.16

The same image and mask, with the edges smoothed, the holes filled, and the Mask Overlay feature active.

Creating a Lens from a Mask

You can create a lens on an editable area. A lens distorts the image beneath it in some way, depending on the type of lens selected.

Select an image and then use the Rectangular Mask tool to create a marquee around an area. Select Object, Create, New Lens. In the New Lens dialog box, select the desired lens type. Figure 24.17 shows a psychedelic lens created from a rectangular mask in the middle of the planet's image.

FIGURE 24.17

The psychedelic lens effect applied to a rectangular mask.

24

Clipping Masks

A clipping mask enables you to modify an object's transparency without affecting the object. If you recall, the Object Transparency tool permanently affects the object to which you apply transparency.

24.1: Create and Modify a Clipping Mask

▼ To Do

In this exercise, you will first select an object and then create and clip a mask.

1. Select the object in the Object Docker so that the thumbnail is highlighted by a red square and so that the name of the object is surrounded by blue.

2. Right-click on the thumbnail and choose Create Clip Mask.

3. Select the kind of clip mask you want to create. To Show All is a clip mask that is all white. To Hide All is a clip mask that is all black. When a pixel in a clip mask is white, it is totally transparent and allows the image pixel to show through. If the pixel is black, it is totally opaque and does not allow any part of the image pixel to show through. Gray pixel values in the clip mask show more of the pixel beneath as the gray value moves from black to white. In other words, the whiter the pixel, the more transparent the mask and the more the image shows through.

▼

▼   4. Click on the clip mask to highlight the clip mask thumbnail in the Object Docker.

5. Select a grayscale value paint from the palette (the uniform palette contains a set of grayscale colors) and select the Paint tool. Paint on the surface of the image.

▲ Painting on the surface image modifies the currently selected clip mask and, depending on the shade of gray that you select, modifies the transparency of the current object.

Figure 24.18 shows an image with a Show All clip mask and a black color. Then, with the clip mask selected, a coil pattern was painted on the image. This procedure effectively creates an opacity paintbrush.

> To delete a clip mask from an object, right-click on the clip mask and select Remove Clip Mask. To make the clip mask modify the transparency of the object permanently, select Combine Clip Mask.

FIGURE 24.18

Painting on the clip mask to affect the transparency of an object.

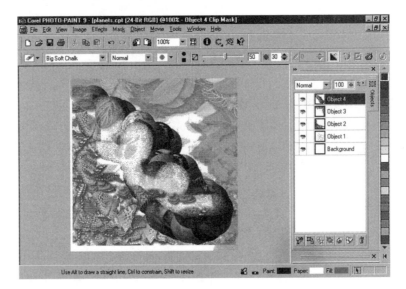

Clipping from Mask

The mask marquee on top of an object can be used as a window on the object. Select a Mask tool and draw a mask marquee on an object. Then, select the object and create a clip mask, but this time select From Mask. The object is then clipped to fit into the mask marquee area.

To move the object so that the clip mask stays stationary, click on the plus sign that is adjacent to the object thumbnail. Then, select the object thumbnail and move the object. The mask marquee now acts as a window on the object moving behind it. Figure 24.19 shows a window created on the planets object.

FIGURE 24.19

A window created from the mask.

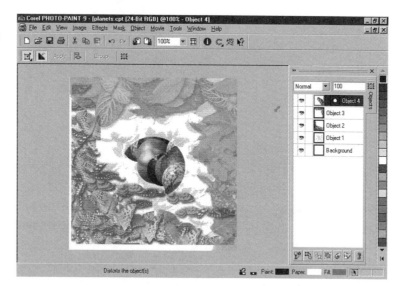

PHOTO-PAINT 9's masking tools have numerous capabilities that expand your creative design capabilities. Experiment with all these tools and effects to learn more about their uses.

Summary

In this hour, you explored some nuances of one of PHOTO-PAINT's most powerful features, the mask. There is much to learn about this feature. Discover, explore, and experiment with masks: You will be richly rewarded. PHOTO-PAINT 9 is a tool that complements CorelDRAW extremely well.

Workshop

The following steps create the image in Figure 24.20. This exercise explores creating and modifying a mask, creating an object from the mask, and adding a drop shadow to the object.

24

FIGURE 24.20

The Workshop image.

1. Start PHOTO-PAINT 9 and select File, New to create a new image.

2. Select a size for your image. In this example, the measurement is 4-by-4 inches, and the resolution is set to 96dpi.

3. Select the Image Sprayer tool from the Paint Tool flyout.

4. Select the raindrops image list from the image list. Use this image list to paint the background of your canvas.

5. Use the Rectangle Mask tool to mask about 80–90% of the image. Create an object from the rectangle area by selecting Object, Create, Object: Cut Selection.

6. Drag the corner of the new object to scale the object down. This will create a white border around the object.

7. Select the Object Drop Shadow tool from the toolbox. In this example, the orientation is set at 315 degrees, the opacity at 100%, and the width of the feather at 20 pixels.

8. Use the Object Picker tool to select the main object and duplicate it by pressing Ctrl+D.

9. Create a mask from the duplicate object by selecting Mask, Create From Object. Select Effects, 3D Effects, Page Curl. OK the Page Curl default settings.

10. Select the Text tool and type R.S.V.P.. In this example, 36-point Edwardian Script was selected, with a black paint. Position the text.

Remember to save your image by choosing File, Save As.

Quiz

Answers to the quiz questions can be found in Appendix A, "Quiz Answers."

1. How do I create an object from a photograph?

2. What is a clip mask?

3. How do I move a mask?

4. What are the different mask modes I can work with?

24

PART VII
Appendix

Hour

A   Quiz Answers

APPENDIX A

Quiz Answers

Hour 1

1. How do you select a line?

   You can select a line by clicking on it with the Pick tool or by using the Tab key to toggle between objects.

2. How do you create a 15-degree angle line?

   By holding down Ctrl after you click to establish the first node in a line, you can constrict the next node to an angle divisible by 15 degrees.

3. How can you tell whether an object is closed?

   Sometimes, it is difficult to see whether an object is closed, or *almost* closed. One way to tell is this: If you have drawn more than one line segment but not created a closed object, you will see the Auto-Close Curve button in the Line Property Bar.

4. How do you create a closed object composed of straight lines?

   You can close an object using the Auto-Close button or by placing the final node of a multiline object on top of an existing node.

Hour 2

1. How do you edit artistic text?

   You can edit artistic text right in the Desktop or the Drawing page by double-clicking on the text frame. For a more powerful editing environment, select Text, Edit Text to open the Edit Text dialog box.

2. How do you rotate text?

   To rotate text, click twice to display rotation angle handles and drag on one of them to rotate the text object. You can rotate text to a precise angle by using the Angle of Rotation box in the Property Bar.

3. What is a quick, easy way to access dozens of clip-art images?

   You can find plenty of commonly used symbols in font sets such as Webdings.

4. What font attributes can you assign from the Font Property Bar?

   You can assign font type and size from the Property Bar.

5. How do you format individual text characters?

   You can format specific characters in artistic text in the Edit Text dialog box (select the text with the Pick tool and press Ctrl+Shift+T). When you view your text in the Edit Text dialog box, you can drag to select characters and assign font attributes from the Edit Text dialog box toolbar. You can also format individual characters in the Drawing area. To do that, use the Text tool to select a text object, select text with the insertion point cursor, and assign font attributes from the Property bar.

Hour 3

1. The Shapes tool flyout enables you to create which additional shapes?

   The shape tool flyout tools are the Spiral and Graph Paper.

2. What shapes can you create with the Polygon tool?

   You can use the Polygon tool to create polygons, stars, or polygons-as-stars.

3. What are the unique features of the Ellipse Property Bar?

   The Ellipse Property Bar has buttons that enable you to convert an ellipse into a pie or an arc.

4. How do you assign no outline to a selected shape?

   You can assign no outline to a selected shape by right-clicking on the X in the color palette.

5. How can you define different radii for the rounded corners in a single rectangle?

   Deselect the Round Corners Together button in the Rectangle Property Bar to define unique radii for different corners in a rectangle.

Hour 4

1. Where can you save objects that you want to be able to quickly get to in any publication?

   You can store objects in the Scrapbook docker window for use in any Corel file.

2. What button on the toolbar cancels your most recent action(s)?

   The Undo button reverses your previous action(s).

3. How do you close those Docker windows?

   You can close a Docker window by clicking on the small x in the upper-right corner of the window.

4. What does the x value in the status bar represent?

   The x value in the status bar represents the distance from the left edge of the Drawing page to the center of the selected object.

Hour 5

1. How do you select more than one object if you cannot draw a marquee around them?

   You can use Shift and click on the objects one at a time to select them all.

2. How do you select a page size?

   The easiest way to define page size is to click on a section of the Drawing area that does not have an object on it and choose the page size from the Property Bar.

3. How do you delete a guideline?

   You can delete a guideline by clicking on it and pressing Delete. Remember, though, that guidelines do not print.

4. Name two ways to align the tops of objects.

   You can align the tops of objects using the Align and Distribute dialog box (Arrange, Align and Distribute). Or you can place a horizontal guideline and turn on the Snap to Guidelines button in the Page Property Bar.

Hour 6

1. How do you define a default outline?

   To define a default outline, define an outline with no object(s) selected.

2. How do you define an outline width to four decimal places?

   Open the Outline Pen dialog box. In the Width spin box, you can type a width setting.

A

3. Name five attributes that you can assign to an outline.

   You can assign outline color, thickness, style, corners, and arrows.

4. Does an object need an outline to be visible?

   No. Objects with fills can be seen, even if they do not have an outline. However, objects with no fill or outline will not print and are not visible unless they are selected or in Wireframe view.

Hour 7

1. How do you define a default fill?

   To define a default fill, define a fill with no object selected.

2. How do you define a Fountain fill path?

   You can define the trajectory of a Fountain fill by dragging the slider that appears when you select an object with the Interactive Fill tool.

3. Can a pattern be used for a fill?

   Yes—you can apply Pattern fills from the Pattern Fills dialog box (select it from the Fills flyout).

4. What are three popular methods for defining mixed colors in CorelDRAW 9?

   You can define mixed colors using CMYK, HSB, or RGB settings.

5. How do you select a color palette?

   You can assign a color palette by selecting View, Color Palette from the menu bar and then selecting a palette.

Hour 8

1. How do you expand the spacing between letters?

   You can expand the spacing between letters by dragging the horizontal shape-sizing handle to the right. Or you can move individual letters using the Shape tool.

2. How can you tell whether a curve is closed?

   You can tell whether a curve is closed by selecting it and checking the Curve Property Bar. If the Auto-Close button is available, the curve is not closed.

3. How do you create a closed curved object while you are drawing it with the Freehand tool?

   You can create a closed curved object by having the curve end where it started.

4. How do you add to and delete nodes from an object?

You can add and delete nodes by right-clicking on an existing node with the Pick tool, and choosing Add or Delete from the shortcut menu that appears.

5. How do you convert Artistic Text to curves? And why would you want to? What's the drawback in converting text to curves?

Right-click on the text and choose Convert to Curves from the shortcut menu. After you convert text to curves, you can edit the shape of individual text characters. You cannot, however, edit the content of Artistic Text in the Edit Text dialog box after you convert it to curves.

Hour 9

1. Where do you find the Bézier tool?

Select the Bézier tool from the Freehand flyout—the second tool in the flyout.

2. What are two main drawing tools in CorelDRAW?

There are two main drawing tools in CorelDRAW: the Freehand tool and the Bézier tool.

3. How do you complete a Bézier curve?

You can complete a Bézier curve by pressing the spacebar.

4. How do you move text from one side of a path to the other?

You can move text from one side of a path to the other by selecting the fitted text and then clicking on the Place Text on Other Side button in the Property Bar.

5. How do you center text on a path? Or right- or left-align it?

With Text Orientation and Vertical Placement selected, you can use the Text Placement drop-down menu to left-align, center, or right-align your text.

A

Hour 10

1. How do you round the corners on a rectangle?

Round the corners on a rectangle by clicking and dragging on a corner node, and pulling in toward the middle.

2. Which tool can cut a shape into two?

The Knife tool can cut a shape into two or more parts. Click twice on edges of the object to create a dissection line. Then select either of the two new objects and edit (or delete) either one of them.

3. How do you transform a selected line or shape into a curve?

When you select a shape node with the Shape tool, a Convert To Curves button appears on the Property Bar. Click on that button to transform your shape into a curve. You can convert all the nodes in a shape to a curve by selecting the shape with the Pick tool and then choosing Arrange, Convert to Curves from the menu bar.

4. How do you add nodes to a curve?

When you select an object with the Shape tool, you can add nodes by clicking anywhere on the shape and then clicking on the + symbol in the Property Bar. You can delete nodes by clicking on a node and then clicking on the – in the Property Bar.

5. How can you fine-tune the appearance of a curve?

Node curves are determined by the type of curve (Cusp, Smooth, or Symmetrical), and by the distance and location of the control points.

Hour 11

1. What are bitmaps?

Simply put, bitmaps are images that store a location and description of pixels. Pixels are nothing but dots. So, rather than defining images in terms of curves and lines, bitmap images are defined as dots.

2. How do you remove a background from an imported bitmap?

Select the image with the background you want to remove, choose Bitmap, Convert to Bitmap from the menu bar, and use the Transparent Background check box to strip the background from the image.

3. How do you bring bitmaps into CorelDRAW?

You can bring bitmaps into CorelDRAW by importing files, copying images from any program, scanning images, or converting existing drawings to bitmaps.

4. How do you strip several undesired colors from a scanned photo?

You can strip undesired colors from a scanned photo by using the Bitmap Color Mask rollup.

Hour 12

1. How are lens effects different from fills?

Lens effects do not change the appearance of the object to which they are applied. A circle with a magnify lens effect applied to it does not change its own appearance. The effect takes place when that circle is moved over another object.

2. Do PowerClips enlarge (or shrink) to fit the object into which they are injected?

   Neither. PowerClips do not change the size of either the container object or the target object. So, if you copy a large object into a small one, it will get cropped to fit the size of the target object. If you copy a small object into a large object, it will not fill the target object completely.

3. What is so special about the Interactive Transparency tool?

   The Interactive Transparency tool is unique because you can define a graded degree of transparency within the lens object.

4. Can you apply more than one lens at a time to an object?

   Yes. You also can use many lenses in an illustration. However, you'll quickly notice that the intense calculations necessary to create this effect slow down your system.

5. How do you edit the contents of a PowerClip?

   You can edit the contents of a PowerClip by clicking on the (combined) object and selecting Effects, PowerClip, Edit Contents. After you edit the PowerClip container contents, choose Effects, PowerClip, Finish Editing This Level to place the container object back into the target object.

Hour 13

1. What does the Blend tool do?

   The Blend tool fills the area between two different objects with a set of new objects that transform attributes such as shape and color, step-by-step, from the first object to the second.

2. What are the main ways to define the appearance of a blend after the objects have been selected?

   You can control the effect of a blend by defining the number of steps or by defining a path along which the blend will flow.

3. How do you define the line thickness of the lines generated by the contour effect?

   The thickness and color of the generated contour lines is determined by the thickness and color of the original lines.

4. What happens when you edit one of the two objects used to generate a blend?

   Blended objects affect the generated transitional objects interactively. In other words, if you change one of the two blended objects, all the generated intermediate objects change as well.

A

Hour 14

1. How do you move the vanishing point in an extrusion?

    You can move the vanishing point by dragging it around in the Drawing area.

2. What does a straight line envelope enable you to do?

    When you apply a straight line envelope, you create a shape in which you can place other objects. Straight line envelopes are constricted to straight lines between each handle.

3. How do you remove Perspective effects from an object?

    You can clear Perspective effects from an object by clicking on the tool in the Property Bar that removes that effect.

4. How do you mold artistic text to a shape?

    You can use the Envelope effect to mold any object, including an artistic text object, to a preset shape.

Hour 15

1. How do you enter paragraph text, as opposed to artistic text?

    To type paragraph text in the Drawing window, start by selecting the Text tool in the toolbox and drawing a marquee to frame your text.

2. How do you assign font type and size to paragraph text?

    You can format the font type and size for selected paragraph text in the Edit Text dialog box or in the Drawing window. In either case, use the cursor to select the text (in the Drawing window, you have to select the Text tool first). Then choose font type and size from the drop-down menus in the toolbars.

3. How do you shape paragraph text?

    When you select a frame of paragraph text with the Text tool, you can shape it with the Interactive Envelope Tool—the fourth one on the Interactive Blend flyout.

4. If you want to resize your text to fit in a text frame, what's the quick, easy way to do that automatically?

    You can resize text to fit a frame by selecting the text frame and then selecting Text, Fit Text to Frame from the menu bar.

Hour 16

1. How do you make the Object Manager Docker window appear?

   You can work with the Object Manager Docker window by selecting Window, Dockers, Object Manager from the menu bar.

2. How do you add pages to a drawing?

   To add pages, select Layout, Insert Page from the menu bar. The Insert Page dialog box enables you to define how many pages you want to insert, whether you want those pages before or after the current page, and the size and orientation of the new page(s).

3. How do you make a layer nonprinting?

   You can make a layer nonprinting by clicking to deselect the Printer icon in the Object Manager next to the layer.

4. Can you rename pages?

   Yes, you can rename pages. Just right-click on the Page tab and select Rename Page from the shortcut menu.

Hour 17

A

1. What's the difference between importing objects from other file formats and opening files of other formats?

   Importing files from other programs brings those objects into *already open* CorelDRAW files, whereas opening foreign files creates a new drawing.

2. Can you change imported images as you import them?

   Yes. Among other things, you can crop imported bitmap images as you import them.

3. What do you do when your printing service bureau cannot handle CorelDRAW files?

   Almost every printing service bureau can work with EPS files, and CorelDRAW files can be saved to PostScript format. You can also publish CorelDRAW files to the globally recognized PDF file format.

4. What's the quick, easy way to transfer CorelDRAW objects into other Windows applications?

   Most of your transfer problems between CorelDRAW and other programs can be handled by copying and pasting objects. When you select an object, or objects, you can copy them into the Windows Clipboard and then paste them into other applications.

Hour 18

1. Where do you define layout for different size paper such as business cards or labels?

    To define layout for cards or labels, select Layout, Page Setup from the menu. Then double-click on Label in the Options window.

2. If you bring a two-color brochure to a commercial print shop, which color separation process works best?

    Spot color separation is more economical and dependable, and will work fine for two-color output.

3. When you print color separations, how do you know what color is associated with each plate?

    You can print an additional set of your separation masters that have information on them identifying which color goes with that plate.

4. Can you print CMYK color separations if you used process color in designing your publication?

    Yes. To convert spot colors to process colors, click on the Convert Spot Colors to CMYK check box in the Separations tab of the Print dialog box. The spot colors you assigned break down to mixtures of the four CMYK colors.

Hour 19

1. How do you prepare a single object you created in CorelDRAW to be embedded in a Web page you are defining in HTML code, or with a Web page layout program?

    To send CorelDRAW objects to Web publishing programs, export them to GIF or JPEG file format.

2. What does transparency do to GIF images?

    By making a single color in a GIF image transparent, you can get rid of any one color (usually the rectangular background associated with the image). Transparency enables the background of a Web page to show through a part of the GIF image. In most cases, this is the rectangular background, but any one color in a GIF image can be made transparent.

3. How do you assign links to CorelDRAW objects?

    Links can be assigned from the Internet List drop-down menu in the Internet Objects toolbar.

4. What should you watch out for when you convert text objects to HTML?

    Check to make sure you converted all paragraph text to HTML-compatible paragraph text and that you converted artistic text to curves.

Hour 20

1. What is a bitmap?

   A bitmap is an image divided into a grid of squares called pixels.

2. What does dpi mean?

   The size of a bitmap image is usually expressed in dpi—dots per inch. A bitmap image can also be measured in inches, centimeters, or other units of length.

3. How do you know what resolution size to set?

   Resolution is best determined by the destination of your image. For instance, if the image is going to be displayed on a monitor, set it at 72 to 96dpi.

4. How do you create a new PHOTO-PAINT image?

   To create a bitmap image in PHOTO-PAINT simply click the "New" icon from the Standard tool bar at the top of the screen (located just below the menu items) or choose File, New. PHOTO-PAINT opens a dialog box asking for the type of bitmap image to create.

Hour 21

1. When should the paint and fill colors be selected?

   Select both paint and fill colors before painting on the image.

2. Can you easily change the color of a text object?

   Yes. Select the new paint color (left-click on a palette color) and use the Text tool to select the text object again.

3. What is the Objects Docker?

   The Objects Docker window contains a list of all the objects in the current image.

4. How do you turn on anti-aliasing?

   Choose anti-aliasing by clicking the Anti-aliasing button on the Property Bar.

Hour 22

1. What does a mask do?

   A mask selects a portion of an image which can then be modified, while the rest of the image is protected.

2. How do I place a border or outline on an object?

   Choose a paint color (which determines the border color), select the Shape tool you desire, and enter a dimension in the width property box on the Property Bar. The higher the dimension, the thicker the border.

A

3. Can I change the color of a rectangle object after I paint it?

   Trick question. Yes and no. You cannot modify the rectangle like you can in CorelDRAW, but you can modify it using the Fill tool.

4. What determines the color of a line?

   The paint color, not the fill color.

Hour 23

1. What is the difference between grouping and combining objects?

   Grouping keeps the objects' identities. Combining the objects creates a new object from the existing objects.

2. What if I want to put an object behind an area that is not a floating object?

   You have to create an object area—that is, use one (or more) of the Mask tools to create a mask around the area of interest. Then, select Object, Create, Object Cut Selection. This will lift off the area that is masked and create an object that contains the area. Then place an object behind the new object using the Object, Arrange commands or drag the objects around in the Object Docker.

3. What is the difference between the Paint tool and the Effect tool?

   Paint tools add color to your image in a way determined by the type of paintbrush and color you choose. Effect tools modify the existing pixels in different ways.

4. How does the Clone tool work?

   The Clone tool enables you to duplicate part of an existing image—including an image from a source other than the one on which you are working—and use it to paint on your current image.

Hour 24

1. How do I create an object from a photograph?

   By using a mask. Draw a mask around the area that you want to make into an object. You can use any combination of Mask tools to isolate the area of interest. After the mask is created to your satisfaction, select Object, Create, Object: Copy or Cut Selection. A floating object is created from the masked area.

2. What is a clip mask?

A clip mask enables you to modify an object's transparency without affecting the object. Remember the Object Docker and the thumbnail depicting the objects in your image? The clip mask is the little thumbnail image next to an object image. It is created by right-clicking on the object thumbnail and choosing Create Clip Mask. The mask can then be modified.

3. How do I move a mask?

With the Mask Transform tool. It is hidden in the flyout of the Pick tool. Select the Mask Transform tool and click on your mask. Object-like handles will appear and you can modify your mask as you can modify any object.

4. What are the different mask modes I can work with?

You can choose from Normal, Additive, Subtractive, or XOR. Select Mask, Mode and choose the mode you want.

A

INDEX